THE
FIRST
WORLD WAR
IN 100 OBJECTS

THE STORY OF THE GREAT WAR
TOLD THROUGH THE OBJECTS THAT SHAPED IT

GARY SHEFFIELD

ANDRE
DEUTSCH

THIS IS AN ANDRE DEUTSCH BOOK
Published in 2013 by André Deutsch Limited
A division of the Carlton Publishing Group
20 Mortimer Street
London W1T 3JW

10 9 8 7 6 5 4 3 2 1

Text © Gary Sheffield 2013
Design © André Deutsch Limited 2013

A CIP catalogue for this book is available from the British Library

ISBN: 978 1 780 97396 8

Printed in Dubai

Pages 6–7: A soldier attends a colleague's grave near Mametz
Wood, 1916.

CONTENTS

Introduction

The First World War decisively changed the course of history. The scale and bloodiness of the battles were greater than anything that had been seen before. The war placed states and societies under unprecedented strain, and the impact of the experience is felt to this day. Above all, it destroyed the balance of power that existed in 1914. Germany, Europe's strongest power, lost swathes of territory and suffered national humiliation, but its eclipse was temporary: within two decades it once again went down the road of aggression. The multi-lingual, multi-ethnic Austro-Hungarian Empire was shattered into component national fragments. Modern Turkey emerged from the Ottoman Empire. The victor states enjoyed variable fortunes. France was victorious on the battlefield but weakened. Nationalist forces had been unleashed by the war that within two generations were to destroy Britain's empire. The United States of America, having started to act as a great power, temporarily withdrew into isolationism.

In retrospect, the collapse of Imperial Russia in 1917 was a particularly significant event. A Marxist revolutionary group seized power and, against the odds, survived and eventually thrived. The new government promoted a hugely influential ideology, founded on international proletarian revolution, that spent much of the next 70 years in competition with another ideology, the capitalist liberal democracy championed by Britain, France and – especially – the United States of America. The period 1914–91 has been called the "Short Twentieth Century", a period of two "hot" world wars and a "cold" one. Not until 1989–91 was this ideological struggle to be concluded, with the end of the regime founded in 1917 and the termination of the Cold War. The significance of the war is such that it demands to be understood. Yet popular views on the war are encrusted with myths, particularly in the Anglophone world.

When asked to write a book on the First World War constructed around the discussion of 100 relevant objects, I was intrigued by the challenge. It gave the opportunity to explore some unfamiliar facets of the war, and to approach better-known aspects from an oblique angle. I was given complete freedom in selecting the objects, and deliberately chose an eclectic list. I made no attempt to be comprehensive, and cheerfully admit that the list is weighted towards my particular interests. In some cases, my approach has been straightforward. The entry on Sir Douglas Haig's "Backs to the Wall" order covers the man himself and the context in which the order was given. In other cases, the subject matter has been used as a springboard to discuss wider issues. So, the piece on the extravagant war memorial in the French village of Proyart leads into a discussion of life in the part of France and Belgium under enemy occupation.

Although my name appears on the cover of the book, I was assisted by a talented team of authors. Dr Phylomena H. Badsey was primarily responsible for articles 10, 17, 53, 54 and 74; Dr Michael LoCicero for articles 6, 9, 11, 12, 13, 25, 26, 28, 38, 69, 84 and 86; and Dr Spencer Jones for articles 20, 22, 30, 36, 40, 41, 43, 44, 48, 52, 55, 58, 60, 63, 72, 73, 77, 90, 98 and 100. My thanks go to all three co-authors, and also to my editor at Carlton, Vanessa Daubney; it has been a pleasure to work with her. I would also like to thank my extremely patient literary agent, Peter Robinson, and his assistant, Alex Goodwin. Finally, as ever my greatest debt is to my family, and I dedicate this book to my nephew, Jack.

Gary Sheffield

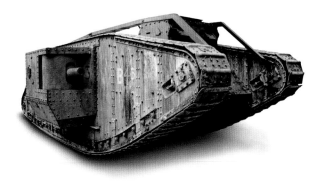

01 Archduke Franz Ferdinand's Car

Abullet-marked car in the Museum of Military History is a stark reminder that the immediate origins of the First World War lay in the Balkans. This car, a 32 horse-power, four-cylinder, open-topped 1911 Graf & Sift limousine, featured in an event that triggered the war. On 28 June 1914, Archduke Franz Ferdinand was driven in this car to an official reception in Sarajevo, the capital of Bosnia-Herzegovina. Franz Ferdinand was the heir to the Imperial and Royal throne of Austria-Hungary, and everyone expected that he would soon be Emperor: his aged uncle, Emperor Franz Josef, was almost 84. For Franz Ferdinand to come to Sarajevo at this time was to take a risk. Bosnia-Herzegovina had been annexed by Austria-Hungary only in 1908, and tensions were still running high. The nineteenth century had seen the triumph of nationalism in places such as Germany and Italy, and the multi-ethnic empire ruled over by the Habsburg family was coming under increasing pressure from nationalists within and without its borders.

The Serbs presented a particular problem. The Balkans was the last remaining sphere of influence for Austria-Hungary, and the independent state of Serbia was, from Vienna's perspective, an insolent upstart rival, encouraging dissension within the Empire in the hope of taking over Imperial territory. Franz Ferdinand's visit to Sarajevo was an assertion of Habsburg authority. It was also a red rag to Serb nationalists, especially as it took place on Serbia's national day. The Archduke would have been aware of the risk, because the threat of assassination was very real for royal figures of the period. Franz Josef's wife, Empress Elizabeth, had been murdered in 1898.

Members of the Serbian nationalist Black Hand group, decided to take the opportunity of killing the Archduke on his visit. They were backed clandestinely by members of Serbian military intelligence, which was a law unto itself; the Serbian government did not authorize the killing.

The assassination attempt was initially bungled. One conspirator on seeing the car lost his nerve, and another threw a bomb that hit the car behind the Archduke's. However when driving away after the reception, the chauffeur took a wrong turn, and one of the conspirators, Gavrilo Princip, happened to be standing by. As the car reversed, Princip shot both Franz Ferdinand and his morganatic wife, Duchess Sophie. Both were fatally wounded. Princip was apprehended before he could kill himself.

Only a little over a month passed between Franz Ferdinand's murder and the outbreak of a general war in Europe. In that time the crisis changed from a localized clash in the Balkans into a conflict that would eventually involve all the Great Powers and kill millions. The other factors which were at play – a German bid for hegemony, Anglo-German naval rivalry, and Russia's desire to reassert itself on the world stage, to name but three – should not be allowed to obscure the fact that Austria-Hungary's reaction to the events in Sarajevo precipitated the war. After the assassination, the decision was taken to punish Serbia through war, regardless of the consequences. On 23 July, Austria-Hungary issued an ultimatum, and although the Serbs agreed to almost all of Vienna's demands, war was declared five days later. Austria's decision to attack Serbia involved an extremely high risk of involving Russia, Serbia's patron, and France, Russia's ally, thus widening a Balkan conflict into a general war. Austria-Hungary's fateful gamble, and Germany's decision to support their ally in this endeavour, meant that the primary responsibility for unleashing the First World War rests with the small group of decision-makers in Vienna and Berlin.

OPPOSITE: Gravilo Princip fires the shots that killed Archduke Ferdinand and his wife Sophie. Hemmed in by the crowd, he was unable to prime the bomb he was carrying and resorted to his pistol, shooting without taking aim.

ABOVE: Archduke Ferdinand and his wife Sophie outside the town hall in Sarajevo, moments before their assassination. The two had survived an assassination attempt earlier that day, when a bomb had bounced off the folded hood of the convertible, exploding under a car behind.

▪02 Gare de l'Est

The Gare de l'Est was one of two major railway stations in Paris that acted as gateways to the Western Front. Historian Adrian Gregory has written that "Neither the First World War nor the capital cities of 1914–1918 would have been recognizable or even conceivable without the railway." He is correct. Aided by staff work that was greatly superior to that of its enemies, the Prussian Army in 1870 used the country's extensive network of strategic railways to make a rapid concentration of forces on the border with France and seize the initiative. The army of Napoleon III never recovered from this initial setback.

The lesson about the importance of speed in initial deployment, and of not sacrificing the initiative to the enemy, was taken to heart. In the 1960s, the controversial historian A. J. P. Taylor went so far as to argue that the rigidity of mobilization plans was a critical factor in the outbreak of war by denying governments flexibility during the 1914 July crisis.

Taylor stated that war was "imposed on the statesmen of Europe by railway timetables. It was an unexpected climax to the railway age". This was an exaggeration, but it contained a grain of truth; the German Schlieffen Plan, for instance, relied on strategic railways to move forces to the West in order to defeat the French, and then to move them east to face the Russians.

Once the shooting war began, railways were essential for supplying the front line in 1914. The waging of such a war of materiel was dependent on an efficient transport system delivering men, munitions, food, post and the like to railheads from where they could be moved to the front, sometimes by means of light railways. Railways were also used by soldiers going home on leave, and on occasions for large-scale troop movements such as the redeployment of German divisions from Russia to France prior to the Kaiserschlact of March 1918. Major railway stations such as the Gare de l'Est were thus highly significant in military terms.

In autumn 1914, many refugees from the battle-zone arrived at the Gare de l'Est. One woman recorded "the lamentable procession of poor wretches" arriving there, "carrying all the possessions that they still have. It is hard to imagine a sadder spectacle". The military controlled both this station and the Gare du Nord. After the flood of refugees had died down, civilians were rarely seen at either. Instead, the stations were filled with huge numbers of soldiers coming home on leave and returning to the front – the Gare de l'Est was the transit point for up to 6,000 men each day in late 1916. In October 1917, five daily leave trains came into the Gare de l'Est, and six left for the front. An official and unofficial infrastructure grew up around this and other stations, not only in Paris but in London, Berlin, and in other major cities across Europe – military police posts, canteens, bars, brothels (and large numbers of "freelance" prostitutes), and shady dealers where soldiers could get much needed funds by (quite illegally) selling their equipment. Voluntary agencies proliferated: at the Gare de l'Est, among others, the American Red Cross operated a "Soldier's Restaurant". Not surprisingly, as soldiers arrived at the station on trains that were not equipped with lavatories, one soldier recalled that, on arriving at the Gare de l'Est, "you are always greeted by the fading odour of steam and coal, mixed with the scent of urine".

OPPOSITE: Newly mobilized soldiers on board a train leaving the Gare de l'Est in August 1914. By this point, some 2.9 million French men had been mobilized.

ABOVE: Crowds watch reservists departing from the Gare de l'Est in August 1914. The terminus of a railway network running eastwards through France, it was a major staging post for troops heading to the Front.

03 German *Pickelhaube*

The *Picklehaube* ("spiked bonnet"), the helmet of the soldier of Imperial Germany, came to symbolize German militarism and was first introduced into the Prussian army in the 1840s. The version in use in 1914 was made of leather, lacquered black, with a metal spike rising from the centre. It was adorned with a brass front plate, commonly the Imperial eagle, but with many variations. The Imperial army consisted of contingents from many different states, and helmet plates of Bavarian troops, for example, bore the Bavarian coat of arms. Artillery helmets had a ball rather than a spike. The lower part of *Uhlun* (lancer) helmets resembled the *Pickelhaube*, but rose to form the classic square-topped *czapka* (lance cap).

Usually worn with a cloth cover on active service, the *Pickelhaube* rapidly fell victim to the British naval blockade. Supplies of leather could no longer be imported, and so *ersatz* (substitute) helmets of lacquered steel and other materials were produced.

Military fashion tends to reflect military success, and following the victory over France in 1870–71 the army of Germany was

Ausdauer, Kraft und Energie

Kola-Dallmann

Dallkolat

Geit 25 Jahr beim Militär bewährt

recognized as the world leader. Many armies adopted the Prussian style. Marking the shifting of military reputations, British soldiers dressed in a broadly French style before 1870, with a *képi*, but adopted German fashions in subsequent years. Ironically, the colourful full dress of many British infantry regiments in 1914 featured a spiked helmet that bore a distinct family resemblance to that worn by their enemies, and was an unspoken criticism of the performance of their

allies in a previous war! Fortunately, this uniform was replaced by khaki and a soft, peaked cap on the Western Front.

The *Pickelhaube* was a favourite "souvenir" of Allied troops (this word entered the English language during the war). There are many photographs of British soldiers with captured or looted spiked helmets, and many eventually found their way into military museums. On the Eastern Front, on occasions when German troops were sent to reinforce their Austro–Hungarian allies, characteristic items of uniform such as the *Pickelhaube* were concealed to avoid alerting the Russians to their presence.

Although the spiked helmet is synonymous with the German soldier of the First World War, it was gradually replaced by the more prosaic *Stahlhelm* (steel helmet), on general issue from early 1916 onwards. The "coal scuttle" steel helmet offered more protection to the head, and in a modified form came to symbolize the German soldier of the Second World War. The *Pickelhaube* did not vanish from the battlefield entirely. Officers continued to wear it in 1917, albeit with the spike removed (the spike identified the wearer as a high value target to Allied snipers). By 1918 it had disappeared from the front lines, although it continued to be sported by officers in rear areas. Like the equally emblematic French *képi*, which was replaced by the steel "Adrian" helmet, the *Pickelhaube* proved unsuitable for the new conditions of trench fighting. Thus the demise of the Pickelhaube is a potent symbol of the emergence of mass industrialized warfare.

OPPOSITE: A German poster from the First World War advertising candles, which emphasized their "Endurance, Strength and Energy".

ABOVE: A German *Pickelhaube* with the Imperial eagle emblem on the front.

04 Proyart's Arc de Triomphe

The Arc de Triomphe, located on the Place Charles de Gaulle in Paris, is a symbol of French military glory. Finally completed in 1836, it is a monument to Napoleon I and his army, and after the First World War, the French Unknown Soldier was buried beneath the Arc. An eternal flame burns in memory of those French soldiers killed in both world wars who have no known grave.

The unwary traveller can be surprised to encounter, in a small village in Picardy, a miniature version of the Arc de Triomphe. Many similar communities chose, in the aftermath of the war, to have a statue of a *Poilu* in greatcoat and Adrian helmet. But Proyart chose to model its war memorial on the grand monument in Paris. It is as if a tiny community in Norfolk or Arkansas had based their war memorial on Nelson's Column in Trafalgar Square or the Washington Monument in Washington D.C. Under the arch is a statue of a *Poilu*, with a foot symbolically treading on a German helmet. Updating Petain's battlecry at Verdun, *"On les aura!"* ("We'll get 'em"), the memorial bears the words *"On les a"* ("We got 'em").

Proyart was one of many towns and villages that, through a geographical accident, found itself in the war zone. The French and Germans fought an action there in August 1914. Four years later, in the aftermath of the Battle of Amiens, a sharp action took place around the village. A British war correspondent recorded that when 10 Australian Brigade, supported by tanks, came close to Proyart "the enemy's machine-gun fire was so heavy that the Australians did not attempt to proceed ... The [subsequent] advance ... was difficult and tedious". Proyart was taken when pressure on the flank forced the defenders to withdraw. By that stage of the war, the local population would have been compulsorily evacuated, "under terrible conditions", to Germany or Belgium, adding to the vast number of French and Belgians displaced from their homes since 1914.

The fate of French and Belgian civilians under German occupation is yet another example of the brutality and violence inherent in a total war like the 1914–18 conflict. As French historians Stéphane Audoin-Rouzeau and Annette Becker have written, "A genuine reign of terror was instituted as of 1914 and maintained throughout four years of conflict ... The idea was to keep people in a state of shock with the systematic use of exceptional, violent measures, based on a desire to humiliate." Food was in short supply, and very expensive when available. French civilians – who were mainly women, children and older men (as men of military age would have been called up for the army in 1914) – lived in a permanent state of fear. Armed German soldiers were everywhere. Movement was restricted by strictly enforced pass laws. Hostages were taken, reprisals inflicted. Many civilians were conscripted for forced labour. Some 120,000 Belgians were shipped to Germany to work in war factories in 1916–17. An American recalled seeing Belgian forced labourers. They were "skeletons, with blue flesh clinging to their bones, too weak to stand alone, too ill to be hungry any longer. This was only a miniature venture into slavery, a preliminary to the epic conquest and enslavement of whole peoples in 1940, but it seemed hideous and unprecedented to us in 1917."

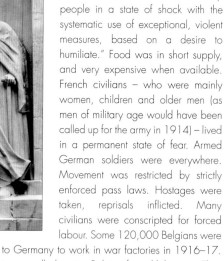

As this quotation indicates, there were strong continuities between the behaviour of Imperial Germany and its Nazi successor when it came to the treatment of occupied peoples. The Kaiser's Germany was not, in this instance, consciously genocidal, but it was bad enough.

OPPOSITE: This panel, *Le Départ*, depicts a soldier saying goodbye to his family before leaving for the front.

ABOVE: The Proyart Memorial stands on ground donated by the Normand family, who lost their only son in the war. It includes a replica of the Arc de Triomphe in Paris, which honours those who have fought and died for France.

05 Tannenberg Memorial

The German victory over the Russians in East Prussia in August 1914 was laden with symbolic value. Although the battle was fought near the town of Allenstein, it was given the name "Tannenberg" after a wooded hill some miles away, where in 1410 the Teutonic Knights had suffered a decisive defeat at the hands of an alliance of Poles and Lithuanians. This was a powerful use of propaganda that linked current struggles against a Slavic enemy to those of the past.

Tannenberg 1914 was not a decisive victory in terms of numbers. The Russian army was large enough to absorb losses of some 50,000 dead and wounded, and 90,000 prisoners. In the short term, it went on to achieve military success against the Austro-Hungarians, and as late as 1916 the Russians launched the "Brusilov Offensive", which initially achieved striking success. Yet Tannenberg was an important psychological victory. It laid to rest Germany's fears that the "Russian steamroller" would remorselessly advance from the East while the bulk of its army was engaged in Belgium and France. Moreover, the confidence of the Russian government in its army received a blow, and Britain came to see that Russia and France needed the direct support of British troops on the ground, thus pushing London towards greater involvement on the Western Front.

After the war Tannenberg, above all other Eastern Front battles, took on a highly symbolic role. It was important that the German forces had been under the nominal command of General (later Field Marshal) Paul von Hindenburg, a national hero (although his subordinates Erich Ludendorff and Max Hoffman had greater influence on operations). Moreover, Tannenberg came to be seen as the epitome of German military excellence, the prime example of where skilful generalship

and manoeuvre had defeated sheer numbers. Because the battle had been in response to the Russian invasion of East Prussia, it could be presented as defensive, important at a time when German aggression and responsibility for the war had been enshrined in Article 231 of the Treaty of Versailles, the so-called "War Guilt Clause". It was also symbolic of the Teutonic victory over Russian "barbarism", a motif that became particularly important after Hitler came to power in 1933.

In 1927, a memorial to the battle was opened. It had taken three years to build, and Hindenburg was present at the laying of the foundation stone. Designed by Walter and Johan Kruger, it resembled a castle. It was octagonal in shape, 100 m (325 ft) across, with eight towers, 23 m (75 ft) tall, connected by walls that were 6 m (20 ft) high. The monument contained not one but twenty "unknown soldiers" – the remains of men killed in the battle. Atop their tomb was a 12-m (40-ft) high cross. The Nazis transformed the Tannenberg Monument into Hindenburg's tomb. His status as national hero had been further enhanced by his time as the President of Germany – he had appointed Hitler as Chancellor in 1933. In August 1934, the unknown soldiers' tomb was replaced by one in which Hindenburg and his wife were interred, in Hitler's presence. Thus the Tannenberg Memorial became a symbol of National Socialism, linking Hitler's regime with past glories.

In January 1945, the Soviet Red Army was advancing into East Prussia, and the German authorities removed the remains of Hindenburg and his wife and partially destroyed the monument. After the war the territory on which it stood became part of Poland; "Allenstein" became Olsztyn. Today, the few ruins of the monument give mute testimony to the destruction of the Germanies of Hindenburg and Hitler.

OPPOSITE: Horses lie dead among the remains of a Russian ammunition column destroyed outside Puchalow, East Prussia. German forces had been grossly outnumbered in the battle, the ratio of Russian to German soldiers being 29 to 16.

ABOVE: This aerial view of the Tannenberg Memorial was taken in 1933. In August of that year, the Nazis held a demonstration there

to commemorate the battle. They were able to do so because the Polish Government allowed them to travel through the Polish Corridor to reach it.

OVERLEAF: The unveiling of the Tannenberg Memorial on 18 September 1927. Hindenburg stands in the middle.

06 Big Bertha Howitzer

The opening German attack of the First World War struck at the formidable Belgian fortress of Liège on 4 August 1914. General Otto von Emmich's Army of the Meuse was tasked with storming the bastion as a necessary preliminary to the invasion of France and Belgium. By 7 August, this composite force of six infantry brigades managed, with heavy losses, to push between the defences east of the river and enter Liège regardless of the fact that 11 of the 12 forts ringing the city still held out. At this point an enormous Krupp 420-mm howitzer came into play. Supported by eight Austrian 305-mm Skoda siege mortars, the howitzer mercilessly shelled the remaining forts into submission during 13–16 August. Fortress commander General Leman was discovered stunned in the shambles that had once been Fort Loncin. "I was taken unconscious," he told his captors; "be sure to put that in your dispatches." The opening phase of the Schlieffen Plan, its first major obstacle effectively reduced to a heap of smoking ruins, commenced the following day.

The 420 mm howitzer had its origins in the Russo-Japanese War (1904–05), when the besieging Japanese Army employed 280-mm coastal guns against Russian fortifications at Port Arthur. The demonstrated potential of transportable heavy siege batteries against an established fortress position was not lost on contemporary German and Austrian observers. Drawing on years of experience with the design and development of coastal trench mortars, the Krupp firm introduced the first prototype heavy howitzer (30.5-cm Beta-Gerät) in 1908. Five more years would elapse before a comparatively mobile example was produced. By August 1914, two wheel-mounted "42-cm M-Gerät 14" – popularly known by its literal sobriquet *Dicke* or "Fat Bertha",

normally rendered into English as "Big Bertha" (supposedly in honour of steel and armaments heiress Bertha Krupp) – were ready for service with the western armies. Test-fired the previous February at Kummersdorf proving ground in the regal presence of a delighted Kaiser Wilhelm II, the 75-ton monster howitzers required a combined crew of 280 men to maintain a fire rate of 10 rounds per hour. Firing semi-armour piercing projectiles weighing 930 kg (2,052 lb), it had a maximum range of 12.5 km (15,530 yards). At Liège, the succession of discharged shells were observed to rise to an arc of 1,200 m (4,000 ft) before reaching the target in approximately 60 seconds.

Hailed by the German press as Krupp's *Wunderwaffe* for its remarkable success against the Liège forts, the mobile 420-mm battery went on to support the subsequent reductions of Namur, Antwerp, Maubeuge and other Allied fortresses. In all, 14 M-Gerät's were built and deployed on the western and eastern fronts. Its considerable reputation for fortress demolition was nevertheless somewhat diminished during the long drawn-out battle for Verdun during 1916: there the French forts had been constructed of reinforced concrete and steel, unlike the poorer quality Belgian citadels encountered in 1914, and they successfully withstood serious damage from the squat siege cannon's massive projectiles. The less-than-spectacular results and consequent introduction by both sides of guns and howitzers with longer ranges led to the decommissioning of the *Dicke Bertha* batteries by 1917.

ABOVE: German artillery troops with a shell, 1916. It is inscribed, "Bertha's greetings to Joffre", a reference to the French general.

ABOVE: A "Big Bertha" in firing position on the Western Front, 1915. Artillery dominated the First World War battlefields.

OVERLEAF: German soldiers with a "Big Bertha" in Liège, Belgium on 7 August 1914.

07 French Soldiers' Red Trousers

French soldiers went to war in August 1914 wearing some of the most splendid uniforms of any of the belligerent armies. Elsewhere over the previous decade or so, the tendency had been for colourful uniforms to be kept for home service and the parade ground. The British wore very practical khaki, the Germans field grey, the Austrians pike grey (a greenish shade), and the Russians light khaki, all colours intended to rendered their wearers less conspicuous on the battlefield. This trend was of a piece with the abandonment of close-order tactics in favour of dispersed formations as the range and accuracy of rifles and artillery grew dramatically greater from the mid-nineteenth century. The French were an exception to the rule. Although a sombre "horizon blue" uniform was authorized in July 1914, on mobilization in the following month the infantry wore blue greatcoats, a red *képi* (usually with a blue cover) and red trousers. In the cavalry, the cuirassiers looked very similar to those who had fought at Waterloo, 99 years previously, with their "classical" style, maned helmets and steel breast plates (albeit both worn with a cloth cover); their red trousers were redolent of the Second rather than the First Empire.

French soldiers had worn red trousers since the 1840s. One theory is that they were introduced as a result of the French conquest of Algeria, to provide a market for the red madder dye produced in North Africa. Sixty years later, proposals to reclothe French soldiers in less conspicuous uniforms were rejected, in part because of fears that if the men were forced to exchange their iconic trousers for more prosaic dress, their élan would suffer. In 1913, the Minister of War stated that

"Red Trousers are France". Élan was seen as crucial to the French way of warfare, based on the *offensive à outrance*: the all-out offensive. Inspired by the ideas of Lieutenant-Colonel Loyzeau de Grandmaison and General Ferdinand Foch, this saw moral factors – highly motivated soldiers imbued with the will to conquer and, of course, the spirit of the offensive – as the key to success on the battlefield. At the strategic level, the primacy of the offensive was reflected in Plan XVII, which was put into effect in August 1914. The French have often been ridiculed for this fixation on the offensive, but similar ideas of the primacy of *the offensive* and the critical role of morale were held by all armies in 1914. The lesson of recent military operations, such as the Russo-Japanese War (1904–05), seemed to be that in spite of the destructiveness of modern firepower, attacks could prevail provided they were delivered by determined troops with high morale. As historian Paddy Griffith argued, this emphasis on moral factors seemed "solidly based in the psychological and racial sciences of the day".

The result of the French approach to the Battle of the Frontiers in August 1914 was casualties in the order of 200,000, including in excess of 4,700 officers, who had suffered from leading from the front. In fighting on 22–23 August 1914, 3rd Colonial Division lost 11,000 out of 16,000 men. By the end of 1914, 400,000 French soldiers had been killed.

One eventual result of the vast losses was that the exotic Second Empire uniforms of the French army were replaced in 1915 by clothing of less conspicuous "horizon blue" colouring. This sartorial change was paralleled by the adoption of more realistic tactics that were to make French troops formidable opponents on the deadlocked Western Front.

Patience, Courage, Espérance
Mon cœur est près de toi

Myosotis

76

EME

OPPOSITE: French soldiers rest in the forest during the First Battle of the Marne, September 1914. The army did eventually replace the red trousers as part of the move to a less conspicuous uniform.

ABOVE "Patience, courage, hope / My heart is close to you" reads the copy on this card. It is worth remembering the patriotic significance of the traditional uniform: "Abolish red trousers? Never! Red trousers are France!" declared Eugène Etienne, the French Minister of War in 1913.

◼ 08 Belgian Machine Gun dog

Horses and mules were not the only quadrupeds to take their place on the battlefield. Belgian army machine-gunners used pairs of dogs, Belgian mastiffs, to pull the wheeled carriages on which the weapons were transported. Dogs were much used for transport in Belgium. A contemporary work claimed that a 50-kg (110-lb) dog could pull a load of up to 400 kg (880 lb) and that the dog was "intelligent and docile, and puts all his heart into serving his master faithfully under all circumstances … on the march, and under fire, one can rely on his working till absolutely exhausted or mortally wounded".

Despite being a significant part of the coalition that defeated Germany, Belgium played a role in the First World War that is often overlooked. Neutral in 1914, Belgium had an army of 117,000 men organized into six infantry divisions and one cavalry division – about the same size as the initial British Expeditionary Force. The Schlieffen Plan directed the main axis of the German advance through Belgium, and the Belgian army, although initially overwhelmed, recovered to fight alongside French

and British forces and delay the German advance. On 25 October, the canal locks at Nieuport were opened, halting German attacks on the River Yser but inundating fertile ground – a tangible symbol of Belgium's will to resist the invader. By the time stalemate set in on the Western Front in mid-November, most Belgian territory had been captured by the Germans. Both the capital, Brussels, and the main port, Antwerp, had fallen. Ypres was the only major Belgian city that remained out of German hands. This was a factor in the tenacious Allied defence of the awkward "Ypres salient" during the war.

King Albert I of the Belgians commanded his armies in person, maintaining his headquarters at La Panne, on the coast. Having lost most of his country, Albert himself declared that "the Army was practically the only remaining emblem of Belgian nationality". Casualties were extremely difficult to replace and Albert husbanded his troops, refusing to commit them to the bloody attritional battles of 1915–17. Albert maintained a semi-detached position vis-à-vis the coalition. It is conceivable, if not likely, that the Germans could have reached a compromise peace with Belgium. This would have placed the rest of the coalition in a very awkward situation. But the Germans – who had stripped industrial plants from Belgium, and shipped Belgian forced labourers back to the Reich – never pursued this option with the seriousness it deserved.

During the final Hundred Days campaign in 1918, the Belgian army joined in the Allied offensive. King Albert commanded the Flanders Army Group (GAF), with a French officer, General Jean Degoutte as his Chief-of-Staff. The British Second Army, under General Sir Herbert Plumer, formed part of Albert's command, and eventually took on a spearhead role. On 28 September the GAF in front of Ypres advanced right across the old 1917 battlefield, which Allied troops had struggled across for three-and-a-half nightmarish months, in a single day: Belgian troops captured Passchendaele Ridge, with the British taking Messines. Thereafter the Belgian army's inexperience showed itself, particularly in logistic matters. When King Albert entered his capital, Brussels, at the head of Belgian, British, French and American troops on 22 November, this represented a political as well as a military triumph, a reassertion of Belgian national sovereignty and independence.

OPPOSITE: This illustration of dogs dragging machine guns was printed in the French newspaper *Le Petit Journal* before the war, on 8 June 1913. Dogs were easier to handle than pack horses, and their lower profile enabled them to stay close to the guns in action.

ABOVE: A gunner stands alongside two Belgian Mastiffs, both muzzled and harnessed to the carriage of this Maxim gun, 1914.

09 French Adrian Helmet

Attired for frontline service in Sam Browne belt, heavy field boots and oil-skin trench macintosh, Lieutenant-Colonel Winston Churchill gazes with inimitable bulldog defiance from beneath the protruding visor of a French Adrian helmet in an iconic photograph dating from late 1915. His political career seemingly in ruins as a result of the Gallipoli fiasco, the future prime minister was appointed to command the 6th Battalion Royal Scots Fusiliers on the Western Front. Displaying that celebrated maverick approach to all things, he had, in addition to a Colt 1911 automatic pistol and portable bath with boiler for heating water, managed to obtain an example of the distinctive "Casque Adrian" as part of an already cumbersome officer's kit. Head protection thus assured, Churchill wore this unique acquisition until his short-lived time at the front ended with a return to the uncertain realm of politics in May 1916.

Consisting of four separate metal components (front visor, rear visor, bowl and deflector crest), leather liner, corrugated tin liner band and adjustable chin strap, the Casque Adrian or M15 steel helmet was, when compared to the basin-like British Brodie "tin hat" or the markedly gothic German Stalhelm, a striking combination of Gallic functionality and style. Its design and development originated with the urgent need to protect the head from low-velocity shrapnel balls discharged with lethal effect by exploding artillery shells. The noticeable increase in skull-related injuries led to the conclusion that some sort of standard-issue steel headgear might greatly reduce fatal casualties in the trenches. Equally, consideration of mounting casualties sustained in large-scale offensives and the consequent need to conserve the nation's dwindling manpower resources contributed to the growing demand for what would be the first modern combat helmet.

Based on the ornamental brass helmet worn by the Parisian fire brigade, the Casque Adrian (named after its designer Intendant-General August-Louis Adrian) was officially adopted for service in the spring of 1915. It was fabricated from mild steel and weighed only 0.765 kg (1 lb 11 oz.), with a four-part riveted seam construction that created potential weak spots which were almost wholly absent from the stamped steel process employed to manufacture weightier British and German designs. Comparatively cheap and easy to make, the new helmet provided sufficient protection against shrapnel. Painted in a matte blue-grey or khaki finish, it was adorned with easily identifiable badges indicating arm of service. The infantry and cavalry wore a flaming bomb (or grenade); the élite chasseurs, a bugle; gunners, crossed artillery barrels; classical helmet and cuirass for engineers; and an anchor badge for colonial troops. Over three million M15s were produced before the armistice. Affectionately known as the "blue hat" to African-American units brigaded into French formations, Adrian's ubiquitous helmet also saw service with Belgian, Italian, Russian, Romanian and Serbian armies during the First World War, and a modified version was used by the French army of the Second World War. Its lasting legacy as an emotive symbol of France's struggle for survival is best expressed by the pink granite demarcation stones that mark the limit of the German advance in France and Flanders. Surmounted by carved representations of an Adrian or Brodie helmet, depending on the army that held the sector, they bear the moving inscription: "Here the invader was brought to a standstill".

OPPOSITE: Maurice Létang, a soldier of the 19th Battalion Chasseurs, took this view of a machine-gun post in a trench at Melzicourt, France in 1916. The village of Servon-Melzicourt was entirely destroyed by the fighting.

ABOVE: The Adrian helmet was lighter than its British and German equivalents.

◼10 War Bonds

War Bonds were a financial mechanism used by all belligerent governments to raise money to fight the First World War by getting their citizens to lend to the government. The bonds offered a "fixed" but low return on the funds invested, but did provide a safe and secure form of saving for the general population. In the United Kingdom, they were primarily aimed at the working-class (whose wages were paid weekly) and lower-middle classes (whose salaries were paid monthly), many of whom had not had any spare money for savings before the start of the conflict. As the war progressed, the demand for labour increased and the working population expanded. The government became concerned about the rise of inflation and consumer spending. War bonds encouraged the habit of saving and a sense of being a "shareholder in the Empire", which in turn provided the government with fiscal capital to fight the war and also limited the danger of wartime inflation within the economic system.

Germany issued nine war loans, at half-yearly intervals. The most enthusiastic level of take-up came in March 1916, with 5.2 million subscribers. It has been argued that the less enthusiastic response to the September 1916 loan reflected the fact that the confidence of the German middle-class had begun to waver at a time of heavy losses at Verdun and on the Somme. In all the German war loans raised "100,000,000,000 marks, or two-thirds of the war cost". In historian David Stevenson's words, "The European middle classes proved willing to gamble with their own prosperity as well as with their children's lives".

British war bonds were available in a range of denominations, so that all classes in the United Kingdom and in the Empire should be able to afford to purchase a "War Savings Certificate". Advertising posters, which were phrased like an instruction, and other written material constantly stressed the patriotic nature of the purchase and the duty of each citizen to support both the government and armed services in time of conflict. The popular mass media of silent film and cartoons was used to promote their sale in *There Was A Little Man and He Had A Little Gun* (1918), in which the symbols of Great Britain, John Bull with his bulldog, face down the Kaiser and Hindenburg, with the help of war bonds. Garish posters appeared at banks, post offices and on large bill-boards, forming a visual display around the temporary platforms erected in many town squares to raise funds for various "Battleship" or "Tank Weeks".

When the United States joined the First World War in 1917, the posters produced by the American government to raise "Liberty Loans" stressed the beastly nature of the Prussian and the "Hun" in general, but also reinforced the sense of pride and honour that purchasing a Liberty bond would bring to all citizens, and that indeed it should be a duty to do so, if one could not enlist to defend one's country. The Canadians issued posters to "Buy Victory Bonds" with the images of a female winged angel and a Union Jack flag. War bonds were purchased by millions of people and the posters which promoted them provide evidence of how the First World War entered everyday domestic life.

THE TANK TOUR

BUY NATIONAL WAR BONDS (£5 TO £5000) AND WAR SAVINGS CERTIFICATES 15/6

OPPOSITE: This Austrian poster from 1917 depicts a soldier holding a grenade, ready to go "over the top". The question asks simply: "And you?"

ABOVE: A British poster featuring the ever-popular tank. Note that it seeks to appeal to investors with only modest sums to contribute.

OVERLEAF: A rally in Trafalgar Square in London to promote the sale of war bonds, December 1917. A tank was a draw for the crowds.

National War Bonds SOLD HERE

⒒ Ross Rifle

The much-maligned and inefficient series (Mk I, Mk II, Mk III) of .303 calibre Ross rifles were formally adopted by Canadian military authorities in the decade before the First World War. It was designed and aggressively marketed by Scottish inventor and entrepreneur Sir Charles Ross, but its subsequent poor performance in the wet and muddy conditions of France and Flanders was followed by almost wholesale replacement with the battle-proven British Short Magazine Lee Enfield in 1916.

The Ross rifle had its origins in the refusal of the British, during the height of the Second Anglo-Boer War (1899–1902), to allow the manufacture of Lee Enfields in Canada. This unexpected manifestation of wartime Imperial discord provided a welcome opportunity for Ross to present his weapon as a readily available alternative to the British government's choice of service rifle. Gruelling testing of the rival designs occurred on the windswept Plains of Abraham outside Quebec in August 1901; the result was that the Lee Enfield pattern proved, with the notable exception of range accuracy, far superior to Ross's straight-pull action design.

The latter's explanations for his rifle's many shortcomings were nevertheless accepted by Canadian ordnance officials in order to keep Militia Minister and enthusiastic Ross rifle advocate Sir Frederick Borden content. Thus the Ross rifle, despite reservations expressed by London and in other militia quarters, was officially accepted for Canadian service in March 1903.

Complaints dogged the Ross rifle throughout the period leading up to 1914. The earliest, filed by the Royal North West Mounted Police commissioner in 1906, cited "many weak points" including an eye injury sustained when the bolt assembly blew back into the shooter's face. One critic scathingly claimed, "it kills as much behind as in front".

Making use of a wide variety of political connections and a demonstrated willingness to address the increasing clamour by implementing a major overhaul of the original design allowed Ross to weather the storm and maintain his lucrative contract with the Canadian government.

The Canadian armed forces were almost wholly equipped with the Mark III variation at the outbreak of war

in August 1914. This new design, introduced earlier that year, included an extended box magazine and rear sight mounted behind the charger bridge instead of the barrel. On 10 August, Militia Minister Sam Hughes ordered a further 30,000 units to equip the assembling Canadian Expeditionary Force. Consequent deployment on the Western Front in early 1915 quickly exposed inherent weaknesses in the chosen service rifle. It was in the immediate aftermath of the German gas attack at Ypres (22 April 1915) that the dubious value of the Ross rifle was first exhibited on a large scale with deadly consequences; comprehensive weapon jams resulted from the all-pervasive muck of the battlefield and extensive use of British ammunition not manufactured to more exacting Canadian standards. The need for standardization commenced in an unofficial capacity when hard-pressed Canadian soldiers discarded their useless rifles for Lee Enfields gathered from British dead and wounded. Official recognition took more time. In the shadow of Canadian pride and nascent nationalism, the Ross rifle continued to have some advocates back in Canada, but it was replaced by the Lee Enfield in September 1916. The discredited rifle nonetheless remained popular with snipers due to the undeniable accuracy that barely compensated for its questionable acceptance and issue.

OPPOSITE: Two sergeants (standing) instructing soldiers on a firing range. Sniper teams usually consisted of a sniper and a spotter, and for them the Ross rifle proved accurate. It was during the First World War that sniper teams proved their worth, their ability to demoralize troops meaning that they had significant impact.

ABOVE: The Ross rifle was simply inadequate for use in the trenches: its screw threads couldn't tolerate dirt, which often jammed the weapon open or closed. Always more popular with politicians than frontline soldiers, it was withdrawn in 1916.

◼12 Barbed Wire

Barbed wire was one of the pieces of "low technology" that helped create deadlock. The other was the spade, used to dig holes which offered some protection against enemy fire. By contrast, an attacker had to expose the whole of his body as he advanced to attack a trench, and barbed wire presented a further obstacle that had to be negotiated. Being faced by belts of uncut wire was a sadly common experience of British infantry on the First Day on the Somme, 1 July 1916. One Highland infantry man recalled, "I could see our leading waves had got caught by their kilts. They were killed hanging on the wire riddled with bullets, like crows shot on a dyke."

Wire obstacle erection and maintenance, one of the many onerous routines of trench warfare, were dependent on wiring parties that would enter no man's land under cover of darkness, lay out wood or steel corkscrew pickets (2 ft 8 in [81 cm] or 3 ft 6 in [1.07 m] in height) and connect them with wire strands reeled-out using burdensome spools obtained from supply dumps. This dangerous task – sometimes carried out within yards of the opposing trenches – required equal measures of patience and skill. Special tools (padded wooden mallets, reinforced gloves, manual winches, wire cutters, etc.) were distributed to expedite the process. Ideal placement was generally 18 m (20 yards) from the front trench with another entanglement situated 35–45 m (40–50 yards) ahead to keep enemy bombers at bay.

Wire fields varied greatly in composition and extent, those protecting the vaunted German *Siegfriedstellung* or "Hindenburg Line" consisting of successive tracts of up to 90 m (100 yards) in depth. The British relied on the "standard double apron fence" as their primary obstacle configuration.

Generally composed of one or more parallel wire and picket barricades reinforced with random coils of wire, it was the "basic building block" upon which their equivalent fields were constructed. Relatively easy to replace and often sowed in a way that "killing zones" could be established for the benefit of defending machine-guns and artillery, barbed wire provided a cheap and effective defence.

Like so many other tactical problems, solutions appeared in time. While simple wire cutters could be effective (see Wire Cutters, page 150), one effective mechanical barbed wire crusher was introduced in September 1916 in the form of the tank. The British Number 106 fuse was another. Previously, wire cutting had been attempted by 2-in mortars, which could work well but had only a short range and in 1916 experienced an alarmingly high proportion of "duds", or firing shrapnel shells timed to burst at the optimum distance above the wire. The 106 was a "graze" fuse, sensitive enough to explode on contact with wire. Combined with the high-trajectory plunging fire of the howitzer, which proved to be more effective for wire cutting than the flat-trajectory field gun, the 106 fuse had provided a partial solution to the problem of barbed wire by the spring of 1917. Nevertheless, attacking infantry helplessly caught up on the wire remains a powerful image of the First World War, as expressed in a famous soldier's song:

"If you want the old battalion, I know where they are,
They're hanging on the old barbed wire.
I've seen them, I've seen them, hanging on the old barbed wire,
I've seen them, I've seen them, hanging on the old barbed wire."

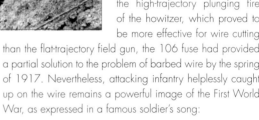

OPPOSITE: Barbed wire is strung across a trench, where French soldiers are lined up for inspection, 1916. By the war's end, a vast quantity of barbed wire had been laid across a front some 645 kilometres (400 miles) long.

ABOVE: Barbed war defences at Quéant, part of the Hindenburg Line, the German defensive position, 1918. The difficulty of crossing barbed wire was one reason for the introduction of a new battlefield weapon: the tank.

13 Lebel Rifle

When France went to war in 1914, its infantry were armed with the *Fusil Modèle 1886* – better known as the "Lebel" rifle. Born from the ashes of defeat in the Franco-Prussian War (1870–71), the "Lebel" was the world's first small-bore, smokeless powder military rifle. With this ground-breaking weapon, the French Republic gained a fleeting technological edge in the race to develop a modern and efficient long arm. Previously, official adoption of bolt-action rifle designs was, more or less, based on keeping pace with advanced models produced in Germany. It was with the acceptance of the 1886 Model Lebel into French service that German small-arms manufacturers found themselves scrambling to come up with an equivalent challenge to this latest entry into the pre-1914 European small-arms race. The Lebel was a generally accurate, dependable and robust mainstay of the French army for many years, from Algeria to Indochina, the Marne to Verdun and beyond.

The advanced Lebel rifle had its technological roots in the almost simultaneous inventions of smokeless gunpowder by the

French chemist Paul Vieille in 1884 and the advanced small-bore "full metal jacket" cartridge by a Swiss officer, Eduard Rubin. In January 1886, War Minister General Georges Boulanger, with a remarkably astute recognition of the likely impact on future small-arms development, urgently requested that these revolutionary discoveries be incorporated into the design of a new service rifle. The desired prototype was, from drawing board to evaluation, subsequently produced in less than five months – an almost unheard of feat for any of the ponderous military bureaucracies of the day. Erroneously named after Lieutenant-Colonel Nicolas Lebel, who contributed to the design of its component flat-nosed projectile, the *Fusil Lebel* was officially adopted on 22 April 1887. Its revolutionary mechanics, contrived and tested by controllers Albert Close and Louis Verdin at the state weapons factory at by Châtellerault, created quite a stir. Incorporating a turn-bolt action of rather conventional construction, the rifle featured, in addition to the state-of-the-art 8mm calibre and encased smokeless bullet, an eight-round tube-fed magazine running the length

of the barrel and forestock and it was this that drew the most attention when potential rates of sustained individual fire were taken into account. Surmounted by the intimidating needle-like, 46-cm (18-in) *Épée-Baïonnette Modèle 1886* (known as "Rosalie" to the *Poilu*), the Lebel at 1.72 m (5 ft 8 in) was longer than the height of many of the soldiers that carried it. It went into immediate production at the Third Republic's three main state arsenals (Chatellerault, Saint-Etienne and Tulle). Approximately 2,880,000 units were manufactured in a 53-year period from 1887 to 1940.

Any advantage gained by acceptance of the cutting-edge design proved, as with all innovative military technology, to be somewhat transitory. With the introduction of the *Gewehr 1888* or "Model 1888 commission rifle", Imperial Germany once again took the lead in military firearms development, although a slightly improved version of the Lebel was produced in 1893. This 1886/93 model *Fusil Lebel* remained the standard French infantry rifle at the outbreak of war in August 1914, despite being outmoded by latter designs. One problem lay with the way that the magazine was constructed, which tended to unbalance the weapon as rounds were fired. By 1918, men armed with the Lebel were only one part of the infantry team. Like other armies, the French evolved sophisticated infantry tactics that also incorporated grenades, rifle grenades and automatic weapons.

OPPOSITE: This machine turned the buttstocks of the Lebel rifles, which were being manufactured in America by 1917, the date of this photograph. The Lebel was durable and reliable, making it popular with troops despite its small sights and a tube magazine that took time to reload.

ABOVE: This Lebel rifle was made in 1888 and much of the original bluing remains. Below it is a first pattern bayonet, designed to be mounted below the barrel.

Alfred Leete's "Lord Kitchener" poster

Lord Kitchener's stern, luxuriantly moustachioed face and pointing finger, along with the words "wants YOU", feature on what is quite possibly the most famous poster of all time. Designed by the illustrator Alfred Leete (1882–1933) and issued in September 1914, it gave birth to a number of copies. To this day it remains iconic, its fame extended through many parodies. Back in the First World War, James Montgomery Flagg took the basic idea but replaced Kitchener with a top hatted, goatee-bearded "Uncle Sam", the slogan reading "I want YOU for US Army". This design, too, was hugely influential and popular, being parodied savagely in anti-war posters during the Vietnam War. Leete's "Kitchener" also had an influence on the Italian artist Mauzan's design for a war-loan poster. Featuring an Italian soldier clutching his rifle and pointing dramatically at the viewer, it had the caption "Do your whole duty!". Posters were widely used as a means of mobilizing civilian populations to participate in the war effort, an essential facet of waging total war: the British Parliamentary Recruiting Committee issued some two million by the end of March 1915.

Field Marshal Earl Kitchener of Khartoum was appointed Secretary of State for War for War shortly after the outbreak of hostilities. A national hero who had spent much of his adult life in the far reaches of the Empire, he was a somewhat secretive man and a serving soldier who did not find it easy to work with professional politicians in Asquith's Liberal Cabinet. He clashed with the likes of Lloyd George and by the time he died on 5 June 1916, drowned when the ship he was travelling in struck a mine, he had been stripped of some of his power. But in September 1914, his prestige was immense. His decision to raise a mass army from civilian volunteers transformed British strategy. Gone was the idea of Britain relying primarily on sea-power and financial muscle, while keeping the army small and relying on her allies to do most of the land fighting. "K of K" believed that the war would be long, not short. It would be an attritional struggle, which might be decided by "Kitchener's Army" taking the field in about 1917, by which time the armies of allies and enemies alike would be exhausted. Kitchener's insights were largely accurate, but ultimately his strategy failed. The realities of coalition warfare meant that the new armies had to be committed in support of her allies long before 1917. However, Kitchener's foresight was important in providing Britain with an army big enough to make a vital contribution to the defeat of Germany on land.

By the end of 1915, 2,466,719 volunteers had joined the army. Ironically the influence of Leete's famous poster in hurrying men to the recruiting office has been overrated. September 1914 saw the best recruiting figures of the entire war: 462,901 men volunteered. Although Leete's design was used on the cover of a magazine on 5 September 1914, it appeared in poster form only at the end of the month. Recruiting in October plummeted to a figure of 169,862, and the surge of recruiting in September 1914 was never repeated. Faced with a crisis in keeping up the strength of the army, conscription was introduced in 1916.

BRITONS

"WANTS YOU"

JOIN YOUR COUNTRY'S ARMY!

GOD SAVE THE KING

Reproduced by permission of LONDON OPINION

Printed by the Victoria House Printing Co., Ltd., Tudor Street, London, E.C.

OPPOSITE: Lord Kitchener, the Secretary of State for War, leaving the War Office in London on 2 June 1916, just three days before his death. By this time, Kitchener's power was waning.

ABOVE: This image first appeared in black and white on the cover of the London *Opinion* magazine on 5 September 1914. Its equally famous copy "Your Country Needs You" was the work of Eric Field, a writer for Caxton Advertising.

▪ 15 Sir Douglas Haig Toby Jug

S ome senior First World War British generals achieved celebrity status, with their image appearing on postcards, badges, in cartoons, and even on toby jugs. The toby jug, a pottery vessel in the shape of a seated person, was first made in Staffordshire in the mid-eighteenth century. The name may come from a poem of that period about a soldier with a punning name: "Toby [a toper is a heavy drinker] Philpott [i.e. fill pot]" – described in a mid-eighteenth century song as "a thirsty old soul". A toby jug could make a political statement. In 1899, during the Second Boer War, the French firm of Saareguemines produced a head-and-shoulders treatment (technically, a "character" jug) of Paul Kruger, the President of the Transvaal. To many in Britain and the Empire, Kruger was an arch-villain, but he was a hero to opponents of British imperialism elsewhere in Europe and in the United States. During the First World War, patriotic British manufacturers produced toby jugs of, among others, Sir John French, Lord Kitchener, David Lloyd George, Admiral Sir John Jellicoe, and of course Sir Douglas Haig.

The toby jug of Douglas Haig (1861–1928), the most controversial British general of the Great War, repays careful study. It was based on a design by Sir Francis Carruthers Gould (1844–1925), a famous political cartoonist and satirist of Liberal persuasion. The toby jug, made by Royal Staffordshire Pottery, is 26.5 cm (10.5 in) in height, and it shows Haig clutching a jug painted with the Union Flag while sitting perched on a small tank. The handle of the toby jug is formed by an aeroplane propeller. Inscribed on the base are the words "push and go" – a contemporary phrase denoting energy and dynamism.

In part, Haig's poor popular reputation rests on the idea that he was a horse-obsessed technophobe. This view is highly inaccurate. The toby jug depicts Haig as a general on top (literally) of the latest technology. The tank made its debut at the Battle of Flers-Courcelette on the Somme in September 1916, the year before this toby jug was made. Haig was a strong supporter of the tank, and also, as the propeller suggests, of the Royal Flying Corps. He was a keen supporter of machine guns (contrary to myth) and a staunch backer of artillery, which was the cutting-edge technology of the war. In 1915, he had championed the development of chemical weapons, structuring his plan for the Battle of Loos (25 September) around the use of poison gas. At Loos, Haig expected too much from primitive technology, and the attack failed; much the same criticism could be made of his expectations of tanks a year later. So receptive was Haig to technology, that he considered the potential of a death ray, only later to discover that he had been taken in by a charlatan.

Perhaps Haig's greatest achievement was to oversee the transformation of the large but poorly trained army of 1916 into the highly effective war-winning force of 1918, a process that involved the incorporation of advanced technology and the evolution of doctrine and tactics to harness it.

PUSH AND GO FCG

OPPOSITE: Haig commanded the British Expeditionary Force from December 1915 until 1919. One of the most successful generals in British history, he is also one of the most controversial.

ABOVE: Eleven military leaders and politicians were immortalized as toby jugs in World War I, and only 350 copies of the Haig toby jug were made during its years of production (1915–1920).

OVERLEAF: Wounded French soldiers tended to at a farmhouse after the 1915 Champagne Offensive. The simultaneous British Battle of Loos led to Haig becoming Commander-in-Chief of the British Army on the Western Front.

16 Rum Jar

One of the most welcome sights in British trenches during the First World War was an earthenware grey and brown coloured jar stamped with the initials "S.R.D." This probably stood for "Supply Reserve Depot", although sources differ. These initials were jocularly interpreted by soldiers as meaning "Soon Runs Dry" or "Seldom Reaches Destination", the latter in reference to dark suspicions that rear area troops helped themselves to rum destined for the front line. The rum tot had to be consumed there and then, in the presence of an officer, to prevent it being hoarded. Some very unpopular teetotal officers objected to issuing their men with alcohol and instead provided an innocuous substitute. Often rum was administered on a large spoon, or sometimes added to tea. The official ration was one sixteenth of a pint (30 millilitres), a quarter of a gill, but as historian Alan Weeks has pointed out, soldiers actually received roughly half of this amount. Rum could give a soldier "Dutch courage". Opinions differ on how important alcohol was in maintaining morale and helping soldiers cope with the fear and stress of battle, but it certainly played a role.

One major difference between the First World War and earlier conflicts was the hugely increased exposure of soldiers to acute danger. Except in very specific circumstances, such as siege warfare, soldiers had fairly rarely been placed in life-threatening situations for prolonged periods. Battles, although dangerous and terrifying, generally lasted for a period of hours, after which soldiers would enjoy comparative safety. The long range and enhanced lethality of First World War era artillery, combined with the trench deadlock and the introduction of bomber aircraft, meant that soldiers had to cope with high levels of stress for long periods. The result was a dramatic increase in what would now be termed "psychiatric casualties", inaccurately known then as shell shock.

However, some things could ameliorate the stress. One factor was paternal leadership by officers and NCOs. Lack of this in the French army contributed to the serious mutinies that broke out in spring 1917. Rest and relaxation, and little luxuries like tobacco, tea and coffee were important. The connection between home front and fighting front was crucial. Morale invariably dipped when mail was late. In 1918, German soldiers' morale was also damaged by getting letters from home telling of the hardships, such as food shortages, being suffered by their families. Conversely, a sense of fighting for "home" could be a powerful and positive element in troop morale. Home leave was also an important factor.

Finally, patriotism and belief in the cause, which often intertwined with simple self-interest, should not be underestimated as an influence on morale. Serbs, French and Belgians fought to defend their homeland, as British and Dominion troops fought to defend theirs, at one or two removes. During the Gallipoli campaign, Turks were fighting on their own soil. Even Germans could believe that they went to war to prevent encirclement and a Russian invasion. One reason why working-class British soldiers fought was to prevent the social, political and economic gains of the last few decades from being taken away from them. Rum played a part in maintaining morale, but it was far from being the only factor.

OPPOSITE: Troops in France issued with their rum ration, 1916. The ration was issued during or after the dawn "stand to".

ABOVE: The abbreviation "S.R.D." probably stands for "Supply Reserve Depot" – though soldiers interpreted it variously as "Seldom Reaches Destination", "Service Rum Diluted" and "Soon Runs Dry".

17 Soap

Cleanliness and hygiene were of vital important to all armies fighting in the combat zones of the First World War; with so many men living in crowded and unsanitary conditions for long periods of time, any type of infection or infestation could undermine both the morale and effectiveness of a fighting unit. The British made special provision out of the line for mobile bath-houses and cleansing stations, which washed and sprayed uniforms to kill and remove the lice that cause epidemic typhus and their eggs, always a great cause of concern.

There was also a stress on personal cleanliness and many soldiers of all ranks requested soap from their families to supplement issued items. The commercial soap manufacturers of the time, who made brands such as Pears', Lifebuoy, Sunlight and Wright's Coal Tar created sophisticated marketing campaigns (using posters and newspaper advertisements) which emphasized the purity of their products and the patriotic duty of families to provide extra comforts for the troops. One advertisement for Sunlight soap claimed "The British Tommy" was "The cleanest soldier in the world". Mothers and wives were often featured in these advertisements, the provision of soap being an extension of their domestic duties and an expression of their affection. An advertisement with the heading "For Her Boy at the Front!" depicted three women making up a parcel: "Only the BEST is good enough [,] that is why she always includes in her parcel a few tablets of Pears' Soap. Thoughtful gifts of this kind mean so much to the brave boys fighting for England and Home".

Smell is one of the most powerful triggers of human memory; the gift of soap from home may have reminded the recipients of ordinary civilian life, but evidence also exists that many returning solders could no longer tolerate the sight or smell of the red toilet soap Lifebuoy, which contained carbolic acid, a disinfectant that gave the soap a very distinctive smell. This ingredient was the reason it was used widely in hospitals both on wounded patients and for general cleaning purposes.

Other items frequently requested by soldiers included toothpaste, tooth brushes and foot powder, for the prevention and treatment of "Trench Foot", a particularly severe medical problem on the Western Front. The condition is caused by soldiers having to stand for hours in cold, waterlogged trenches. Cuts or grazes could quickly become infected and if left untreated this would cause gangrene (the death of living tissue due to lack of blood flow), which could require the foot and often part of the leg to be amputated. The only effective treatment was prevention, by keeping feet warm and dry; this required changing socks several times a day and their careful washing and drying, together with boots. The British army implanted a rigorous foot inspection scheme, with officers examining their men's feet. Poor foot care could result in loss of leave or disciplinary action. From 1917 onwards, this practice was followed by the United States Army, which, as part of its hygiene policy issued its troops with the new Gillette "safety" razor instead of the "cut throat" razor. This also created a demand in the British Army and helped to change shaving habits forever.

LIFEBUOY SOAP

DON'T FORGET
to send HIM a tablet of
LIFEBUOY SOAP
It Cleans and Disinfects.

THESE POST CARDS CAN
BE OBTAINED HERE FREE.

LEVER BROTHERS LIMITED, PORT SUNLIGHT.

OPPOSITE: The text on the front of the postcard (bottom right) reads: Said the bold Grenadier, "To me it is clear Disease is a dangerous foe; So I'll lead the attack, LIFEBUOY SOAP in my pack, My body with HEALTH all aglow."

ABOVE: This block of soap was issued in a German hospital to Private H. H. Gurdin, a British prisoner of war captured after being badly wounded on 7 March 1918.

◼18 French 75-mm Field Gun

The First World War, especially on the Western Front, was dominated by one weapon. Despite popular belief, this was not the machine gun. Artillery was the king of the battlefield, causing more casualties than any other weapon. Perhaps the most famous artillery piece of the war was the French 75-mm calibre gun, *the Canon de 75 Modèle 1897*, or "*Soixante Quinze*". Some 21,500 were produced, 17,500 during the First World War. Served by a six-man crew, the 75mm threw shells (High Explosive or shrapnel) out to a maximum range of 6,900 m (7,500 yards) and in its day it was a revolutionary weapon.

Artillery had been devastating enough in earlier periods of history. Napoleon, a gunner by background, had made effective use of massed gun batteries. But from the mid-nineteenth century a series of technological developments greatly increased the lethality of artillery. The introduction of breach loading, rifled, steel guns firing High Explosive with smokeless propellants made the guns of 1890 much more formidable than their predecessors of Napoleon's day. However, the introduction of the French 75-mm in 1897 was a step-change. It solved the problem of recoil. Previously, every time a round was fired, the gun was thrown backwards. It had to be laboriously manoeuvred back into position before it could be fired again. Recoil thus reduced the rate of fire and the accuracy of the gun. The 75-mm used a hydraulic system which absorbed the recoil, and so the gun snapped back into place, with the barrel

still trained on the target. This eliminated the need to re-lay the piece, and meant that it could fire an unprecedented 15 accurate rounds a minute. It came into service with the French army in 1898 and gave French artillery a distinct advantage, gaining almost legendary status in the process.

The 75mm proved highly effective against German infantry in the open in the initial battles of 1914. By that time other nations had developed equivalent weapons, such as the British Ordnance 18 pounder Q. F. ("Quick Firing") gun, and the German 77-mm (properly, 7.7-cm FK 96 n.A). Added to machine gun and even rifle fire (the infantryman could fire faster, further and more accurately than his equivalent a generation earlier), the battlefield in 1914 was an unprecedentedly lethal place. The response was recourse to the spade, with infantry digging down to provide a measure of protection against the massive weight of firepower. Thus trench warfare came to the Western Front, the *Soixante Quinze* playing a major role in bringing about tactical deadlock.

Under the new battlefield conditions, the 75mm, like its British and German equivalents, proved to be less effective. Under conditions of siege warfare, much heavier guns were needed to pound enemy positions. However, in the mobile operations of 1918, the *Soixante Quinze* once again came into its own as a remarkable field gun. In 1915, the gun was immortalized in the 'French 75', a cocktail invented in the New York Bar in Paris.

OPPOSITE: French 75-mm field guns in operation during the Second Battle of the Marne, July 1918.

ABOVE: The 1897 75-mm field gun. The flaps at the bottom of the shield were lifted up during transportation.

■19 Turkish Pith Helmet

The Turkish fighting man had no great reputation in 1914. In the recent First Balkan War (1912–13) the Turks had suffered a series of defeats, and consequently the Ottoman Empire had been forced to yield significant territories to its enemies. The unstated assumption behind the attack by British and French Empire forces at the Dardanelles in 1915 was that the Ottoman forces would not put up much of a fight. Indeed, Sir Edward Grey, the British Foreign Secretary, candidly admitted that it was hoped that the appearance of a powerful force off the Ottoman capital, Constantinople, would provoke an uprising in the city which would overthrow the Turkish government. This pessimistic view of the capabilities of the Ottoman soldier was unfounded. "Johnny Turk", or "Little Mehmet", proved to be a tenacious enemy, and the Ottoman army possessed a level of military effectiveness that came as an unpleasant shock to its opponents.

The Turks of Anatolia provided the backbone of the army of the multi-ethnic, polyglot Ottoman Empire, but other nationalities, such as Arabs and Armenians, also served, in addition to irregular units of Kurds and Caucasian Turks, among others. The record of non-Turkish troops was mixed. Arab units fought extremely well at Gallipoli in 1915, but from 1917 onwards, desertion to the enemy became a serious problem. At the outset of the war, many Armenians took the opportunity to desert to the Russians in order to fight the Ottomans. From before the war, the Turkish army had been heavily influenced by the Germans; German doctrine and equipment was prevalent, and German officers and NCOs served in Turkish units. However, as historian Edward J. Erickson has recently shown, there was a much more equal relationship between the German and Ottoman high commands than many historians have depicted.

As a result of pre-war military reforms, Turkish soldiers wore a khaki uniform with a *Kabalak* – a sort of pith helmet, constructed from a cloth wrapped tightly around a light frame; this was the headgear most closely associated with the Ottoman army of the First World War. Officers sometimes war a sheepskin *kalpak*, and Arab head-dress and even the pre-1909 red fez were not unknown. Later in the war, some Ottoman troops were equipped with German-style "coal scuttle" steel helmets. Depending on the period of the war and the unit in which a soldier served, uniforms and equipment ranged from very good to dire. Boots were often a problem. British and Anzac soldiers at Gallipoli recorded enemy infantrymen with strips of cloth bound around their feet, or even going barefoot.

The Ottoman army's offensive into the Caucasus in late 1914, although initially alarming their Russian enemies, was ultimately a failure. By far the most successful Ottoman campaign was the defence of the Gallipoli peninsula in 1915–16 against the invading Anglo-French forces. Defending their homeland, often inspired by their Muslim faith, harshly disciplined, and commanded by a number of competent Ottoman and Turkish officers, ordinary Turkish soldiers gained wary respect from their enemies for their sheer toughness. Later, unsuccessful campaigns, such as those in Palestine (1917–18), showed that the Allies had become more effective than the Ottomans, not least by applying the lessons of the Western Front. But during the First World War "Little Mehmet" generally belied his reputation as a poor soldier, instead showing himself to be a formidable opponent.

OPPOSITE: Turkish soldiers in Cairo, wearing Enver Pasha helmets. Prisoners of war, they are being marched away by the British.

ABOVE: Three turkish reserve cadets: an infantryman (left), cavalryman (centre) and a member of the signal corps.

Body Armour

The growing power of gunpowder weapons meant that body armour had all but vanished in Europe by the end of the eighteenth century. The exceptions were some cavalry regiments, such as the French, Saxon, and Russian cuirassiers of the Napoleonic Wars. However, at the turn of the twentieth century the increased deadliness of rifles, machine guns and artillery had prompted military thinkers across Europe to consider the possibility of reintroducing some form of combat armour. In early 1914, the British Army experimented with large bullet-proof steel shields, but they proved too heavy and difficult to move. The outbreak of war in August 1914 prevented further trials.

The heavy casualties suffered in 1914 and 1915 prompted British, French and German designers to give serious thought to the creation of new body armour. The British Experimental Ordnance Board tested a wide variety of materials for the purpose, including various combinations of thick rubber, dense fabric and steel plate. Fabric-based body armour showed promise, but

was found to degrade very quickly in the wet and muddy conditions found in the front line. Metal body armour was inevitably heavy and seriously reduced a soldier's mobility. Steel plates incorporated into a fabric jacket offered a compromise between the two materials, but they remained heavy and were costly to produce. Ultimately, the Board decided that a combination of practical drawbacks, financial costs and limited protective value made body armour impractical for widespread use. Nevertheless, small quantities of armour were made available for specialist troops from 1917 onwards.

In the absence of widespread army-issued armour, private manufacturers produced protective suits for those with sufficient purchasing power. This typically limited ownership to officers or better-off soldiers, but in some cases local groups or concerned family members would purchase armour for distribution to the front line. This privately manufactured body armour came in a variety of designs, but all suffered from the drawback of being heavy, while few offered truly reliable protection.

In the same period, the German army experimented with metal composite armour that included full body suits and face-plated helmets that caused wearers to resemble warriors of a bygone age. British troops nicknamed these large suits "lobster armour". The heavy kit offered protection, but its great weight made it a specialist item. Various versions of the armour were issued to troops in static positions, such as machine-gun crews and snipers, where it proved of some value in battle. In 1917, the Germans devised new metallic armour that covered the body and groin. The suit weighed approximately 9 kg (20 lb). This body armour was distributed to units of *Sturmtruppen* (storm troops) in 1918, but the weight of the breastplate made it a poor match for troops expected to carry out mobile and rapid attacks.

Ultimately, despite substantial testing and experimentation, neither side was able to devise a truly effective set of body armour in the First World War. The combined drawbacks of cost, weight, durability and uncertain protective value seriously limited the potential of personal armour until the advent of Kevlar in the 1960s.

OPPOSITE: Three Irish Guardsmen wear captured German body armour to examine a German machine gun. Photographed at Pilckem, site of the opening attack of the Third Battle of Ypres, 31 July 1917.

ABOVE: German helmet and body armour from 1915–16. Note that the armour does not fully enclose the body.

21 Zeppelin

In 1908, H. G. Wells published a novel *The War in the Air*, which portrayed cities being destroyed by airship fleets. Within seven years, enemy airships were indeed dropping bombs on British soil. Just prior to the First World War, as Wells's imaginative fiction suggests, it was by no means clear that the future of manned flight belonged to the aeroplane. The airship – a lighter than air machine consisting of a gas-filled "envelope", at least one "gondola" for the crew, and an engine – predated the Wright brothers' first successful flight in 1903 by some 50 years. Manufacturers in France, Britain and Italy produced airships, but the most famous designer was a German nobleman, Ferdinand, Graf von Zeppelin.

Zeppelin began serious experiments with airships in the 1890s, producing the *Luftschiff* (airship) LZ1 in 1900 and a much-improved version in 1906. The name Zeppelin became synonymous with airships in Germany; and indeed Imperial Germany itself. There was considerable patriotic pride in Zeppelins, with some regarding it as a quintessentially "German" weapon, as opposed to the "French" aeroplane. For all that, the Zeppelin failed to sweep all before it in Germany. Aircraft development continued there, while the Zeppelin was hampered by setbacks including crashes, the sheer difficulty of operating the craft in poor weather and underfunding (airships were expensive: 34 aeroplanes could have been constructed for what it cost to build a Zeppelin in 1914). Nevertheless, both the army and navy retained some faith in lighter-than-air craft.

On 19 January 1915 two Naval Zeppelins – L3 and L4 – were sent across the North Sea to bomb targets in Britain, with a third being forced to turn back. Originally, the target was Humberside, but bad weather meant that East Anglia was hit instead. Great Yarmouth and King's Lynn were bombed, with five people being killed and a number of buildings damaged. The raid caused outrage in Britain, being treated as another example of Hunnish barbarism.

London was first attacked in May 1915 and raids on Britain continued intermittently until August 1918. However, it became increasingly clear that the costs of the Zeppelin fleet exceeded the results it was able to deliver, and from 1916 the aeroplane supplanted the airship as the primary method of bombing. Moreover, British air defences improved and on the night of 2–3 September 1916 Captain William Leefe Robinson of the Royal Flying Corps became the first British pilot to shoot down a Zeppelin in British air space – an act for which he was awarded the Victoria Cross.

Airships proved more useful in the maritime reconnaissance role, having greater endurance than aeroplanes. The Royal Navy used them with some success in protecting shipping from U-boat attack. But as ever, airships were susceptible to the vagaries of the weather. During the Battle of Jutland in May 1916, the German High Seas Fleet received only minimal support from the scouting force of Zeppelins.

The airship proved to be an evolutionary dead-end in military aviation. It was designed to operate in benign environments, and once serious battles began to be fought to achieve air superiority over the battlefield in 1915, it was at a massive disadvantage compared to the aeroplane. Also, as air defences improved, it became less effective as a strategic bomber. But nonetheless, the Zeppelin, with its ability to bring death from the skies to the enemy's homeland, was a potent symbol of total war.

OPPOSITE: This photograph was taken from Hendon of a Zeppelin raid on London on 8 September, 1915. Aeroplanes were also used in raids on Britain later in the war.

ABOVE: *L48* was the last German Zeppelin to be shot down over English soil. It came down in flames on Holly Tree Farm, Therberton in the early hours of 17 June 1917, killing all but three of its 19-man crew.

OVERLEAF: A Zeppelin flying above a river and through smoke from fires smouldering in Balkan terrain.

■22 Leaning Virgin of Albert

Prior to the First World War, the small French town of Albert had achieved a measure of fame as a place of pilgrimage. A medieval legend told how a farmer had discovered a statue of the Virgin and child in a nearby field and stories of miraculous cures became associated with the area. Albert developed a reputation for healing that made it a minor rival to Lourdes. In the late nineteenth century, it was decided to take advantage of this reputation with the construction of an impressive statue atop the basilica, the "Golden Virgin", a representation of Mary offering up the infant Jesus. The Golden Virgin was visible from a great distance and was the first landmark of Albert that would become visible to any approaching traveller.

In January 1915, the Virgin was hit by German shellfire, which knocked it loose and left the statue leaning at a precarious angle to the ground. French engineers secured the Virgin in its unsteady position until it could be formally repaired and it remained in this state when the British took over the area in the summer of 1915. The incongruous sight of the leaning statue immediately generated comment and it gained the nickname "The Leaning Virgin". In 1916 passing Australian troops referred to the statue as "Fanny Durack", a famous Olympic swimmer who had won gold for Australia in 1912, as the statue looked like it was diving into a swimming pool.

However, over time the sight of the Virgin developed a superstitious hold over the minds of many soldiers. The British Army had a strange fascination with the religious imagery seen on the churches of France and Belgium. This, in turn, fed legends amongst the troops. During the Battle of Mons in 1914, there had been widespread and sensational British reports of the appearance of angels on the battlefield. In later years, the imagery would become darker, with persistent rumours of captured British soldiers being crucified by the Germans.

The British developed a legend about the Golden Virgin (apparently shared by the French) which stated that the war would not end until the Virgin fell from her perch. There also seems to have been a general belief that when she did fall, the war would end in defeat for the Allies. The Virgin's commanding position meant that it was also visible from the German side of the lines. Although Albert itself was frequently shelled, there was a degree of superstition amongst the German gunners that whichever side knocked the Virgin off the basilica would actually lose the war.

The Germans captured Albert during the 1918 spring offensive and found the Virgin still in place. German artillery observers used the tower to direct fire, prompting British gunners to target the position and destroy it. In the process, the Virgin finally fell and the remains of the statue were never found. Albert was retaken by the British a few months later and the war ended later the same year.

Following the war, the basilica was rebuilt to match its pre-war likeness and still stands to this day. It is said that during the rebuilding process a British officer wrote to the town chiefs urging them to rebuild the Golden Virgin complete with its lean. Understandably, this suggestion was rejected, but the fact that it was made at all reveals something of the affection that the passing British troops held for the famous landmark.

OPPOSITE: British cavalry pass by the ruins of the Basilica in Albert, France. The photograph was taken in late 1918 after the Virgin had been knocked down.

ABOVE: The ruins of the Basilica, 1916. Five kilometres (3 miles) from the front lines, it was a familiar sight to the British soldiers passing through Albert to fight at the Somme.

◼ 23 Merchant Ship

The merchantman *Clan Mactavish* was carrying cargo, including frozen meat and rubber, from New Zealand to Britain when it was attacked and sunk by the German surface raider SMS *Möwe* off the African coast on 16 January 1916. Launched in 1913, and operated by the Glasgow firm of Cayzer, Irvine and Company, *Clan Mactavish* was a ship of 5,816 tons, 137 m (450 ft) long, and had a speed of 24 km/h (13 knots). Seventeen crew were lost, and the Master, Captain William Oliver, taken prisoner. Statistically, *Clan Mactavish's* loss contributed to the 81,259 tons of merchant shipping (62,645 tons British, the rest Allied and neutral) lost in January 1916. The fate of *Clan Mactavish* was indicative of the dangers faced by merchant seamen in the two world wars. In October 1942, a later *Clan Mactavish* was sunk by a U-boat off the coast of South Africa.

In both world wars, Britain's Achilles heel was its reliance on merchant shipping to bring supplies from overseas. Britain was not self-sufficient in a range of key resources, from oil to food. While by the end of the war home-based factories were turning out truly impressive numbers of munitions, the voracious appetite of the British army for shells and the like could be satisfied only by importing materiel from North America. Neutral vessels, including those of the United States before April 1917, also played a vital role in keeping Britain in supply. In early 1917, Britain came perilously close to being forced out of the war. The ravages of the German U-boats in the Atlantic and coastal waters around the British Isles were at their height, and by April Britain was reduced to a mere six weeks' supply of food. The introduction of the convoy system for merchantmen in May 1917 enabled the Allied navies to gain the upper hand.

In wartime, the merchant seaman's life, which was ordinarily hard and dangerous, was even worse. Hours were long and the work exhausting. Wartime conditions exacerbated these conditions: 14,679 merchant seamen were killed in the First World War. Some were sunk multiple times, and when a ship was sunk, the seaman's pay was stopped. Merchant seamen worked hard and played hard. When in port, heavy drinking, which was central to the culture of the merchant seaman, and to a much lesser extent, sex with prostitutes, were favourite leisure activities. Merchant seamen were not generally under military discipline – although they could be subjected to it under certain circumstances – but rather operated under the discipline that was inherent in seamanship, operating as part of a ship's team. That did not prevent men jumping ship when in port, particularly in the United States, where seamen could be paid far more for doing the same job on an American ship. The crew of the *Chepstow Castle* deserted virtually *en masse* in a US port in 1915.

The men who manned Britain's merchant ships came from many different places. As historian Tony Lane has pointed out, "crews were *normally* cosmopolitan and war made little difference to this". The *Cabotia*, sunk in the Atlantic in 1916, "included Greeks, Italians, Portuguese, Americans, Danes and Norwegians" as well as British in its 74-strong crew. In any case, the category "British" included Indian "lascars", Hong Kong Chinese, and a host of men from other parts if the Empire. As many as "40 per cent of seaman killed in British ships were not natively British". These men have certainly not received the recognition that they deserve.

OPPOSITE: The SS *Clan Mactavish*, which was sunk by the German ship SMS *Mowe* on 16 January 1916.

ABOVE: A British standard built merchant ship in dazzle camouflage. Developed by artist Norman Wilkinson, dazzle did not disguise but rather made it difficult for the enemy to estimate a target's range and speed.

◼ 24 Askari's Hat

European conquests of colonial empires in Africa and Asia in the eighteenth and nineteenth centuries were made possible by the large-scale use of indigenous soldiers. The loyalty of such troops was no less important in allowing European powers to retain their grip on their colonies. The continuing political and military reliability of key non-European units, notably the Sikhs and Gurkhas, was a significant factor in allowing British rule to survive the Indian Mutiny of 1857–58. More than 50 years later, the loyalty of African Askari soldiers to their colonial rulers enabled Germany to wage a guerrilla campaign in East Africa that lasted beyond the end of the war in Europe, and tied down disproportionate numbers of troops from the British Empire, some 160,000 in all.

This achievement looked unlikely in 1914. The Royal Navy isolated Germany's colonies from Europe, so it was almost impossible to reinforce them. It seemed just a matter of time before the Allies conquered them. Sure enough, although the Allies' offensives were no simple matters, German possessions in West Africa had been captured by early 1916. In German East Africa, thanks to a determined commander, Colonel Paul von Lettow-Vorbeck, things were different. His *Schütztruppen* (protection force), never more than 14,000 strong, consisted of 3,000 German troops and 11,000 Askaris. They were reinforced in 1915 by the crew and guns from the German cruiser *Königsberg*, which had been scuttled. Von Lettow-Vorbeck's campaign included an audacious raid into British-held Northern Rhodesia (now Zambia) in 1918. When he surrendered, on 25 November

1918, Lettow-Vorbeck had 155 white and 1,156 African soldiers, together with 137 machine guns.

In 1914, Askaris wore a khaki uniform. Their headgear was a red fez, made of felt, with a back tassel. On active service this was replaced by a "tarbush", a hat consisting of a frame of wicker covered with khaki cloth that extended down the back to protect the wearer's neck. On the front was worn a metal badge of a German Imperial eagle.

During Lettow-Vorbeck's long campaign, uniformity became something of a relative term. A German serving with him wrote of Askaris in 1917. One "had on an ordinary felt hat, and something that had once been a shirt, but it was so tattered and torn that his gleaming black skin showed through". Another wore an "askari cap and neckcloth [i.e. tarbush]" but no shirt; while a third had "an English khaki shirt, but otherwise more or less regulation German uniform", but carried a British rifle.

This ill-dressed force enabled Lettow-Vorbeck to maintain a guerrilla campaign that was far from defeated even when news of the end of the war in Europe prompted him to surrender. His strategic achievement was measured not only by the number of British Empire committed to operations in East Africa, but also by the fact noted by Professor Sir Hew Strachan that at the peak of the U-boat menace in 1917 merchant ships had to undertake "long haul voyages when they were badly needed elsewhere". Lettow-Vorbeck's Askaris had their counterparts in the African and Asian troops deployed by the British and French Empires, who made a major, if little remembered, contribution to the Allied war effort.

OPPOSITE: An Askari patrol in German East-Africa (now Tanzania), 15 July 1915. The men were reporting back after the attack on the Uganda railway.

ABOVE: A fez worn by an Askari serving with the 1st Depot Company of the German Protectorate troops for the Cameroons, at Duala in 1914.

25 Observation Balloon

The use of observation balloons for artillery spotting and intelligence gathering purposes reached its pinnacle during the First World War. The first practical military application of the pioneer Montgolfier brothers' eighteenth-century manned flight novelty was by French revolutionary forces during the Battle of Fleurus in 1794. Widespread use during the American Civil War, Franco-Prussian War, Second Anglo-Boer War and Russo-Japanese War had demonstrated the value of this early "eye in the sky" technology. The balloon comprised a sturdy fabric envelope filled with hydrogen, and the First World War observer took up position in an attached basket and then ascended with the assistance of steel cables to ensure stability. Balloons were rendered extremely vulnerable by their highly flammable content, and it was not until after the Armistice that non-flammable helium was recognized as a safe and suitable lighter-than-air substitute. By 1914, an improved aerodynamic lozenge design and accompanying motorized winch had been adopted by all the major powers.

Ascending to some 900 m (3,000 ft) in height, stationary lines of sausage-shaped observation balloons were a familiar sight on the battlefronts of 1914–18. Such a balloon gave its name to "Sausage Valley", on the Somme. Balloons were often the target for destruction by roaming fighter aircraft, though fatalities amongst designated observers were somewhat alleviated by the issue of parachutes. By contrast, airplane pilots were, more often than not, denied this vital life-saving device by higher headquarters. The almost universal issue of parachutes to balloon officers and men did not always guarantee a descent to safety, as the death of Captain Basil Radford tragically illustrates. Born in 1889, this talented music hall artist – known to Edwardian theatregoers by the stage name "Basil Hallam" or "Gilbert the Filbert, the Kernel of the Knuts" – enlisted in the Royal Flying Corps shortly after the outbreak of hostilities. Assigned to No. 1 Army Kite Balloon Section, he was tragically killed in August 1916 when his balloon broke loose from established moorings before it could be hauled in. Having jettisoned telephone, binoculars, maps and books overboard, Radford stood momentarily poised on the basket edge, a black figure silhouetted against the clear summer sky, before leaping to earth. Unfortunately, the cumbersome pack chute became entangled with the rigging and, to the horror of those watching below, he fell to his death.

The importance placed by all combatant nations on the elimination of enemy observation balloons was epitomized by United States Army Air Service ace Lieutenant Frank Luke. He was second in rank (with 18 confirmed victories) amongst American Expeditionary Forces (AEF) aviators, his unceasing pursuit to destruction of the ubiquitous stationary targets earning this maverick, rough and tumble south-westerner the contemporary sobriquet "Arizona Balloon Buster". The celebrated nickname was in reference to a unique run of aerial victories achieved while flying a Spad XIII. These amounted to 14 balloons and four aircraft during 10 sorties in just *eight* (in the period 12–23 September 1918) days. Luke's luck ran out following the destruction of three more balloons on 29 September, when he was forced down behind enemy lines. Seriously wounded by ground fire, he defiantly emptied rounds from a Colt automatic into approaching German infantry before expiring in the cockpit of the grounded Spad XIII. His balloon-busting career brought to an untimely end, the valiant Luke was posthumously awarded the highest United States decoration, the Congressional Medal of Honor.

OPPOSITE: The observer in this kite balloon is testing the telephone before ascending. The photograph was taken in 1916, at some time during the Somme offensive, from July to November.

ABOVE: A US Army balloon in France, 1918. The ascent of an observation balloon was often the precursor to a bombardment, so it is possible that this is the origin of the phrase "The balloon's going up!", meaning that trouble was ahead.

OVERLEAF: British troops going over the top from the trenches during the Battle of the Somme in 1916. Observation balloons gathered intelligence for operations in the area.

26 *Bouvet*

At about 3.15 p.m. on 18 March 1915, a British officer on HMS *Prince George* witnessed a naval disaster unfold. Watching the French battleship *Bouvet*, he "saw a tremendous quantity of black smoke arise just abaft of funnels on starboard side. Then she commenced gradually to roll towards us, we were about 400 yards to starboard of her. The roll steadily continued until she was keel uppermost then her stern steadily settled down and just as steadily she went under in about 3 minutes from when first struck. It was awful & unnerved us all in the top. There was no time to do anything".

Another Royal Naval officer, Commodore Roger Keyes, thought *Bouvet* had been hit by a shell fired by a shore battery, which had touched off her magazine. "Within a minute of the explosion there was nothing to be seen but a few heads in the water". In fact it is likely that *Bouvet* was hit by a heavy shell, but within a few seconds had also struck a mine, sown by the Ottoman minelayer *Nusrat*. Only about 50 men, out of the ship's company of 710, survived.

Bouvet was part of an Anglo-French naval fleet commanded by Rear Admiral John de Robeck, which was attempting to force its way through the Dardanelles, the narrow strip of water separating the mainland of Asia Minor from the Gallipoli peninsula, which is in Europe. The ultimate aim was to reach the Ottoman capital, Constantinople, and knock Turkey out of the war — perhaps by prompting a revolution in the city.

Bouvet was built in the mid-1890s, being commissioned in 1898. Thus she was a pre-Dreadnought: the launch in 1906 of the eponymous "all big gun" British battleship with steam turbine propulsion had made ships like *Bouvet*

obsolescent. With a displacement of just over 12,000 tons, maximum armour thickness of 18 in (45 cm), and speed of 18 knots (33.3 km/h), *Bouvet* had a main armament of two 305-mm (12-inch) and two 274-mm (10.8-inch) guns. She had a substantial secondary armament, consisting of eight 138-mm, eight 100-mm (3.9-in) and 12 1.5-kg (3.3-lb) guns. The theory was that after long range gunnery, ships would close to administer the *coup de grace* using lighter, more accurate guns capable of rapid fire.

At the outbreak of the war, navies still had substantial numbers of pre-dreadnoughts, and they were used in secondary theatres. Commanders were prepared to take chances with them; the risks taken with the 18 pre-dreadnoughts in attempting to force the Dardanelles can be compared to the care lavished on HMS *Queen Elizabeth*, the state-of-the-art "super dreadnought" that was sent to the theatre. When a pre-dreadnought, HMS *Goliath*, was sunk by a Turkish torpedo boat on 12 May, thus further demonstrating the vulnerability of large warships in inshore waters to such weapons, *Queen Elizabeth* was promptly recalled to home waters, being judged far too valuable to risk.

The battle of 18 March was a clear Ottoman victory. The Allied navies had lost three capital ships (HMS *Ocean* and *Irresistible* in addition to *Bouvet*) sunk and three (HMS *Inflexible*, and French ships *Gaulois* and *Suffren*) crippled. So the decision was made to launch a joint attack on 25 April, with amphibious landings being carried out on the Gallipoli peninsula in order to clear the coastal defences. Thus the land portion of the Dardanelles campaign would begin; it was to be of much longer duration than the naval assault, but from the Allied perspective ultimately no more successful.

OPPOSITE: Shortly before the battle, the waters in the Dardanelles had been mined – a fact unknown to the Allies. The defensive victory of 18 March 1915 is famous in Turkey to this day.

ABOVE: *Bouvet* had been out of date since 1906 and the launch of the Royal Navy's *Dreadnought*. Twenty-nine years old and in poor condition at the time of the battle, she took less than two minutes to sink, for the loss of 660 crew.

■27 Winston Churchill's Cigars

Winston Churchill (1874–1965) is one of the most easily recognizable figures of the twentieth century, and was seldom seen without a cigar. He picked up the cigar-smoking habit in Cuba in 1895, and his favourites included the Romeo y Julieta brands. Never one to deny himself the finer things in life, Churchill made sure that cigars took their place alongside champagne, brandy and fine food as everyday essentials – although he would often let the cigar go out and chomp on the butt. So identified did cigars become with Churchill that the historian A. J. P. Taylor unkindly coined the phrase "cigar butt strategy" to explain First World War British expeditions such as Gallipoli (1915): "Someone, Churchill or another, looked at a map of Europe; pointed to a spot with the end of his cigar; and said 'Let us go there'". This image of Churchill as an amateur strategist, sending men to die almost on a whim, did great damage to his reputation during and after the First World War. Only with his great success as Prime Minister in the Second World War was the memory (mostly) expunged.

The First World War was Churchill's apprenticeship as a warlord. The son of a prominent aristocratic Conservative politician, Winston was regarded as an *enfant terrible* by 1914. He was reviled by Tories as a class traitor for joining the Liberals and pushing through radical social policies, and many of his Liberal colleagues distrusted his judgment as a gung-ho Home Secretary and First Lord of the Admiralty (political head of the Royal Navy). His behaviour in October 1914 reinforced this distrust. Churchill went out to Antwerp, which was being menaced by German forces, and made himself look foolish to his

Cabinet colleagues by offering to take command there – if only he could be made a general. However, this must be set against his prompt reactions in July and August 1914, which ensured that the Fleet was not dispersed at the end of its annual exercise and meant that the Royal Navy was very well prepared for the outbreak of war.

Churchill was one of the principal originators of the Gallipoli campaign, which was intended to strike at Turkey by attacking the Dardanelles, the narrow straits that connect the Mediterranean ultimately to the Black Sea. He certainly deserves criticism for championing what proved to be an unworkable project against professional naval advice; but he was not responsible for the poor execution of the plan. In the Second World War, the ill-conceived and disastrous Norway campaign of 1940, which was his brainchild, showed that Churchill could still be accused of cigar-butt strategy.

In May 1915, Churchill was sidelined from power. Temporarily abandoning politics, he went to the Western Front later that year and commanded an infantry battalion for a few months. Returning to politics, he was an outstanding success as Minister of Munitions in 1917–18, providing the guns, shells, tanks and the like with which Haig's army won the war. It is noteworthy that as he was outside the War Cabinet, his ability to influence strategy or to interfere in other's departments was severely limited.

1914–18 showed Churchill's strengths and weaknesses as a war leader. Intensely charismatic, he was a brilliant organizer, but too often indisciplined and impetuous. The cigar butt was never very far away.

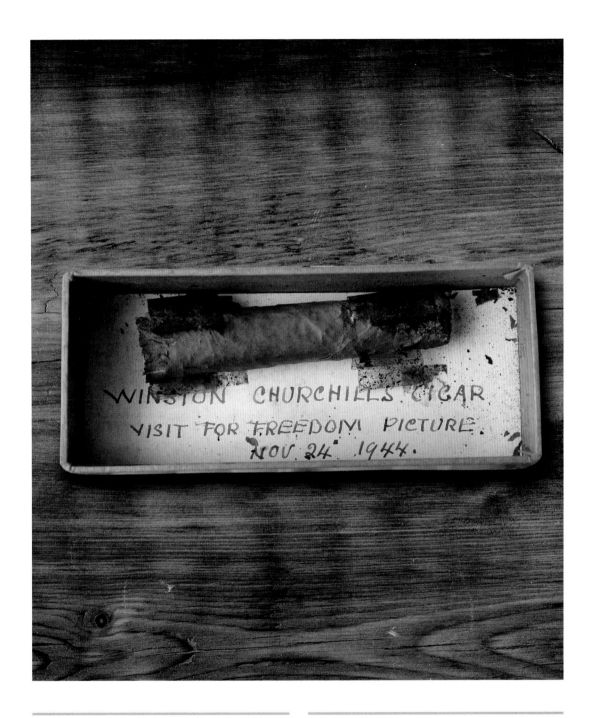

WINSTON CHURCHILLS CIGAR
VISIT FOR FREEDOM PICTURE.
NOV 24 1944.

OPPOSITE: Churchill, plus cigar, leaving the Japanese Embassy in 1914. In May 1915, he would be sidelined from government.

ABOVE: As Prime Minister in the Second World War, Churchill's cigar-smoking habits became even more famous. This cigar stub was collected as a souvenir.

■28 German *Flammenwerfer*

On 30 July 1915, British troops holding the frontline at Hooge, near Ypres, discerned a faint hissing sound emanating from the German trenches moments before cascading sheets of smoke and flame forced the stunned Tommies to abandon their positions in the wake of a follow-up infantry attack. The enemy had managed to gain a footing on a commanding ridge by deft use of a novel liquid fire apparatus, which combined physical with psychological effect. Shocked and dismayed, British high command ordered the vital high ground to be retaken without delay. Repeated efforts to reclaim the lost territory were, however, repelled with heavy loss.

Design and development of the German flamethrower commenced during the first decade of the twentieth century. The pioneer was Richard Fiedler, who collaborated with Leipzig Fire Chief Hermann Reddeman (the latter would become an officer in a flamethrower unit on the Western Front). Their invention evolved into two basic designs: the two-man *Kleinflammenwerfer* and the unwieldy and impractical *Grossflammenwerfer*, which discharged burning fuel oil up to a distance of 40 m (130 ft). The two-man unit, comprised of a firing tube and steel tank, was by far the most commonly used device. Strapped to the back of one man, the fuel-filled reservoir discharged its contents for as much as 18 m (60 ft).

Specialist pioneer battalions were formed to operate with the new weapon. The first field tests occurred near Verdun in late 1914. While patchy in their effect, they nevertheless demonstrated the demoralizing physical and psychological

impact of blistering streams of burning oil when employed against an entrenched enemy.

Hooge was the flamethrower's first notable success. The British, at a cost of 31 officers and 751 men, managed to stabilize their broken line before nightfall, but the lost ground remained in enemy hands in the face of determined counterattacks. This local victory led to widespread adoption of the *Flammenwerfer* throughout the German Army. Normally operating in groups of six, flamethrower teams were most often employed to clear Allied positions at the opening stage of an assault. The Germans launched some 650 *Flammenwerfer* attacks during the war. Their overall effectiveness gradually diminished as initial alarm coalesced into practical defensive measures to deal with the recognized menace. Indeed, the distinct possibility of a well-placed bullet or random shell fragment piercing the weighty fuel cylinder ensured a flamethrower operator's life expectancy was, more often than not, a short one.

The use of flamethrowers – or "liquid fire", as the British called it – was at one level simply the application of technology to the battlefield in an attempt to seek a tactical advantage. But it was also regarded as a "diabolical" weapon by the Allies, of a piece with Germany's use of poison gas and the submarine, and as such part of the moral contest between the two sides. This did not stop the British and French from developing their own flamethrowers, just as they developed their own chemical weapons, but they did so with the moral advantage of not having used them first. This was important in the battle for neutral – especially American – opinion.

OPPOSITE: Cumbersome and difficult to operate, the flamethrower usually held only about two minutes' worth of fuel.

ABOVE: German soldiers training near Sedan, France in 1917. There were usually six men in a team of flamethrowers.

29 Simpson's Donkey

Outside the Australian War Memorial in Canberra is a striking statue of a man with a donkey. Sculpted by Peter Corlett in the mid 1980s, the donkey is depicted as carrying a wounded soldier on its back. The man leading the donkey was known as "Simpson" and the presence of his statue outside an institution that is a combination of national war museum, archive and cenotaph reveals much about how the First World War is remembered and mythologized in that particular country.

Simpson landed on Gallipoli on 25 April 1915 as stretcher bearer with the 3rd Australian Field Ambulance. The popular story has him saving the lives of many diggers, perhaps as many as 300, using a donkey ("Murphy" or "Duffy") to take men from the trenches down the beach. His conduct is seen as so brave that there is a campaign to have him awarded a posthumous Victoria Cross for Australia.

However, "Simpson" was not the man's real name. He was born John Simpson Kirkpatrick in 1892 in South Shields, in north-east England. Rather than an Aussie twang, he would in all likelihood have spoken with a strong regional "Geordie" accent. A merchant seaman, Kirkpatrick seems to have deserted from his ship in Australia in 1910. He enlisted under the name "Simpson" in September 1914, one of a sizeable number of British-born men in the original Australian Imperial Force.

While his conduct on Gallipoli was certainly brave, there is nothing to suggest that Simpson deserved a VC – or even that he did anything above and beyond the tasks carried out by other stretcher bearers. Historian Graham Wilson, who has published the definitive book on Simpson, plausibly suggests that the mythical figure "could well have been an amalgam of Simpson and other men who used donkeys to evacuate lightly wounded men". Certainly, a well-known photograph and a painting based on it, popularly supposed to be of Simpson, are actually of a New Zealand soldier.

The "Simpson" story is wrapped up with the Anzac myth, which the Australian official war correspondent and official historian, Charles Bean, played a large part in fostering. This involves the idea that Australian soldiers are characterized by courage, "mateship" and "larrikinism" (scallywaggery, and disdain for authority). All of these virtues reflect Australian values, which were demonstrated at Gallipoli, popularly regarded as the birthplace of Australia as a nation.

For some Australian nationalists, Gallipoli has a drawback as a foundation myth: it was a campaign fought for the British Empire, at the behest of Britain (and it was also a defeat). In the 1990s, the Kokoda Trail (or track) was promoted as an alternative to Gallipoli. This campaign was fought in New Guinea in 1942, when a small force of Australians fought the Japanese. Kokoda had a number of advantages compared to Gallipoli. It was fought to defend the homeland against Japanese invaders who were threatening to invade Australia proper, and so had none of the unfortunate associations with British imperialism that Gallipoli did.

But while Australian troops fought well under atrocious conditions, it was the failure of Japanese logistics that was the major cause of their failure. Indeed, as leading Australian historian Peter Stanley has shown, the Japanese never had any plans to invade the mainland. In any case, while Kokoda has rightly become better known and an object of national pride, it has failed to displace Gallipoli. As the continuing fame of Simpson and his donkey shows, Gallipoli remains central to Australian national identity.

OPPOSITE: Simpson, shown centre, assisting an unidentified British soldier wounded in the leg. The donkey was known by various names, including "Murphy", "Duffy" and "The Donk".

ABOVE: The sculpture *Simpson and his Donkey*, at the Australian War Memorial in Canberra. Generations of schoolchildren have learned of Simpson's bravery in the weeks before his death.

30 Cossack Uniform

In 1914, the Russian army entered East Prussia for the first time since the Napoleonic Wars 100 years before. Cossacks were in the vanguard. Often wearing a khaki greatcoat and fur cap, their fearsome reputation preceded them and caused panic among the civilian population. While looting, murder and rape was certainly carried out by Russian forces, it seems that this was on a relatively small scale.

"Cossack" is the collective name given to a diverse group of peoples based in the Ukraine and southern Russia who shared a broadly similar horse-based, warlike culture. The Cossacks had become notorious as brigands and mercenaries. As the Russian state expanded its influence in the eighteenth century, it forged alliances with key Cossack tribes, taking advantage of their traditions as mercenaries and rewarding them a degree of status within the empire.

By the nineteenth century, Cossacks retained their semi-autonomous status but had become incorporated into the Russian army. Their culture made them ideal light cavalry. Armed with sabre, lance and carbine, they were capable of fighting mounted or dismounted. They became famous throughout Europe for their role in the Napoleonic Wars; Napoleon himself praised them as the finest light troops in the world, but they also gained notoriety for their brutality. In Russia, their reputation for violence and their cultural distinction from the majority of the population meant that they were often used to suppress civil unrest. They were employed extensively in this role during the unsuccessful 1905 Revolution against the Tsar, with their violent conduct forming a centrepiece of the famous film *Battleship Potemkin* (1925).

Cossacks performed poorly in the Russo-Japanese War (1904–05), prompting one British observer to dismiss them as "pretty well useless for war purposes". In the aftermath of the

conflict, the Russian army retained large numbers of Cossack troops for scouting and skirmishing, but recognized that their formally trained cavalry was of greater value in battle.

Nevertheless, on the eve of the First World War the image of the wild and dangerous Cossack fired the imaginations of other Europeans. The spectre of hordes of Cossacks descending on East Prussia was a vivid propaganda image. In Britain, Cossacks were frequently used as a personification of the Russian army, being seen as untamed yet ultimately noble. Germany also used the image of Cossacks to personify the Russian military, but portrayed them as Slavic barbarians bent on rape and murder.

From late 1914 onwards, the Russian war effort steadily crumbled under a combination of military pressure at the front and social unrest at home. Cossack formations fought throughout the conflict, achieving some notable successes against Austro-Hungarian cavalry in 1914–15 and Ottoman forces in 1915–16. However, Cossack units were amongst the first to join the revolution in February 1917, a devastating blow for Tsar Nicholas II, who had trusted them with internal policing in the past, and a key factor in his decision to abdicate. As the Russian state collapsed, some Cossack tribes took the opportunity to declare their independence. These Cossacks formed the core of the White Russian armies that fought in the Russian Civil War (1917–22), but a minority of Cossacks fought on the side of the Bolsheviks. Bolshevik victory was followed by violent persecution of the recalcitrant Cossack population in the 1920s and 1930s.

However, pro-Bolshevik Cossacks retained their place in the Soviet military and played an important role in the Second World War. The image of the pillaging Cossack, which had proved mostly illusionary in 1914, ultimately became a frightening reality for Germany in 1945.

OPPOSITE: A Cossack sergeant of the Lifeguards Composite Cossacks Regiment, 3rd company, stands in full dress uniform beside his horse, 1914.

ABOVE: A modern reproduction of the Cossack uniform. The uniform was based on traditional tribal dress and had not changed greatly over the previous century.

31 SS *River Clyde*

The Dardanelles campaign of 1915 took place in an area rich in history and myth. In classical times, the Dardanelles, the narrow straits dividing Turkey-in-Europe from Asia Minor, was known as the Hellespont. Here Xerxes, the Persian King of Kings crossed using a bridge of boats in 480 BC. On the Asian bank, a little way inland, lay the site of Troy, which had been excavated by Heinrich Schliemann in the late nineteenth century. For many classically educated British officers, serving where Hector and Achilles had fought was a great thrill. "I only hope I may be able to nip over and have a look at Troy," wrote Patrick Shaw-Stewart of the Naval Division. Some historians have argued that while a public school education produced excellent colonial administrators, and junior infantry officers, it did not equip the leaders of British society to face the economic challenges of the twentieth century. While this argument can be pushed too far, it has some merit.

It was perhaps inevitable that someone – actually Commander Unwin, RN – would come up with the idea of making use of what historian Robert Rhodes James called a "modern Trojan Horse". The idea was for 2,000 troops to be embarked on a collier, SS *River Clyde*, which would be customized by cutting "sally ports" in the ship's sides. It would be run aground on V Beach at Cape Helles, and the troops, having been protected from the defender's fire, would emerge from the sally ports, and get on to the beach. It was a bold idea, which in practice proved to be disastrous.

Fundamentally, the problem faced by the assault troops landing on V beach on 25 April 1915 was the failure to suppress the fire of the Ottoman defenders. To achieve this, a sufficient weight of fire, mainly shells, had to be delivered on to their positions so as to kill or disable them, or at least compel them to desist from using their weapons. This simply failed to happen. As men emerged from *River Clyde*, they saw many men of the Royal Dublin Fusiliers, who had been rowed ashore in "tows", dead or dying. The steam pinnace that was intended to bring lighters into position, which would then form a bridge of boats with planks to allow the men to move from the collier to the beach, broke down. Unwin himself went into the sea and tied the lighters together with rope. As the soldiers of the Hampshire Regiment and the Royal Munster Fusiliers came out of *River Clyde*, they were cut down by Turkish fire. By end of the day, the British had only a toe-hold on V Beach, and elsewhere on Helles. Stalemated trench warfare was about to begin.

It was one of the first amphibious assaults in history to be launched against a coastline defended by an army equipped with modern high-power weapons. Previously, if a landing place was defended, the attackers tended simply to sail elsewhere until they found a more lightly guarded place. At Y Beach on Helles, a small force landed unopposed, but thanks to command problems, lack of initiative and plain incompetence, no advantage was taken of this favourable situation.

Gallipoli stands as an object lesson of the problems inherent in amphibious landings. Planning for an abortive amphibious landing on the Belgian coast in 1917 drew upon the lessons of Gallipoli, but the most thoroughgoing analysis was carried out between the wars by the United States Marine Corps. The ill-fated Gallipoli landings thus had a positive influence on American amphibious operations in the Pacific theatre during the Second World War.

OPPOSITE: Men of the Royal Navy Armoured Car Division prepare for the landings, fixing machine guns in position on the SS *River Clyde* and building protections.

ABOVE: A view of V Beach, taken from the *River Clyde*. On 25 April

1915 boats launching towards the beach took such casualties that the water was red with blood, while the troops left inside the ship heard bullets ricocheting off the hull.

OVERLEAF: The *River Clyde* at V Beach, April 1915.

■ 32 Flying Helmet

The airman's flying helmet became one of the most familiar and distinctive items of uniform during the First World War. Made of leather, and worn with goggles, the helmet was intended to protect the aviator from the elements and was introduced prior to 1914. On their pioneering flight in 1903, the Wright brothers had merely worn their everyday cloth caps, turned backwards, with safety goggles. This style began to be superseded by the familiar close-fitting helmet in the years before the war. The French aviator Louis Blériot wore a woollen variant on his cross-channel flight in 1909. One of the many types used was the leather Spalding helmet, developed for American football, which was adapted for use by pilots. By the end of the war, some sophisticated flying helmets had been introduced. The Dunhill helmet, a British design, incorporated a speaking tube, allowing crew members to shout to each other, and an oxygen mask. Typically, aircrew would wear multiple layers of clothing to protect them from the cold in their open cockpit aircraft; also heavy flying mittens; and a long, heavy coat. Their job was critical to the success of the land battle.

At the beginning of the war, military aviation was in its infancy. By the end, the aircraft was at the centre of a transformation in the conduct of war, so profound that it has been classified as a Revolution in Military Affairs (RMA). Indeed, there is a strong case that only two other RMA have taken place since: the introduction of nuclear weapons, and the computer-based IT RMA, which came to prominence during the 1991 Gulf War and is continuing.

The importance of the military aircraft lay in the fact that it greatly enhanced the capabilities and effectiveness of artillery. Before 1914, indirect fire was rare. Targets needed to be visible in order to be hit. Observers in aircraft were able to spot targets and correct the fall of shots, with the result that gunnery became more accurate and "depth fire", across a wide area, became possible. Gunnery became a more scientific activity, and innovative gunners such as the German Georg Bruchmüller and the Briton Herbert Uniacke established methods of using artillery that long outlived the Great War. This made possible the great bombardments of the later years of the war, such as at the Battle of Messines, 7 June 1917, when the British used 2,266 guns, one for every 6.5 m (7 yards) of front. These bombardments were not only destructive but effective; Bruchmüller's bombardment of British positions on 21 March 1918 involved 6,473 guns, integrated into a sophisticated fire-plan.

While "aces" such as Manfred von Richthofen (Germany – see The Red Baron's Triplane, page 174), the Frenchmen René Fonck and Georges Guynemer, the Englishman Albert Ball VC, and the American Eddie Rickenbacker became famous for shooting down large numbers of enemy aircraft from their scout (fighter) aircraft, the backbone of the air services were the largely unsung pilots and observers of reconnaissance and artillery co-operation aeroplanes. Fundamentally, the job of the fighter pilot was to prevent enemy aircraft from observing friendly trenches while facilitating the observation of the enemy. It was the men flying slow, vulnerable machines such as the British R.E. 8, or the German Halberstadt C.V, rather than the glamorous fighter pilots, who were the key aviators.

OPPOSITE: Eddie Rickenbacker at the controls of his Nieuport 28 fighter plane. The American "Ace of Aces" secured 26 victories.

ABOVE: This British, chamois-lined leather flying helmet dates from c.1920. It is very similar to those in use during the First World War.

33 *Daily Mail* Report of the Shell Scandal

Alfred Harmsworth (1865–1922), created Lord Northcliffe in 1905, was the most successful British press magnate of the Edwardian period and launched the *Daily Mail* in 1896. A new type of middle-brow, right-wing, patriotic paper aimed at a mass market, it rapidly put on circulation. Acquiring more newspapers, Northcliffe was an influential figure by 1915, with strong views on how the war should be conducted. He turned against Lord Kitchener, Secretary of State for War, but his clumsy intervention in politics backfired. On 21 May 1915, copies of *The Times* and the *Daily Mail*, Northcliffe papers both, were burned on the floor of the London Stock Exchange. The normally buoyant sales of the *Daily Mail* plummeted by 200,000 copies in a week. These actions were prompted by the *Mail's* leading article boldly headed "The Shells Scandal: Lord Kitchener's Grave Error". Northcliffe's political press had already had a hand in bringing down H.H. Asquith's Liberal government, but this attack on the hugely popular Kitchener was more than the market would bear.

A coalition had been formed on 26 May, again with Asquith at its head. By the spring of 1915 it had become very evident that a war of materiel was being waged on the Western Front. In this struggle the British army was at a clear disadvantage. The British Expeditionary Force (BEF)'s stockpile of shells, calculated on the basis of expenditure during the Boer War, was quickly shown to be grossly inadequate. The failure of the attack at Neuve Chapelle (10–12 March) was followed by increased concern among the political class about the army's "shell shortage", as it became known, with Field-Marshal Sir John French, commander of the BEF, stirring the pot by means of intermediaries. Although a parliamentary debate was held on 21 April, many were still dissatisfied. In truth, although much could (and later was) done to speed the production of shells, a major munitions industry could not be improvised overnight.

A fresh attack was mounted by the BEF on 9 May at Aubers Ridge. So complete was the failure that French tried to blame the shortage of shells, briefing Colonel Repington, the Military Correspondent of *The Times*. The subsequent coverage in the newspaper on 14 May asserted that "The shortage of high explosive was a fatal bar to our military success." This helped trigger a major crisis that led to the formation of the coalition government – another major factor was the eccentric behaviour of Admiral "Jacky" Fisher, who had resigned as First Sea Lord, the professional head of the Royal Navy, over a dispute with his political counterpart, Winston Churchill. The combination of events seems to have been enough to persuade Asquith that it was time to form a coalition.

Northcliffe, the very model of a newspaper proprietor who enjoyed wielding political influence, had a significant role in these events. The collusion of Sir John French is also noteworthy. French was an enemy of Kitchener, the Secretary of State for War, and he stepped well beyond the bounds of acceptable behaviour for a serving soldier in actively working to undermine the elected government of the country. But in attacking Kitchener, French and Northcliffe overreached themselves. David Lloyd George was appointed to run a new Ministry of Munitions, and made his name as a war leader in the process, while Kitchener remained a key member of the government. If anything, the attacks in his reputation reinforced his hold on public affections. The Shells Scandal of May 1915 demonstrated the power, but also the limitations, of the press in wartime Britain.

OPPOSITE: Taken in January 1915, this photograph shows women munitions workers making shell cases in the Vickers factory.

ABOVE: So popular was Kitchener at the time that this issue badly affected the *Daily Mail*'s circulation. However, the newspaper's sales recovered in time and Northcliffe remained an influential player in British politics.

34 Lenin's Train

On 16 April 1917, a railway train pulled into Finland Station in the Russian capital, Petrograd. On board was a party of 32 Russians returning from exile. They had arrived in their home country thanks to the government of Germany, a state with which Russia was at war. The decision to allow this "sealed train" to pass through Germany and Sweden was taken in order to deliver a strategic blow at Russia; for among the returning exiles was a prominent revolutionary, Vladimir Illyich Ulyanov (1870–1924), better known by his *nom de guerre*, Lenin. Germany hoped to destabilize the Russian Provisional government that had replaced the Tsar's regime the month before. The German ploy ultimately led to one of the defining events of the twentieth century, the Russian "October Revolution".

Lenin had had a long career as a socialist revolutionary, and in 1917 he was in exile in neutral Switzerland. He was a powerful, influential, charismatic but divisive figure within the Russian Social Democratic Worker's Party (RSDWP). Largely as a result, the Party broke into two factions in 1912: the Mensheviks (the "minority", although it was actually the larger of the two) and Lenin's "majority" Bolsheviks. Lenin's ideology was a variant on the theories of Karl Marx, which saw progressive struggle between economic classes as eventually bringing about revolution and the overthrow of capitalism. In contrast to his rivals, he was utterly opposed to co-operation with "bourgeois" groups to bring about a preliminary revolution that could then be exploited by the RSDWP. The situation in Russia did not fit Marx's theories very well, as it was not an advanced capitalist state and lacked the large industrialized proletariat upon which the revolution was supposed to be based, although the rapid industrialization experienced by Russia in the years immediately prior to

the First World War created a growing, and increasingly discontented, working class.

The outbreak of war in August 1914 brought a superficial level of unity to Tsarist Russia. Defeat on the battlefield and the domestic strains of waging the war soon heightened the tensions within the state. Tsar Nicholas II unwisely assumed personal command of his armies in September 1915 and proved ineffectual. Socialist agitators in factories and military units were finding increasingly sympathetic audiences. Discontent with conditions on the home front and the progress of the war grew to such an extent that in March 1917 serious strikes in Petrograd (as St Petersburg had been renamed) led to a rebellion, which included elements of the army. Nicholas abdicated on 15 March, and the Tsarist regime was succeeded by a liberal Provisional government.

Russia entered a period of political instability, with changes of government (as Mensheviks entered the government) and councils ("soviets") of soldiers, peasants and workers filling power vacuums. Earlier, Lenin had called for "Revolutionary Defeatism" as a way of creating the conditions for revolution. Now he saw his chance. Risking the accusation of being a German stooge, Lenin took the sealed train back to Petrograd. He forged an alliance with Leon Trotsky, and pushed for a radical programme of peace and "All Power to the Soviets". Although he was forced to take refuge in Finland, Lenin planned to mount a coup against the government, now led by Alexander Kerensky. He returned to Russia in late October, and on 7–8 November (25–26 October by the Russian calendar) Red Guards attacked and seized the Winter Palace in Petrograd. Lenin emerged as leader of a Bolshevik government. Although his grip on power was precarious at first, Lenin established a regime that was to rule for 70 years.

OPPOSITE: *V. Lenin in the train to Petrograd. April 1917* by Petr Vasilyev. The painting is in an idealized, heroic, Soviet-era style.

ABOVE: The train that carried Lenin to Finland Station in September 1917. Permission to travel through wartime Germany had been difficult to obtain and was granted on condition the train was sealed.

■ 35 Krupp Factory

In the late nineteenth and early twentieth centuries, the name "Krupp" became synonymous with German military might. The steel works founded by Friedrich Krupp in the early years of the nineteenth century grew, under his son Alfred, into an industrial empire, part of which was one of the most important arms manufacturers the world has ever seen. Krupp artillery equipped the Prussian army during the Franco-Prussian War (1870–71) and this established the reputation of the firm, which developed a lucrative export trade. The context of the rise of Krupp was the emergence of Germany as one of the leading industrial powers in the world. Between 1870 and 1913, steel production grew so that it amounted to a significant and growing proportion of Europe's output. By the time of the First World War, Germany had eclipsed Britain as an economic power, with its major rival being the United States.

Although Germany presented an outward appearance of readiness for war in 1914, it was unprepared for the type of war it found itself fighting. Like the other belligerents, it was forced to undertake radical and unexpected mobilization of state and society to match the demands of total war. The "War Raw Materials Office", set up by Walther Rathenau of AEG, played a major role in this transition. In all the belligerent states, established munitions factories like Krupp were joined by many others to churn out the myriad things needed to fight a modern industrial "total" war, although inexperienced firms tended to produce the simpler munitions. The Russian jewellers Fabergé made grenades, for instance. For the likes of Krupp, it was a boom time. As historian Roger Chickering has shown, some parts of German industry "did very well during the war … net profits of the Krupp steel works had increased two and a half times over the prewar average" by 1917.

In August 1916, Germany's mobilization of its workforce and industry for was stepped up. General Erich von Falkenhayn, the de facto head of the German army, was replaced by Field Marshal Paul von Hindenburg and his hugely influential deputy, Erich Ludendorff. Falkenhayn had been one of the few high commanders in any state to contemplate an end to the war that fell short of complete victory. The duumvirate that was appointed in August 1916, and which effectively took over the government of Germany, had very different ideas. The Hindenburg Programme was a hugely ambitious attempt to build a war economy that would sustain the German armed force in a bid for total victory.

In the event, not only did the Hindenburg Programme fail to achieve its aims, the impact it had on ordinary Germans' lives helped undermine support for the Kaiser's regime. The governments of Britain and France, while calling upon their peoples in 1917–18 to bear heavier burdens and endure further losses to win the war, also began a process of what has been called "remobilization": for example by emphasizing democratic war aims and domestic reform. Their counterparts in Germany saw little of the carrot, but plenty of the stick. The failure of their government to do some very basic things, such as ensure that supplies of food reached the cities, contributed to the breakdown of faith in the regime. Imperial Germany collapsed in defeat and revolution at the end of 1918. Although the Kaiser was forced into exile, some other pillars of the Wilhelmine state – such as the Army General Staff and the Krupp organization – survived to play an important role in the resurgence of German militarism under Hitler.

OPPOSITE: The Krupp steelworks and arms factory in Essen, photographed in 1912. The plant had been established a century earlier in 1811.

ABOVE: Indicative of the social changes caused by the number of men conscripted into the armed forces, this photograph shows women operatives making munitions.

OVERLEAF: The First World War was a war of materiel in which industrial production wa s vital to supply the armies at the Front.

36 RMS *Lusitania*

RMS *Lusitania* was a luxury cross-Atlantic passenger liner owned by the Cunard Line. When it was completed in 1907, the size of the ship and the opulence of the accommodation caused a stir and was a major influence on the design and construction of her cross-Atlantic rival, RMS *Titanic*. Both vessels would meet a tragic end.

At the outbreak of the First World War, the Admiralty allowed *Lusitania* to continue her role as a passenger liner on the condition that it would also carry government cargo. In February 1915, Germany announced the implementation of unrestricted submarine warfare, declaring that the waters around the British Isles would constitute a war zone and that any non-neutral shipping in the area, either military or civilian, was liable to be attacked without warning. This was a radical departure from the submarine warfare of the early months of the war, when U-boats had been expected to halt merchant ships and carry out a formal search for contraband before sinking them.

The announcement of the policy had little immediate effect on cross-Atlantic traffic and the *Lusitania* continued her usual Liverpool–New York route. On 22 April 1915, the German embassy in the United States issued a series of newspaper adverts warning American citizens of the risks of sailing aboard the *Lusitania*, and stating that any passengers travelled at their own risk.

On 1 May, *Lusitania* departed from New York on her final voyage. On the morning of 7 May she was some 19 km (12 miles) off the south coast of Ireland when she was spotted by the German submarine *U-20*, which struck her with a single torpedo at approximately 2.10 p.m. The damage was catastrophic and the *Lusitania* sank within 18 minutes. The ship developed a severe list as it sank, which hampered the launching of lifeboats, a factor that contributed greatly to the loss

of life. Of 1,959 passengers and crew aboard the ship, 1,195 perished; 128 American citizens were amongst the dead.

German propaganda justified the sinking on the grounds that the ship was carrying weapons and ammunition. Although the cargo manifest revealed the *Lusitania* was carrying rifle cartridges, the allegation that it was transporting high explosive shells or other war material has never been proven.

The sinking caused international outrage. The vehemence of American anger was such that there was hope in Britain that the United States would declare war on Germany. However, President Woodrow Wilson limited himself to a series of strongly worded notes to the German government, warning that Germany would face "strict accountability" for any further attacks on American citizens. American diplomatic pressure combined with limited military results caused Germany to abandon unrestricted submarine warfare in September 1915.

The sinking of the *Lusitania* became a linchpin of British propaganda, particularly in its attempts to sway American public opinion towards support for the Allies. The incident returned to the forefront of public debate when Germany announced a second unrestricted submarine campaign in February 1917. Wilson, conscious of hardening American opinion on the issue, immediately severed diplomatic ties with Germany and on 6 April 1917 the United States declared war.

"Remember the Lusitania!" became a popular slogan for the American war effort and was featured in numerous recruitment posters. In a newspaper report of 7 July 1918, journalist Phillip Gibbs described an American assault: "The Americans were not tender-hearted; they went forward with fixed bayonets, shouting 'Lusitania!' as their battle-cry … The Germans might well be terrified, for 'Lusitania' is a call for vengeance."

OPPOSITE: *The New York Times* from the day after the sinking of the *Lusitania*. The paper published details of the military cargo – facts withheld from the British public.

ABOVE: The *Lusitania* arriving in New York, 1907. Torpedoed in 1915, the ship sank quickly and only six out of 48 lifeboats were launched successfully.

OVERLEAF: The *Lusitania* steaming into New York harbour, 1907.

■37 Primitive Gas Mask

Looking across No Man's Land at about 5 p.m. on 22 April 1915, Allied soldiers holding trenches in the Ypres salient saw a strange greenish-yellow cloud drifting towards them. It was chlorine gas. In defiance of the 1907 Hague Convention, the Germans had initiated the large-scale use of lethal chemical weapons on the Western Front. The British, French and Canadian soldiers manning the front line had no protective equipment. Urinating on a cloth such as a handkerchief and clasping it about the nose and mouth was a rough-and-ready, and not very effective, form of protection.

Chlorine gas had been developed by a team led by the German chemist Fritz Haber (1868–1934), who was awarded the Nobel Prize in 1918 for work in another area. The gas is heavier than air, and soldiers who had been affected by it suffered from vomiting, breathing difficulties and a terrible burning in eyes and lungs. In large doses it is fatal.

Although chemical weapons had been used on a limited scale before 22 April – the French had used tear gas (xylxl bromide) in August 1914, for instance – Germany's decision to use lethal gas was evidence that a "total war" mentality was setting in. In total war, moral constraints on the use of weapons, and on the targets selected, are disregarded, usually as part of an incremental process. By making the first use of chemical warfare, the Germans ensured that they would have to bear the moral opprobrium. This, taken alongside such acts as the sinking of the passenger liner *Lusitania* just a few weeks after the first release of gas, gave credence to Allied propaganda that Germans were barbarians.

The failure of German High Command to provide an effective reserve, thus throwing away what was by definition a unique opportunity to capitalize on the surprise occasioned by the first chemical attack, must rate as one of the greatest blunders of the War. The Allies recovered from the initial shock and setback, and attritional fighting followed (the Second Battle of Ypres) until 25 May. The Germans had gained ground, but the Allied lines remained intact.

The Allied response was two-fold. First, gas protection equipment was introduced. At first, this was nothing better than a cotton pad soaked in chemicals. One British version was known as the "Black Veil", consisting of a length of veiling material that held in place a piece of cotton soaked in a chemical solution. In July 1915, this was succeeded by the gas helmet invented by a doctor from Newfoundland, Cluny Macpherson. This consisted of a canvas hood with transparent eyepieces and a tube through which the soldier breathed. Treated with chemicals that absorbed chlorine, this was a pioneer gas mask. Second, while loudly denouncing the German use of gas, the Allies quietly got on with developing their own chemical weapons, now that the enemy had conveniently opened Pandora's box. General Sir Douglas Haig, commander of British First Army, saw the potential of gas as a shock weapon. Thus the British attack plan at Loos (25 September 1915) was predicated on the use of gas. Unfortunately, the primitive nature of the wind-borne gas weapon meant that the direction and speed of the wind was critical. As neither proved favourable, the use of chemical weapons proved ineffective, or even counterproductive: in some sectors the gas blew back onto the attackers. For all that, gas was firmly established in the armouries of the belligerent armies by the end of 1915.

OPPOSITE: French troops in the trenches with basic protection against poison gas: goggles and facemasks. The impact of gas lay less in the number of casualties it caused and more in the terror it provoked.

ABOVE: A German soldier with protection from gas. Men who survived a gas attack were often left blinded or severely incapacitated.

38 Mills Bomb

With its serrated cast iron body, steel striker lever and retaining pin, the Mills bomb "No. 5" became the standard issue British grenade of the First World War. This instantly recognizable "pineapple" was patented by inventor William Mills of Birmingham in September 1915. Over 70 million – including two subsequent variants – were produced during the conflict. A proficient thrower could lob what one wartime instructor termed as the "dark, satanic Mills" approximately 15 m (50 ft) with a reasonable degree of lethal accuracy that was further extended by fragmentation following detonation. Mills bomb components functioned with notable mechanical efficiency. The internal striker spring was held firmly in compression by the ringed retaining pin. Removal of the pin released the striker lever, which ignited the detonator cap at the base. The resultant discharge of its Baratol filling (a formidable mixture of TNT and barium nitrate) was extremely deadly, especially in confined spaces.

The new hand bomb, based on its convenient size, relatively light weight (765 g / 1 lb 11 oz) and overall reliability from a user safety standpoint, was ideal for trench fighting and quickly found favour with combat troops in France and Flanders. A number of minor modifications to the original design simplified the process of mass production in a Great Britain retooling for industrial war. By May 1915, four months before government acceptance of the Mills patent, the "Grenade Hand No. 5" was universally adopted for service, although it remained in short supply until the end of the year. Waterproofed bombs ("23 M" and "36 M") with an alternative explosive filling were also manufactured with the often harsh conditions encountered in the Mesopotamian theatre of operations in mind.

British military authorities, concerned over the large number of bombs being tossed about the trenches, produced a small pamphlet (*The Training and Organisation of Grenadiers*) in summer 1915. This first primer of "bombing party" organization and tactics was similar in content to those issued to French and German armies. Potential grenadiers or "bombers" (the Grenadier Guards successfully argued that the term "grenadier" should be reserved for members of their regiment) were to be selected from the fittest and most aggressive soldiers. Height and reach were desirable, so preference was to be given to tall men. The first step in training was to overcome fear of the Mills by its user. This was to be followed by repeated practice of a series of established "action drills" in which the basic unit was an NCO, two bayonet men and two bombers. The importance of the Mills bomb to British tactics can be gauged by the fact that the new platoon organization introduced into British and empire infantry units in early 1917 had a section of bombers, one firing rifle grenades, one of riflemen and one of Lewis Gunners.

One of the most murderous engagements involving the ubiquitous Mills grenade and the trained personnel tasked with its use took place at "Munster Alley" near Poziéres on the Somme in July and August 1916. The vicious ding-dong bomb fight for the tactically important communication trench forced the attacking British and Australian troops to expand some 73,000 hand grenades before the position was finally cleared of the enemy. Such sustained usage explains why so many millions of Mills bombs were produced before the armistice.

OPPOSITE: George V, holding a telescope and standing by captured German trenches, watches the Battle of Pozières, fought during the middle stages of Battle of the Somme.

ABOVE: A Mills bomb grenade, manufactured in 1916. The segmented "pineapple"-like body caused the grenade to splinter, making it an excellent weapon for trench clearing.

◼39 Rising Sun Badge

The "Rising Sun" cap badge, along with the slouch hat to which it was pinned, became emblematic of the "Digger", the Australian soldier. First issued in February 1902, the Rising Sun badge probably owes its existence to Major-General Sir Edward Hutton, the British Commander-in-Chief of the Australian Forces. It was modelled on a shield he had been given, which alternated words and rifle bayonets in a semi-circle around a crown. The third pattern of the badge, the one worn by Australian soldiers in the Great War, had a scroll with the words "Australian Commonwealth Military Forces", and was issued in 1904. Currently in its seventh version, the badge is seen as an important part of the Australian Army's heritage.

This heritage was largely forged in the Great War. Although Australian troops had served in the Boer War, and men from New South Wales been on Imperial service in the Sudan as early as 1885, the Australian Imperial Force (AIF) in 1914 had been a largely unknown quantity. Arriving in Egypt for training, Australian soldiers earned an unenviable reputation for indiscipline. By the end of the war, after distinguished service on Gallipoli, in the Middle East and on the Western Front, the

Diggers had still not lost that reputation: their crime rates were much higher than those of British troops and soldiers from the other Dominions. However, the five-division-strong Australian corps, formed in late 1917 and commanded by an Australian officer, Lieutenant-General Sir John Monash, and with a largely Australian staff and subordinate commanders, was recognized as an elite formation.

So closely has slouch hat and Rising Sun badge become intertwined with Australian national identity, which in turn rests in part on being different from the British (and in extreme cases on rejection of the British heritage altogether), that it is easy to forget that the way in which Australians see the world has changed greatly since 1914. Then, while some Australians resented the Imperial link – those of Irish extraction, for example – most saw themselves as in some sense "British" as well as Australian. Thinking of oneself as "Australian", as opposed to being from New South Wales, Victoria or wherever, was a comparatively new idea. Australia itself had existed as a state only since 1901 when the group of disparate colonies federated. In 1914, the vast majority of Australians considered themselves as being loyal subjects of King George V and citizens of the Empire. As historian Craig Wilcox has shown, the ordinary British soldier was much admired. A magazine cover from 1914 depicted a ghostly Redcoat of Wellington's day informally saluting a slouch-hatted Digger going off to fight in the First World War. The illustration was captioned "The spirit of his fathers". The Digger, the picture implied, had a mighty example to live up to.

A generation later, the army that Australia sent to the Second World War was called the Second AIF. Its battalions had 2/ as a prefix (2/23rd and so on), and the senior Division was the 6th, the junior Division of the First AIF having been the 5th. For between 25 April 1915 and the end of the Great War, in combat on Gallipoli, in the Middle East and on the Western Front, Australian military forces had established a tradition of their own.

OPPOSITE: Three unidentified Allied prisoners of war at Güstrow prison camp, Germany. The soldier seated in the front is wearing a Rising Sun hat badge.

ABOVE: This variation on the Rising Sun cap badge was made to be mounted at Australian Divisional memorials in France and Belgium.

103

◼40 German Potato Masher Grenade

Hand grenades have been a feature of warfare since the invention of gunpowder. Early versions of the weapon were crude devices as dangerous to the user as to the intended target and it was not until the early twentieth century that recognizably modern hand grenades were developed. A Serbian-manufactured hand grenade was hurled at Franz Ferdinand's car on the day of his assassination, but bounced away and detonated under a different vehicle, wounding everyone on board.

At the outbreak of the First World War, hand grenades were seen as specialist weapons that were primarily useful for siege warfare. However, the small stock of grenades available proved valuable in trench warfare during 1914 and all combatant nations began seeking new and improved weapon designs. In 1915, the German army adopted the Model 24

Stielhandgranate. It served as the standard hand German grenade in both world wars. Its distinctive appearance earned it the nickname "potato masher" from British soldiers. It was a high-explosive weapon that relied on the force of its blast to cause injury, rather than on the fragmentation effect that was favoured in British grenades. This made the Stielhandgranate particularly effective when used against confined spaces such as trenches or bunkers.

The Stielhandgranate was primed via a pull cord which ran through the hollow handle. Early versions of the grenade left this cord exposed, running the risk of it snagging on objects and accidently detonating as a result. Learning from this flaw, later designs covered the cord with a porcelain cap. When the grenade was to be used, the cap would be removed, exposing the cord; pulling the cord started a five-second fuse. The stick design made the grenade easy to throw and the handle acted as a lever, giving the grenade an impressive range of between 28 and 37 m (30 and 40 yards). This compared favourably to the British Mills bomb, which had an effective range of between 14 and 28 m (15 and 30 yards).

Tanks made their debut in 1916, and German troops improvised a weapon consisting of a single grenade around which were wired six grenade heads (without handles). This grenade bundle was known as a *geballte ladung* ("concentrated charge") and was capable of knocking out tanks or breaching light fortifications. The bundle would usually be thrown on to the roof of an enemy tank, taking advantage of the thin armour at this point. The danger from these bundles was so great that later designs of British tanks included sloping roofs, which would cause grenades to slide off.

By the end of the war, grenades had evolved from a specialist novelty to an intrinsic part of the infantryman's equipment. The grenade or "bomb" became a key feature of trench warfare. In close-range battles, troops using shell holes and trenches for cover presented a fleeting target for rifle fire but could be rooted out from their positions with grenades. Close-range infantry assaults on trenches would be preceded by a hail of hurled grenades that would force the defenders to break cover or risk being blasted to pieces. Infantry would follow close behind this grenade barrage, leaping into the trenches to finish off any dazed survivors before they could recover. These tactics became common to all armies on the Western Front, and to be "bombed out" of a trench by grenades was a traumatic experience for any soldier.

41 Prisoner of War Camp

The see-saw nature of the opening months of the First World War resulted in both sides taking a huge number of prisoners-of-war (POW). Prior to the outbreak of the conflict, no combatant nations had given any real thought to the problems of holding prisoners, and the sudden influx of POWs meant that a system had to be hastily devised.

The improvised nature of early POW camps caused a number of problems. The Hague convention (1907) stated that all prisoners should be "humanely treated". However, the sudden influx of POWs led to unsanitary and overcrowded conditions. The absence of a centralized system governing guard conduct meant that local abuses of power were common. The camp at Torrens Island off the Australian coast, which held interred German nationals and captured naval crew, became so infamous for its casual brutality that it was closed down in 1915. The POW camps in the Ottoman Empire (which had refused to sign the Hague convention)

were notorious for their harsh conditions. Cruelty against British, Australian and Indian prisoners was commonplace, whilst malnutrition and disease meant mortality rates were high. In Germany, prisoners-of-war endured inadequate rations due to food shortages caused by the British blockade, which led to increased disease. Germany also instituted particularly strict POW camps known as "Reprisal Camps" to punish failed escapees. Future French president Charles de Gaulle spent the latter half of the war in one of these camps.

As the war continued, the problems of overcrowding were slowly addressed through the construction of new POW camps. Conditions in the camps were spartan and life for prisoners was hard. This was especially true of prisoners in Germany, who were often used as a source of manpower for agricultural work and manual labour. Conditions in "officers' camps" tended to be superior to those camps which accommodated private soldiers. In 1916, Britain and Germany reached a reciprocal agreement that allowed POW officers to go for walks outside the camp, provided no attempt was made to escape.

Prison life was characterized by drudgery and routine. Well-behaved prisoners were allowed to send at least one letter per month to their country and the receipt of mail from home was a much anticipated event. In addition, the Red Cross and other humanitarian societies worked tirelessly to provide care packages to prisoners. Other forms of entertainment included reading newspapers, organizing concert parties and learning the local language.

An unusual feature of the First World War was the complex system of prisoner exchanges and neutral internment. Seriously ill or severely wounded prisoners could be sent to a neutral country, where they were either interred or sent home. There were also rules governing the exchange of soldiers who were over 40 years old. Both sides resisted attempts to institute a system that repatriated officer POWs on the grounds that these were too valuable to the enemy.

The prohibition of officer exchanges contributed to the fact that officers were the most likely inmates to attempt an escape. In July 1918, a particularly famous escape took place from the officer's camp at Holzminden, which saw 29 British officers exit through an underground tunnel; 10 of them evaded capture and reached the Netherlands. German records suggest 67,000 Allied prisoners, mainly British and French, escaped over the course of the war.

OPPOSITE: A group of captured Russian prisoners of war, guarded by German soldiers somewhere on the Eastern Front. The date of the photograph is unknown.

ABOVE: German prisoners of war, captured on the Western Front, are marched to camps, 1916.

◪ 42 Ctesiphon Arch

Although warfare has seen dramatic changes over the centuries the magnificent Ctesiphon arch in Mesopotamia (modern-day Iraq) is a reminder that certain factors remain constant. Ctesiphon, the capital of the Parthian and Sasanian rulers of Persia, had seen many armies and many campaigns prior to the First World War. Mentioned in the Old Testament of the Bible, it was captured by Roman armies on five occasions. In AD 198, the Roman Emperor Septimus Severus sacked the city and enslaved the inhabitants. The strategic importance of Ctesiphon lay in the fact that it was located beside the River Tigris, on a natural invasion route into Mesopotamia – and this was as true in the First World War as it had been in Roman times. In November 1915, an Ottoman army occupied positions at Ctesiphon in order to block the British advance on Baghdad, some 32 km (20 miles) to the north.

The great Arch lay in the midst of the Turkish defences. A historically minded Turkish staff officer referred to nearby features as "the confused traces of towns and great cities which endured here for centuries and which the storms of adversity turned into this historical graveyard". Built from baked mud bricks as part of Sasanian King Chosroes's palace in the sixth century AD, the Ctesiphon Arch is an impressive barrel-vaulted audience chamber 30 m (98 ft) high and 43 m (141 ft) long. The Edwardian traveller Gertrude Bell called it "One of the most imposing ruins in the world".

The British had sent an expeditionary force from India to Mesopotamia in November 1914, with the objective of securing the oil fields at the head of the Persian Gulf. Initial success had led to more ambitious plans: an advance of 30 km (20 miles) captured Basra, and another, of 90 km (55 miles), brought the British and Indian troops to the confluence of the two great rivers in the region, the Euphrates and the Tigris. The newly arrived commander-in-chief, General Sir John Nixon, mounted offensives along each of the rivers in spring 1915. Major-General Charles Townshend's 6th Indian Division took Kut, on the Tigris, in September 1915, and then pursued the defeated Turkish army to Ctesiphon. Baghdad was the next objective.

However, the battle of Ctesiphon demonstrated that the British, in their eagerness to secure the chief city of Mesopotamia, had managed to overreach themselves. Townshend's plan, for a night march followed by a flank attack, broke down on 22 November. The attackers reached the second Ottoman position, around the Arch, but, lacking artillery support from gunboats on the river, could go no further. Under the command of the competent Nureddin Bey, the Ottoman forces held on and counter-attacked. Losses were heavy on both sides, but in the end it was Townshend that admitted defeat. On 25 November 1915 he began the retreat to Kut.

At Kut, his British-Indian force was besieged by the Turks from 7 December. Attempts by relief forces to link up with the garrison failed, and after five months the siege of Kut came to an end on 29 April 1916 when Townshend surrendered his 13,000-strong force. Kut was a humiliating defeat for the British Empire, worse even than Gallipoli. But it was to be a temporary setback. Under new commanders, the forces of the British Empire conquered the whole of Mesopotamia in 1917–18. The modern Middle East bears the imprint of the strategic decisions taken in those years.

OPPOSITE: British lines passing under the Ctesiphon Arch, 1917. Inadequate supply lines and an under-staffed medical corps contributed to the British defeat.

ABOVE: The Ctesiphon Arch.

OVERLEAF: British troops on a dusty march in Mesopotamia, c. 1916.

◾43 Gurkha's Kukri

The Gurkhas are one of the most famous military units in the British Army. The British had been impressed by the fighting qualities of the Gurkhas when facing them in the Anglo-Nepal War (1814–16) and subsequently recruited them into the army. They served as part of the Indian Army throughout the nineteenth century. Seen as a "martial race" of natural warriors, they performed well in combat and attracted particularly favourable notice during the Indian Mutiny of 1857.

The kukri is the Gurkha's traditional weapon. Light and mobile, its curved shape greatly magnifies its downward force when used in a slashing motion. The kukri has symbolic significance and may be drawn only if blood is to be spilled. This requirement is met in training by the wielder nicking his thumb or hand before returning the blade to its sheath.

The outbreak of war in 1914 saw the imperial nations of Britain and France look to their empire for manpower. Britain possessed a standing colonial force in the form of the Indian Army and an Indian Expeditionary Force (IEF) was deployed to the Western Front, arriving in time to participate in the First Battle of Ypres in October 1914.

This use of the Indian Army against white opposition caused outrage in Germany, where the Indian troops were portrayed as sub-human savages. A German propaganda cartoon of December 1914 showed hideous caricatures of kukri-wielding Gurkhas preparing to ambush a handsome Aryan German soldier; the caption complained that the British had sent savages to do their fighting for them.

Unfortunately, the Indian Expeditionary Force struggled to cope with the conditions of the Western Front. It was difficult to provide drafts for the army due to the geographical distance from its homelands. The army was led by white officers, who were easy targets for German marksmen and suffered disproportionate casualties. Their replacements often lacked experience of working with Indian troops and were unable to communicate with the troops in their native language. This caused command problems and harmed morale. Indian morale was further reduced by stringent regulations that prevented them from fraternizing with whites behind the lines.

Nevertheless, the IEF fought with considerable courage during battles such as Neuve Chapelle (10–13 March 1915), Aubers Ridge (9 May 1915) and Loos (September–October 1915). However, the problems that beset the force had become so severe by the end of 1915 that it was decided to remove the IEF from the Western Front. Two Indian cavalry divisions remained in France, but the rest of the force was sent to the Middle East, where elements of the Indian Army were already fighting. It was felt that the climatic conditions of the area suited the soldiers better, and resupply was easier due to proximity to India. The Indian Army performed well in this theatre and played a major role in the defeat of the Ottoman Empire.

As part of the wider expansion of the Indian Army, the number of Gurkha battalions was increased from 10 in 1914 to 33 by the end of the conflict. Gurkhas fought in most major combat theatres of the First World War, including the Western Front, Gallipoli, Palestine and Mesopotamia. Including non-combatant roles such as porters, some 200,000 Gurkhas served in the British Army and approximately 20,000 became casualties. A little over 2,000 awards for gallantry were won by Gurkhas during the war, and their reputation as courageous and determined troops was further enhanced. That reputation holds to this day.

OPPOSITE: A Gurkha holding a Kukri, photographed somewhere on the Western front. The weapon has come to symbolize the Gurkha soldier.

ABOVE: Since the blade of the kukri drops forward, its user does not have to angle the wrist towards an opponent, making this an easy weapon to use for stabbing.

◼ 44 Kirchner Pin-Up

Raphael Kirchner (1876–1917) was an Austrian artist who is sometimes known as "The Godfather of Pin-Ups". In the early years of the twentieth century, he earned his living in Paris as a painter for the fashionable magazines of the day. Kirchner soon developed a reputation for his portrayal of feminine beauty, typically caught in an alluring or erotic pose, and his work was in constant demand. At the outbreak of the war, Kirchner relocated to New York because he feared discrimination in Paris due to his nationality. In the event, the popularity of his work was such that his fears were unfounded.

The outbreak of war and the arrival of the British Army in France opened an entirely new market for Kirchner's work. Recognizing the appeal of his illustrations to the lonely soldier, Kirchner altered his style to become more direct. Within the bounds of taste, his wartime illustrations featured more erotic imagery, with the subject often gazing out directly at the viewer. Although there were other French and Italian artists who drew "pin-ups" for the troops, Kirchner's work remained the most popular up to and even beyond his death in August 1917.

Pictures of "Kirchner Girls", either clipped from magazines or purchased in postcard format,

became a much traded commodity amongst the Allied soldiers on the Western Front. Pictures were either kept in pockets or used as "pin-ups" on dug out walls. A poem published in the trench newspaper *The Kemmel Times* in July 1916 in honour of a lost comrade lamented:

O where is Bob of the big moustache?
An alien adjutant shoots,
For the Major-man that I used to know,
With his Kirchner ladies all in a row,
And his seventeen pairs of boots.

However, Kirchner's work did not draw universal approval and elements of polite society in Britain were scandalized by his illustrations. In February 1917, the British magazine *The Bystander* ran a humorous cartoon entitled "Purchase of Foreign Literature" in which a group of eager Royal Navy officers were pictured gathered around a copy of *La Vie Parisienne*, a particularly risqué French magazine in which Kirchner's illustrations were the star attraction. The British Press Bureau did not see the funny side and forbade the cartoon from publication on the grounds that it was a slur on the reputation of Royal Navy officers!

The official disapproval of Kirchner's work mirrored British society's discomfort with the idea of military sexuality. The effects of so-called "Khaki fever", which caused young women to fall into the arms of soldiers, and the well known yet unspoken use of French brothels by officers and men were subjects that were taboo in polite society. It is only in recent years that the hidden history of sex in the First World War has received serious discussion.

Within the context of soaring rates of venereal disease, deep controversy over the use of French licensed brothels and scandals about the issue of prophylactic kits to serving soldiers, Kirchner pin-ups were relatively tame. However, the immense popularity amongst soldiers and the ease with which they could be acquired made them a ubiquitous item within the trenches. The popularity of *La Vie Parisienne* and other saucy magazines with their weekly dose of new pin-ups was enormous. In a cheeky and knowing letter to *The Bystander*, one soldier commented: "The Weekly Illustrateds are as Gin at a mothers' meeting to us here."

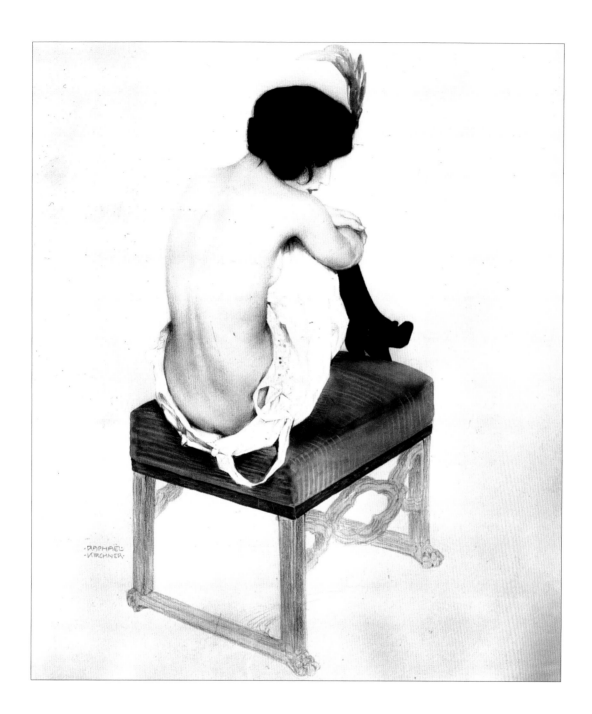

OPPOSITE: *Riquette and her dog, c.*1900. Kirchner's pin-ups were popular with soldiers on both sides of the lines, often available in postcard size.

ABOVE: *Réflexion.* Kirchner's work inspired Alberto Vargas, the man behind the pin-ups of the Second World War, the "Vargas Girls".

45 Sinai Railway

Logistics – the art and science of moving and supplying troops – is a fundamental building block of strategy and operations, but it is surprisingly neglected in much writing on military history. The preparations of the British Empire's Egyptian Expeditionary Force (EEF) for an advance east into Ottoman territory highlights the importance of logistics

By late 1915, traffic on the Cairo-Ismailia railway, which connected the Egyptian capital with the Suez Canal (the effective front line), was becoming increasingly heavy. In December, 15,000 men began work on improving the railway. In 36 days, the line was extended and stretches of single line were doubled. 300,000 cubic metres (400,000 cubic yards) of earth were moved, with the normal number of trains being run, supplemented by a number of special military trains.

The advance in Sinai began in February 1916, after reconnaissance confirmed that the area was largely clear of Ottoman troops. Building a railway line from Qantara to Qatiya began on 10 March, with 26 km (16 miles) of track being laid in about 30 days. However, things were not to go entirely smoothly. An Ottoman force composed of two infantry battalions, an Arab irregular camel regiment, and artillery, commanded by a German officer, Colonel Kress von Kressenstein, raided towards the railway. At Qatiya on 23 April, it inflicted a sharp defeat on British force of Yeomanry (Territorial Force cavalry). The British official historian wrote admiringly of the "speed, skill, daring and success" of the raid, but in truth it delayed the remorseless advance of the rail for only a handful of days. The line to the forward base at Romani was opened on 19 May, and in the following week 1,125 tons of supplies, 815,000 litres (215,000 gallons) of water and 420 tons of railway material were transported. Becoming increasingly anxious at the speed at which the railway was advancing, Kress launched a major attack at Romani on 4 August. The attack was easily defeated, and the Ottoman force suffered heavy losses, including some 4,000 men taken prisoner. Although Kress was able to extract his force and fall back to his base, to the embarrassment of the British military leaders, Romani was an important demonstration of the inability of the Turks to disrupt the advance through Sinai in any serious way.

From September 1916, a pipeline for water was laid beside the railway line. Consisting of 30-cm (12-inch) pipes, it enabled reservoirs at Romani to be filled by mid-November. Since water no longer had to be brought forward by rail, this meant that the railway had more capacity, enabling the rate of building to be increased. A temporary road of wire netting was laid near the track. The steady progress being made by the railway across Sinai enabled the Egyptian Expeditionary Force to approach the "gate of Palestine", Gaza, by March 1917. Although the attack launched by Murray (the First Battle of Gaza) was a failure, the mere fact that the attack was able to be launched at all was testimony to the impressive logistic achievement of building a railway, pipeline and road.

However, more needed to be done. On replacing Murray in late June 1917, the energetic General Sir Edmund Allenby ordered further work on the railway and more provision of water: the latter included, apart from extending the pipeline, the use of 7,000 camels to carry water. Thus, Allenby's successful Third Battle of Gaza (October–November 1917) was underpinned by a robust logistic structure, created by a huge effort that connected the rear area in Egypt with the front line.

ABOVE: An Allied armoured train at the station in Mazar, Sinai, 1916.

OPPOSITE: Men, who in civilian life worked for the New South Wales Government Railways, were recruited for the Railway Supply Detachment.

Railway Men on Active Service

(Photos by the courtesy of Mr. E. Milne, Assistant Commissioner)

A WATER TRAIN EN ROUTE TO
FERRY POST SECTION.

10TH D.U.S. SUPPLY AT MOASCAR
Including Miller, Parke, Tough, King, McIntosh, Reed,
Bruce, Egan, Robertson, Lloyd, McCarthy.

N.S. Wales Railway Supply Detachment

SIGHT-SEEING IN EGYPT
A Group of Railway Men in Leisure Hours

Our Soldiers' Snapshots

AFTER A SWIM, SERAPEUM EAST—April, 1916.
Included in the Group are Boydell, Rigney, Dinning,
Newman and Major Milne.

FIRST TRAIN OF AUSTRALIAN SUPPLIES
To leave from Khatatba to Ber-Hooker, Madi.

■46 SMS *Von der Tann*

SMS *Von der Tann* was a German battlecruiser completed in September 1910. Named after a Bavarian general, the ship had an overall length of 171 m (561 ft), a beam of 26 m (85 ft), and a full load of 21,000 tons. On launching, the ship's company numbered 910. The maximum thickness of the Krupp armour, amidships, was 25 cm (10 in). *Von der Tann* was armed with eight 28-cm (11-inch) guns, with secondary armament of 15-cm (6-inch) guns and 45-cm (18-inch) torpedo tubes. Capable of 52 km/h (28 knots), *Von der Tann* took part in raids on the English coast in 1914–15, the Battle of Jutland (1916) and post-Jutland sorties into the North Sea. The ship surrendered to the British in 1918, and scuttled at Scapa Flow in 1919.

Battlecruisers had the same hitting power as conventional dreadnought battleships (that is, all big-gun battleships; see *Bouvet*, page 70), but were faster, because they were more lightly armoured. They were the brainchild of Admiral Sir John "Jacky" Fisher, the controversial First Sea Lord who held his position from 1904 to 1910, and again in the early months of the First World War. Fisher believed that the battlecruiser's combination of speed and heavy guns would give it a decisive advantage in combat, notwithstanding the potential vulnerability of thinner armour. *Von der Tann* was Germany's response to the new battlecruisers. HMS *Invincible*, *Inflexible* and *Indomitable* were commissioned in 1908–09. By the outbreak of war, Germany had five battlecruisers, with another three being built, to the Royal Navy's nine with a further one under construction. Germany had 15 dreadnoughts, with five being built; the comparable British figures were 22 and 13.

Prior to the rapid expansion of its fleet after 1898, Germany was not seen as a naval threat by the British. As an island state with a vast overseas empire, naval superiority was critical to Britain. Tirpitz told the Kaiser that the idea was to create such a threat that Britain would "concede to Your Majesty such a measure of naval mastery and enable Your Majesty to carry put a great overseas policy". The policy was disastrous. The British accepted the challenge and began a "naval race", while abandoning the previous policy of "splendid isolation" and by reaching agreement with their colonial rivals France and Russia.

Many believed that when war came it would begin with a decisive clash in the North Sea. Instead, both sides behaved cautiously. The commander of the British Grand Fleet, Admiral Sir John Jellicoe, was well aware of the risks to the security of Britain and her empire that he would run in a major battle; even if victorious, substantial loses could alter the naval balance in favour of the Germans. The Germans pursued an attritional strategy, seeking to catch small elements of the British fleet at sea and gradually wear down their strength. On 31 May 1916, off Jutland, the long-awaited battle took place. The British were hugely disappointed by the result. Tactically, the gunnery of the German ships proved superior, and alarming defects in British ship design were revealed. The British lost three battlecruisers, including *Indefatigable*, which was sunk by the 28-cm (11-inch) guns of *Von der Tann*: *Indefatigable's* magazine exploded, but *Von der Tann* itself later took heavy punishment from British battleships, with all of its heavy guns "at least temporarily disabled". A German battlecruiser was lost.

It seemed that the Royal Navy's chance of achieving a great victory had been spurned by timid command. In reality, Jutland was an important success for the British, in that the favourable strategic situation remained essentially unchanged and the Germans never again succeeded in forcing a major fleet action.

OPPOSITE: *Von der Tann*, photographed in 1914. The first German battlecruiser, she destroyed HMS *Indefatigable* at the Battle of Jutland, 1916.

ABOVE: *Von der Tann*, photographed in 1909, the year she was launched. Ten years later, on 21 June 1919, she was scuttled at Scapa Flow.

47 Easter Rebellion Poster

In the words of the old saying, "England's difficulty was Ireland's opportunity." On 24 April 1916, Easter Monday, an uprising began in Dublin. The centrepiece was the reading by Patrick Pearse at the General Post Office in O'Connell Street, Dublin, of one of the most celebrated documents in Irish history: the proclamation of an Irish republic. Appealing to "Irishmen and Irish women" in "the name of God and of the dead generations", the Provisional Government announced the establishment of a "sovereign independent state".

The events of August 1914 had brought about a surprising level of unity. Only the month before, Ireland had been on the brink of civil war. The British Liberal government, with support from John Redmond's moderate nationalist Irish Parliamentary Party, was attempting to bring Home Rule in Ireland. This would have devolved some powers to an executive in Dublin, but the thought of "Rome Rule", as it was derisively known, provoked visceral opposition from the Protestants in Ulster. With both the (Protestant) Ulster Volunteer Force (UVF) and

(Catholic) Irish Volunteers armed and drilling, sectarian conflict seemed imminent. The officer corps of the British army, which contained many Irish Protestants, was split over the prospect of being used to coerce Ulster.

War with Germany brought about an uneasy truce. The UVF formed the core of 36th (Ulster) Division, while 16th (Irish) Division was its Catholic, Nationalist counterpart. Home Rule was put on to the statute books, but immediately suspended for the duration of the war. However, alongside Redmond's constitutional Nationalists, who sought something like Dominion status for Ireland within the Empire and hoped that their loyalty to Britain during the war would help them achieve it, there were more radical groups, including the Irish Republican Brotherhood (IRB). It was the IRB that launched the uprising, supported by elements of the Irish Volunteers and the Irish Citizen Army.

On Easter Monday, the rebels achieved surprise and seized the GPO, St Stephen's Green, and other key sites. The British soon began to counterattack, and bringing up artillery suppressed the insurgency. Ultimately probably 64 rebels and 254 civilian died, along with 116 military and 16 police fatalities. The reaction of ordinary Dubliners to the uprising varied, but many were hostile. The response of the British authorities was to be decisive in tipping popular sentiment in favour of the insurgents. Rebel leaders were executed over a prolonged period, between 3 and 12 May. The outraged response of public opinion to the "policy of dribbling executions", as the Home Rule supporter John Dillon termed it, created sympathy for the rebels. Over time, the Easter Rising and the response of the authorities fatally undermined support for Redmond's constitutional nationalists. In retrospect, the failure to reach a political settlement in the months to come sealed their fate, and that of the Union between Great Britain and Ireland. At the December 1918 British General Election, Sinn Féin took 73 seats, Redmond's party only seven. In Ulster, the Unionists won 22 seats. Sinn Féin, however, boycotted Westminster and set up their own assembly, the Dáil Éireann. In 1919, the British began a concerted effort to reconquer Ireland. The Anglo-Irish War, a guerrilla-based insurgency that was met with a counter-insurgency campaign, continued until a ceasefire in 1921, followed by negotiations that brought about peace based on the partition of Ireland. This was followed by an eleven-month civil war within the new "Free State" between the government that had accepted the compromise with the British, and hard-liners who rejected it. The victory of the government forces brought an end to a period of revolution in Ireland, which had the Easter Rising at its core.

POBLACHT NA H EIREANN.

THE PROVISIONAL GOVERNMENT
OF THE

IRISH REPUBLIC.
TO THE PEOPLE OF IRELAND.

IRISHMEN AND IRISHWOMEN : In the name of God and of the dead generations from which she receives her old tradition of nationhood, Ireland, through us, summons her children to her flag and strikes for her freedom.

Having organised and trained her manhood through her secret revolutionary organisation, the Irish Republican Brotherhood, and through her open military organisations, the Irish Volunteers and the Irish Citizen Army, having patiently perfected her discipline, having resolutely waited for the right moment to reveal itself, she now seizes that moment, and, supported by her exiled children in America and by gallant allies in Europe, but relying in the first on her own strength, she strikes in full confidence of victory.

We declare the right of the people of Ireland to the ownership of Ireland, and to the unfettered control of Irish destinies, to be sovereign and indefeasible. The long usurpation of that right by a foreign people and government has not extinguished the right, nor can it ever be extinguished except by the destruction of the Irish people. In every generation the Irish people have asserted their right to national freedom and sovereignty; six times during the past three hundred years they have asserted it in arms. Standing on that fundamental right and again asserting it in arms in the face of the world, we hereby proclaim the Irish Republic as a Sovereign Independent State, and we pledge our lives and the lives of our comrades-in-arms to the cause of its freedom, of its welfare, and of its exaltation among the nations.

The Irish Republic is entitled to, and hereby claims, the allegiance of every Irishman and Irishwoman. The Republic guarantees religious and civil liberty, equal rights and equal opportunities to all its citizens, and declares its resolve to pursue the happiness and prosperity of the whole nation and of all its parts, cherishing all the children of the nation equally, and oblivious of the differences carefully fostered by an alien government, which have divided a minority from the majority in the past.

Until our arms have brought the opportune moment for the establishment of a permanent National Government, representative of the whole people of Ireland and elected by the suffrages of all her men and women, the Provisional Government, hereby constituted, will administer the civil and military affairs of the Republic in trust for the people.

We place the cause of the Irish Republic under the protection of the Most High God, Whose blessing we invoke upon our arms, and we pray that no one who serves that cause will dishonour it by cowardice, inhumanity, or rapine. In this supreme hour the Irish nation must, by its valour and discipline and by the readiness of its children to sacrifice themselves for the common good, prove itself worthy of the august destiny to which it is called.

Signed on Behalf of the Provisional Government,

THOMAS J. CLARKE.

SEAN Mac DIARMADA.   THOMAS MacDONAGH.
P. H. PEARSE.   EAMONN CEANNT.
JAMES CONNOLLY.   JOSEPH PLUNKETT.

OPPOSITE: Irish rebels lying in wait on a roof, ready to fire, 1916.

ABOVE: The Proclamation of the Republic, which was read by Patrick Pearse outside the General Post Office, Dublin. It had been printed in secret some time before.

48 Sniper's Rifle

The title "sniper" was one given to English huntsmen of the 1770s who had achieved the rare feat of hitting a snipe, an elusive and fast moving bird, whilst it was in flight. The word was adopted by the military in the nineteenth century to denote a crack shot. The First World War would see the emergence of snipers as true battlefield specialists.

At the outbreak of the conflict the German army, in contrast to other combatants, included a proportion of specially trained snipers who carried rifles equipped with telescopic sights. In the static conditions of trench warfare, the snipers proved a lethal foe. The British first became aware of enemy snipers during the deadlock on the Aisne in September 1914, with one soldier recalling, "A German sniper began to annoy us ... Every time anything showed so much as an inch above the crest, it drew fire, and a number of our men were shot passing traverses." Recognizing the effectiveness of these marksmen, the German army greatly

increased its provision of sniper rifles. By mid-1915, German snipers had become a serious threat.

Faced with this problem, the British Army struggled to procure a sniper rifle of its own. Fitting a sight to the standard Lee-Enfield proved difficult, and commercially available hunting rifles were difficult to supply with sufficient ammunition. Small numbers of scoped rifles were issued to the British in 1915, but the snipers received no formal training and were generally ignorant of the technicalities of their sights. The most successful snipers of this period were men who had prior hunting experience and understood the delicate nature of the rifles. Crack snipers with this background included the First Nation Canadian John Ballantyne and the Australian Billy Sing.

In August 1916, the First Army School of Scouting, Observation and Sniping was founded by former huntsman and experienced sniper Major Hesketh Vernon

Hesketh-Prichard. The creation of the school formally institutionalized the art of sniping in the British Army. The syllabus was practical and graduates of the school were praised for their proficiency.

The growing skills of the British were important, as the battle between snipers for dominance of no-man's land was relentless. Sniper activity was constant even in quiet sectors – and on active fronts, such as Flanders, it was particularly intense. Snipers inflicted a steady stream of casualties and could have a highly demoralizing effect on the enemy. In these circumstances, picking off enemy snipers was a priority. Sniper duels were known as "the game" amongst British marksmen, but it was a deadly sport where the winner was often decided by whoever got off the first shot. For this reason, concealment was soon found to be of paramount importance and many novel methods of camouflage were

devised. Other innovations included fake tree stumps that would actually serve as a hide for the sniper and could be surreptitiously located in no-man's land.

It was soon found that, by virtue of their time spent studying the enemy lines, snipers were an excellent source of information. The British considered the observatory role of the sniper as of almost equal importance to his elimination of enemy targets. Snipers were trained to produce accurate sketches of the front line and write detailed reports of enemy activity. This was especially useful when observing the effects of artillery bombardment.

Snipers were a ubiquitous feature of trench warfare. Whilst the British had initially considered the act of sniping to be "unsporting", the war changed attitudes and by the end of the conflict the army had surpassed the German military in the art.

OPPOSITE: Australians and members of the Royal Naval Division in a trench at Gallipoli. One man uses a periscope, another a "sniperscope".

ABOVE: The Mauser Model G98 Sniper Rifle, the type used on the Western Front. It features a leather eye pad and a foresight cover.

49 Indo-Chinese Labourer's Hat

Labourers from French Indo-China, wearing their distinctive hats, were a familiar sight behind the lines on parts of the Western Front. They proved an invaluable source of manpower for the endless tasks that were needed to support the fighting men. Road-building and maintenance, constructing defences and "humping and dumping" supplies were just some of the activities that demanded labour. Men were brought in from overseas to do these jobs, and also to work in war factories and on farms. During the course of the war, these amounted to some 50,000 men from Indo-China, as well as 120,000 Algerians, 82,000 men from neutral Spain and 13,000 Chinese.

In order to satisfy the demand for labour, armies also made use of prisoners of war – 82,000 worked for the French – and also specialized military units, sometimes composed of men unfit for front-line service such as the British Labour Corps, or drawn from overseas empires. The French had such units recruited from Madagascar and sub-Saharan Africa, and the BEF had the South African Native Labour Corps. In addition, the British employed large number of Egyptian and Chinese labourers. Such additional labour provided invaluable services, but very often front-line troops were pressed into service when out of the line. In early 1918, when awaiting the German offensive, the need to use British infantry on improving defensive positions eroded the time available for training, as well ensuring that some were physically tired even before the battle began.

The French army made much use of manpower from their global Empire in combatant as well as non-combatant roles. In addition to the army of metropolitan France, there was also the Army of Africa, whose soldiers were both white and indigenous "Senegalese" (the catch-all term for soldiers from sub-Saharan Africa, but not Malagasies); and the Colonial Forces, which comprised both indigenous and *Coloniale Blanche troops*, the latter drawn from volunteers from France and white Frenchmen from overseas. "At their best," historian Anthony Clayton has written, "when well trained, Armée d'Afrique and Coloniale units contributed a very special élan to the battlefield." Some of these formations were extremely effective. Among many examples, Zouaves and Foreign Legionnaires of the Moroccan Division almost succeeded in capturing the formidable Vimy Ridge on 9 May 1915, while white and black soldiers from Africa (including Somalis) recaptured Fort Douaumont, at Verdun, in October 1916. Without combat troops drawn from its empire, the French army would have been dangerously weak.

The Germans complained about the French use of "savages" in European warfare, and some lurid tales also circulated among the Allies about atrocities committed by French colonial troops, such as collecting German ears. While some were undoubtedly true, such views owed much to contemporary notions of racial and cultural superiority. Lieutenant-Colonel (later General) Charles Mangin, who in 1910 wrote a controversial book, *La Force Noir*, advocating a huge force of African solders to take on the defence of metropolitan France, described African soldiers as having "an underdeveloped intelligence" and "the fault of an infantile character" but that the positive side was their absolute devotion to France and their officers.

The presence in France and Belgium of labourers from Indo-China and South Africa, and Senegalese and North African infantry, underlines the global nature of the First World War, and the ability of the Allies to mobilize huge reserves of manpower from around the world. Without a doubt, the peoples of France's empire overseas made a significant contribution first to staving off defeat and then achieving victory.

OPPOSITE: Indo-Chinese farmworkers lifting potatoes near the front, 1 January 1916. Indo-China was a valuable source of manpower for France.

ABOVE: Marine Infantry (Tirailleur Annamite) resting in a military camp near Salonika, May 1916.

50 Tsetse Fly

Overall, the First World War was the first major conflict fought by the British in which deaths in battle had exceeded deaths from disease. This was a sharp reversal from the situation only 15 years earlier, during the Second Anglo-Boer War. Then, there were 14,000 fatalities from sickness, as opposed to 8,000 as the result of battle. If the influenza pandemic, which was not related to wartime conditions (see Influenza Mask, page 230), is removed from the calculations, the figure of 113,000 "died from disease or injury" of the roughly 1 million British Empire dead would be lower still.

Medical services on the Western Front benefited from enlightened leadership – not least from Sir John French and Sir Douglas Haig at the top of the BEF – good medical facilities (which were aided by the static nature of the fighting for most of the war) and an emphasis on hygiene. The story was not nearly as satisfactory in some other theatres of operations. The East African campaigns of 1916–18 against Colonel Paul von Lettow-Vorbeck's guerrilla force (see Askari's Hat, page 64) were a case in point.

General Jan Christian Smuts, the South African who commanded the British Empire forces (which included Indians and South Africans) in East Africa in the latter part of the war, said that it was a "campaign against nature, in which climate, geography and disease fought more effectively against us than the well-trained forces of the enemy". The tsetse fly proved to be a particularly deadly opponent. This blood-sucking fly is an agent for the transmission of trypanosomosis (sleeping sickness) to animals and humans. The tsetse fly made a sizeable contribution to the casualty lists. The ratio of battle casualties to non-battle casualties in the 1916–18 was 1 to 31.40 among troops and an astounding 1 to 140.83 among "followers", the indigenous porters who supplied logistic support. Whereas approximately 3,650 soldiers and 700 followers were killed, died of wounds, posted missing or taken prisoner in 1916–18, the figures for "died of disease or injury" were 6,300 troops and 43,200 followers.

A recent study by Ross Anderson has assessed malaria as "the greatest plague" for humans, followed by dysentery and pneumonia. The effect of the tsetse fly on animals was "devastating … scarcely a beast survived the rigours of the campaign". The depredations of the tsetse fly on animals had repercussions for humans. Because of the difficulties in keeping beasts of burden fit and well under campaign conditions, there was a great emphasis on human porterage, hence the large numbers of followers who became casualties.

Lettow-Vorbeck's force did not suffer the same rates of sickness. Among the reasons were a comparatively large number of medical personnel, and the rigorous use of quinine to combat malaria, either in conventional pill form, or by drinking "Lettow-schnapps" – an unpleasant liquid produced from boiling Peruvian bark. Better diet, increased levels of fitness, and an effective "system of tropical hygiene" that evolved during the months on campaign all helped Lettow-Vorbeck's German and African troops largely to avoid the fate of their adversaries.

British Empire troops suffered badly from disease on some other fronts. More than 11,000 Indian troops were sick with scurvy in Mesopotamia in the second half of 1916. At Gallipoli in 1915–16, 1,240 troops per thousand were hospitalized through sickness, while the average in France and Flanders was 567 per thousand across the whole war. Unlike on the Western Front, the neglect and indifference of senior officers played a role in this sorry state of affairs. Lessons were learned, however, and by the end of the war medical services were much improved.

OPPOSITE: The tsetse fly, which includes all members of the genus *Glossina*, transmits sleeping sickness

ABOVE: A net worn over the head by soldiers during the First World War to combat insect bites.

51 Verdun Pigeon

On the wall of Fort Vaux at Verdun is a poignant reminder of the military role of animals in the First World War. A plaque pays tribute to a carrier pigeon that carried out the last message from Major Raynal, the commander of the garrison of Fort Vaux. German forces had cut off Vaux from the rest of the French forces and he was reliant on carrier pigeons to maintain communications. As matters grew increasingly desperate, Raynal sent out a final message on 4 June. It said "We are holding on" but a combination of "gas and smoke" had made the situation critical: "We need relief urgently … this is my last pigeon."

Suffering from the effects of gas, the pigeon staggered into the air, disorientated, but eventually flew unsteadily towards the French rear. It arrived at Verdun bearing its precious message, but then expired. Dubbed "Valliant", the pigeon was awarded a posthumous Legion of Honour, and now resides in a museum, a model of the taxidermist's art.

The use of carrier pigeons was part of the military response to the problem that armies, by 1914, were too big and too dispersed to be commanded from horseback, as generals had done in years past. Poor communications affected tactics as well as strategy: it was the single most important factor in producing deadlock on the Western Front. In the process of breaking into enemy positions, troops were invariably weakened through casualties and the need to detach men to hold positions and attack strongpoints. Fresh troops were needed to leapfrog through the assault units and maintain the momentum of the attack. Without radios, armies were reliant on "runners", visual signals, and pigeons. Mostly these methods of communications proved too slow to get reserves at the right place in a timely fashion, and attack after attack faltered.

"AUX COLOMBOPHILES MORTS POUR LA FRANCE"
Une plaque est apposée sur le fort de Vaux rappelant la belle défense du commandant Raynal. — Le départ du dernier pigeon.

The homing instincts of pigeons have been exploited for military purposes since ancient times. During the siege of Paris in 1871, pigeons were used to maintain communications. Perhaps influenced by this experience, the French army was particularly well equipped with pigeons at the beginning of the First World War. "It might be imagined," an article in *Scientific American* from 1913 began, "that the present era of the aeroplane and the wireless telegraph has no use for the swift and faithful winged messengers which rendered such valuable service in the Franco-German and other wars … These views are quite erroneous." The French army had 28 "pigeon houses", specialized units under the aegis of the Engineer Corps, where the pigeons underwent training. Messages were carried in holders made of goose quill that were attached to the bird's tail feathers, or in an aluminium case on the bird's leg.

The assault on Fort Vaux was part of a renewed German offensive in the Verdun sector, launched on 1 June. The Battle of Verdun had begun with a German attack on 21 February 1916. Falkenhayn sought a deliberate battle of attrition, to force the French to the negotiating table. Subjected to intense fire from heavy guns, German troops succeeded on getting on Fort Vaux's roof on 2 June. This was followed by some of the most savage fighting of the campaign, in the corridors and chambers of the fort. The 600-man garrison held out for another five days, but, Raynal's message notwithstanding, he had to surrender, on 7 June. Under pressure from the Allied offensive on the Somme, the Germans were forced onto the defensive in July. In October 1916, the French went onto the offensive at Verdun, and Fort Vaux was retaken in November.

N°	JOUR	HEURE	NOMBRE et MARQUES des pigeons lâchés
15	4-6-16	11h.30	787-15

Nous tenons toujours mais nous subirons une attaque par les gaz et les fumées très dangereuse

Il y a urgence à nous dégager. Faites nous donner de suite communication optique par Souville qui ne répond pas à nos appels.

C'est mon dernier pigeon

Raynal

OPPOSITE: "To all the pigeon-fanciers who died for France": Major Sylvain Eugene Raynal releases the last carrier pigeon during the battle of Verdun, on 4 June 1916. From *Le Petit Journal Illustré*, 7 July 1929.

OVERLEAF: German soldiers preparing a message and the pigeon to carry it, March 1917.

ABOVE: The final cablegram carried by pigeon, sent by Major Raynal on 4 June 1916. Fort Vaux fell to the Germans four days later.

■52 Trench Map

In 1914, most armies carried maps that were little different to those available to civilians. In some cases they were identical. For example, the British army went to war carrying Michelin maps of Belgium and France. After the retreat from Mons had carried the British further south than the map issued at the start of the campaign covered, officers were able to improvise by purchasing new maps from French shops.

The development of complex trench systems from late 1914 onwards necessitated a change in mapping. The maps of earlier wars had been defined by natural geography such as hills, forests and rivers. Trenches changed this, and during the First World War man-made terrain would become the key feature of maps of the Western Front. Early trench maps were crude affairs, but they steadily increased in accuracy and sophistication. By the summer of 1915, the British army had adopted a standard style that would last until the end of the war, although locally produced maps that deviated from this template still remained in use.

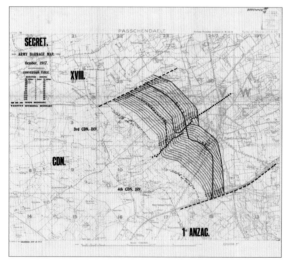

Trench maps served two purposes. First, they allowed the user to navigate the web of trenches that made up the front line. Most sectors of the Western Front had a front line that consisted of two or more major trenches that lay parallel to the enemy position. These lines were further complicated by the presence of dugouts, machine-gun nests and observation posts, all of which were connected by a web of smaller communication trenches that allowed movement between the front and rear areas. The British named trenches as if they were actual streets and even erected wooden name signs so that soldiers moving through the network could establish their position on the trench map.

The second purpose of trench maps was to provide accurate information on enemy positions. Aerial reconnaissance provided photographs that were sufficiently detailed to produce reasonably accurate maps of enemy lines. Although these would provide the layout of the enemy system, ground level observation and reconnaissance was necessary to add important front-line details such as barbed-wire belts and enemy outposts in no man's land. Great time and effort was devoted to ensuring the maps of enemy positions were as accurate as possible. Knowing the layout of the enemy trenches was a prerequisite to any attack and errors or omissions in the mapping process could have fatal consequences once the battle began.

Trench maps came in a variety of forms from large-scale survey maps to detailed tactical maps that covered specific sections of the front. The most meticulous trench maps of all were those used by the artillery. These maps used an alphanumerical grid system to allow the gunners to direct and co-ordinate fire on particular areas of the enemy position. Although the position of enemy trenches could alter, the grid system itself did not change. As the battle ebbed and flowed, gunners shifted their fire accordingly by concentrating on different areas of the grid. This ensured a degree of consistent accuracy even in the midst of battle.

The creation of maps in the British Army was entrusted to the Field Survey Companies of the Royal Engineers. The maps themselves were printed by the Army Printing Section. Field Survey companies were steadily expanded throughout the war, and by May 1918 every British Army on the Western Front had its own Field Survey Battalion, which came complete with its own printing section. By the end of the war the British army had printed an estimated 32 million trench maps, providing a clear testament to their importance and value.

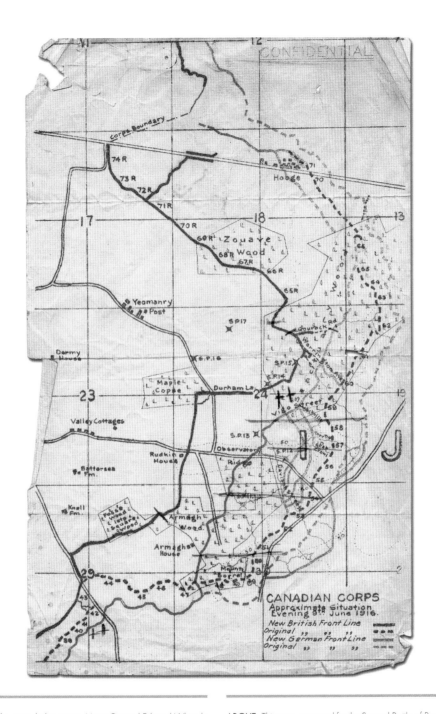

CONFIDENTIAL

CANADIAN CORPS
Approximate Situation
Evening 3rd June 1916.
New British Front Line
Original " " "
New German Front Line
Original " " "

OPPOSITE: This map, belonging to Major-General Edward Whipple Bancroft Morrison, shows the British and Canadian positions in brown and the German positions in red on 4 June 1916, during the Battle of Mount Sorrel.

ABOVE: This map, prepared for the Second Battle of Passchendaele, shows the German trenches in red, correct as of 16 October 1917.

53 Family Photograph

The sepia photographs of wives and children carried by many First World War soldiers represented the civilian and private inner life that they left behind when they volunteered or were conscripted into their respective armed services. Photography had been a "cutting-edge" and popular development, but remained very expensive in the nineteenth century. However the "dry plate" or gelatine photographic process invented in 1871 and greatly refined by 1914, and the No. 3 Autographic Kodak Camera, which was launched the same year, did much to improve the quality of photographs taken and considerably reduced the cost. Across Britain, France, the United States, Germany, Austria-Hungary and even Imperial Russia, families from all social levels could now afford to record important events such as weddings or other family gatherings on photographs. The introduction of the mass-market Kodak Box Brownie in 1900 made "snaps" possible, but there remained a huge market for formal portrait studios.

At the outbreak of the First World War, married men with children wanted photographs of their loved ones, and so a mass market was soon created for the photographic studios. In the United Kingdom, these were often based in the high street and many offered reduced rates for men in uniform to be pictured with their families, often wearing their very best clothes. These photographs often appear staged and lacking in expression. However, contemporary photographic techniques required the sitters to remain motionless for some time and, unlike today, it was considered "poor taste" to smile. For the soldiers, these photographs (often only one or two would be part of an individual's personal effects) were imbued with the warmth of pride and happy memories of home. For some they became a protective talisman, and reminders of the reason that they were fighting. Great care was taken to protect and preserve such photographs as they were carried in wallets, Bibles or wrapped in letters from the family. These precious faces from home would be shared with comrades. It was common practice for individuals going into combat to ensure that their photographs were placed in safe keeping with a fellow soldier or an officer remaining behind, until their return. Often considerable efforts were made to send them to the families of soldiers who did not come back, who were killed or taken prisoner. Best of all was a friend on leave, who could deliver the photographs to the family in person, and tell them of their loved one's last moments (whether truthfully or moderated with a degree of tact).

When a soldier was taken prisoner, all his personal effects were removed (paybooks and the like could be useful for intelligence-gathering purposes), but photographs of family were almost always returned. Indeed, it was common for soldiers to show their captors these family images in an attempt to be regarded as a human being and not just an enemy in a foreign uniform. Something of a taboo existed about destroying photographs. It is significant that so many of them are now in local archives and museums, the names of wives and children and family relationships lost in time. The comfort and hope offered by these images remain strong across the decades.

OPPOSITE: A British soldier saying goodbye to his family, c.1916.   ABOVE: A mother and her two children pose for a family photograph.

∎54 Telegram sent to Soldier's Family

Within British society, one of the cultural legacies of the First World War was the widespread belief that telegrams always brought bad news. The official notification of a soldier's death was by telegram (officers) or Army Form B104-82 (Other Ranks) delivered by Boy Messengers employed by the General Post Office. These messages became for many relatives both a hated and treasured link to their loved one.

Even when families received the "last letter" written by many soldiers to their close relatives "in case of misfortune", and letters of condolence from their comrades and officers, together with personal effects, many still refused to accept the notification of death. The situation was even more traumatic for those families whose loved ones were listed as "missing presumed killed", with no known grave but named on war memorials at home or overseas. They repeatedly demanded more detailed information from the War Office and sought to question men from their husband or son's unit. Rudyard Kipling, who tirelessly sought news of his son John's last moments at the Battle of Loos 1915, was unusual only for his celebrity. This search was often a hopeless task because many men simply disappeared in the chaos of battle. Finding comrades who had survived the fighting was by no means easy, and it was common to lie about how a soldier had died in order to spare the feelings of his relatives. In these circumstances, the telegram acquired for bereaved families the status of a relic, because it held the faint hope that a mistake had been made and their loved

father, brother, son might one day return. Some relatives clung to this illusion for decades.

Bereavement and the process of mourning is a normal and healthy response to death, which at the time followed a well-established pattern, linked to religious and social conventions of the period. But these could not easily be followed if the soldier died overseas. Repatriation of remains was not allowed. The dead were buried "in theatre" in a military cemetery, or sometimes in a civilian churchyard. Many families bitterly resented this policy and had private funerals in their parish churches, but without a coffin or the ability to say a final goodbye.

The actual date of the death of the relative became a fixed point in the year for reflection and memory for many people. The distinguished writer Vera Brittain (1893–1970) was a Voluntary Aid Detachment nurse during the war. She served in Malta and France and suffered four bereavements. Her fiancé Roland Leighton died of wounds in France in 1915. Her friend Geoffrey Thurlow was killed in April 1917 during the battle of Arras in France, and has no known grave; another friend, Victor Richardson MC, died of wounds in June 1917 and is buried in England. Vera's brother Edward Brittain MC was killed in action in June 1918, and buried on the Asiago Plateau, Italy. It was this last date and the telegram that brought the terrible news that haunted both her writings and the rest of her life. When Vera died in March 1970, she left instructions for her ashes to be divided and a portion were buried with her brother in Italy. Vera Brittain was not unique in seeking to continue a dialogue with the dead.

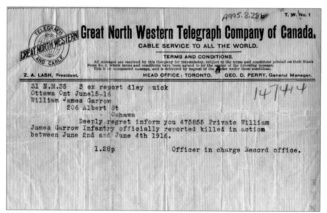

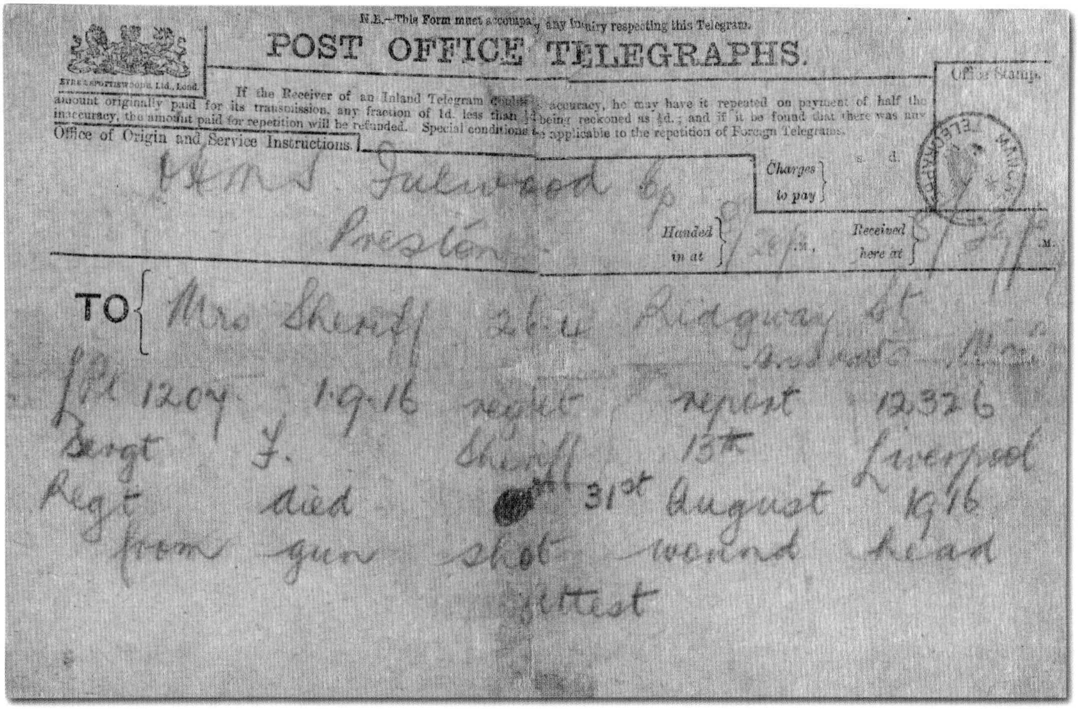

N.B.—This Form must accompany any Inquiry respecting this Telegram.

POST OFFICE TELEGRAPHS.

If the Receiver of an Inland Telegram doubts its accuracy, he may have it repeated on payment of half the amount originally paid for its transmission, any fraction of 1d. less than ½d. being reckoned as ½d.; and if it be found that there was any inaccuracy, the amount paid for repetition will be refunded. Special conditions are applicable to the repetition of Foreign Telegrams.

Office of Origin and Service Instructions.

Charges to pay s. d.

Handed in at

Received here at

Office Stamp.

H M S Fulwood Cp
Preston

TO { Mrs Sheriff 264 Ridgway St
Andrews

Fpl 1207 1.9.16 regret report 12326
Sergt F. Sheriff 13th Liverpool
Regt died 31st August 1916
from gun shot wound head
Littest

OPPOSITE: Telegrams announcing the deaths of loved ones were sent to all parts of the British Empire. This Canadian example gives the fate of Private William Garrow, killed in 1916.

ABOVE: Telegram announcing the death of Sergeant F. F. Sheriff of the 13th Battalion King's (Liverpool) Regiment at Abbeville on 31 August 1916. The cause of death was a head wound.

■55 Prosthetic Limb

The Great War killed millions and maimed more. An estimated eight million servicemen were permanently crippled. Over 750,000 of these permanently disabled veterans were British, and about double that number German. One all-too-typical example was a German former bank clerk, Erich Rehse, who lost both hands and an eye, and with them his independence. The sight of badly wounded men became a common one on the streets of Europe, Australasia, North America and further afield during the 1920s. The unprecedented number of disabled men placed enormous pressure on the prosthetic industry. In Britain alone 41,000 British servicemen had lost limbs, of whom almost 30,000 had lost legs. In June 1918, there were 4,321 men on the waiting list for replacement legs. It would take until the early 1920s until all patients had been fitted and by then many early war amputees were returning to hospital to have their worn-out prosthetics replaced with new designs.

The centre for the British war time prosthetic industry was Roehampton Hospital in London. The hospital was founded by private individuals in 1915 with the intention that it would specialize in the treatment of amputees. Prosthetic limb makers were invited to present their work to the hospital and the best designs were then contracted to produce limbs for the wounded. The hospital incorporated prosthetic workshops so that the limbs could be manufactured on site.

The prosthetic industry expanded dramatically as the war continued. The multitude of manufacturers and the fact that no amputation injury was quite the same limited the progress of standardization. Manufacturers took pride in their own unique design features and each casualty needed to be fitted individually. It was not until 1921 that the British government officially approved a universal prosthetic leg design, which all centrally contracted manufacturers were required to produce.

However, by then, the company Desoutter Brothers had launched the first lightweight metal leg. In terms of weight,

function and appearance the metal leg was adjudged considerably superior to the traditional wooden limb. Under pressure from the public and the Disabled Society, the British government gave Desoutter Brothers a central contract and allowed them to produce their own design rather than the standard wooden leg. The popularity of the new design was such that by the mid-1920s more than half of all prosthetics issued to ex-servicemen were metallic.

The level of innovation in the prosthetics industry during the First World War was remarkable. Individuals and small firms patented a vast range of designs and devices for amputees. These included alternative limb replacements, including some that were made from papier-mâché due to its lightness. In addition, companies also designed clothing and household items for amputees, including coats and suits that accommodated missing limbs, as well as more ingenious devices such as moveable tables for men who were missing both arms. One limb manufacturer stated that the "amazing progress" made in the industry from 1914 onwards "was entirely due to the Great War". The designs produced as a result of the First World War would remain the standard until the invention of plastic limbs in the 1950s.

Compared to their German counterparts, disabled British war veterans received little assistance from the State. In 1922, the government shut down a training programme for the disabled, in spite of 100,000 disabled veterans being without jobs. In historian Deborah Cohen's words, "the rehabilitation of the disabled remained largely the business of voluntarists" while in the new German Weimar Republic it was "the cornerstone of the new democratic order". The 1920 German Law of the Severely Disabled gave preference to crippled veterans in employment. Paradoxically, British veterans became pillars of the establishment in the interwar period, while their opposite numbers in Germany became alienated from the State and helped bring it down.

OPPOSITE: A soldier fitted with an orthopaedic limb, 1915.

ABOVE: A prosthetic arm and leg which were used by French soldiers.

56 8th East Surreys' Football

In the late nineteenth century, Association Football – known to the upper classes and Americans as "soccer" – came to be the most popular sport among the British working classes (there were some regional variations: Rugby Union was dominant in South Wales, Rugby League in parts of northern England). The rules of the game were codified in the 1860s, but the game rapidly developed from its public school, amateur roots to become a proletarian, professional sport. By the turn of the century, football had reached out from its northern base to become established in the south of England. London clubs included Tottenham Hotspur – in 1909 the Spurs team included Walter Tull, who was to gain posthumous fame as one of the first Black officers in the British army – and Woolwich Arsenal. Ending its connection with the great armaments factory, the club moved to north London in 1913, dropped the first part of its title, and went on to dominate English football in the interwar period. Football was equally popular in Scotland. Initially, Queen's Park was the most famous Scottish team, but by 1914 the "Old Firm" rivalry of the Glasgow teams, Rangers and Celtic, based in part on sectarianism between Catholic and Protestant supporters, was firmly established.

The First World War offers many examples of the hold that football had on working-class imaginations. At least one scratch game was played between British and German soldiers in No Man's Land during the Christmas truce of 1914. The entire Heart of Midlothian team joined 16th Royal Scots, raised by an Edinburgh MP, Sir George McCrae. At the height of the Second Battle of Ypres in April 1915, a soldier rushed to tell his officer that Chelsea had won the FA Cup. An officer commented that no matter how apparently exhausted the men were,

they always managed to revive sufficiently to play football – the list goes on and on.

Football was an important factor in maintaining soldiers' morale. One officer who recognized this was Captain W. P. ("Billie") Nevill, a company commander in the 8th East Surreys who provided probably two footballs (the exact number is uncertain) to kick as the battalion went in to action on the First Day on the Somme, 1 July 1916. One ball bore the words "The Great European Cup-Tie Final. East Surreys v Bavarians. Kick off at Zero". Nevill's use of footballs has been seen as an act of public school bravado, but it was more likely an inspired act of psychology, intended to distract his men at a moment of terror by presenting them with a familiar situation. It was one of many ways in which the public school games ethic influenced the British officer corps.

8th East Surreys was part of 18th (Eastern) Division, which, attacking as part of XIII Corps on the extreme right of the British line, captured all of its objectives in the Montauban sector on 1 July 1916. 18th Division, commanded by the formidable Major-General Ivor Maxse, benefited from weak German defences, good training, effective artillery, and excellent support from the French on the flank of XIII Corps. Nonetheless, success came at the price of heavy casualties. Among the dead was Nevill. Celebrated by a poem, press articles and a somewhat fanciful picture by the renowned military artist R. Caton Woodville, the incident rapidly became famous. One of the footballs survived the war and reposes in the regimental museum. The 8th East Surreys were not the only troops to kick a football into battle – the London Irish also did so at Loos in September 1915, for example – but Nevill's action stands as a testament to the centrality of football to British culture during the First World War.

OPPOSITE: The kicking of footballs immortalised the attack of the 8th East Surreys on the first day of the Battle of the Somme.

ABOVE: Captain W. P. "Billie" Nevill of 8th East Surreys, who bought the footballs for the regiment while on leave in Britain.

OVERLEAF: "The Surreys Play the Game" by R. Caton Woodville, which appeared in the *Illustrated London News* on 27 July 1916.

E EAST SURREY REGIMENT.

Football on the Battlefield at Contalmaison.

57 Playing Cards

Playing cards were an essential part of the kit of very many soldiers, regardless of nationality. Small enough to be carried in a pocket or knapsack, cards provided the means of an absorbing game capable of providing instant entertainment, and the usual surreptitious chance of gambling. Doppelkopf, and Skat, a three-handed card game, were popular among German troops. Its popularity is hinted at by the fact that the great artist and war veteran Otto Dix produced a famous Dadaist painting in 1920 entitled *The Skat Players*. A powerful comment on war and the state of Germany following the defeat of 1918, it showed, in grotesque form, three disfigured, disabled war veterans playing cards; in *All Quiet on the Western Front,* (see *All Quiet on the Western Front*, page 248) Erich Maria Remarque depicts soldiers playing the game.

Other armies had their own card games. French soldiers enjoyed Manille, Piquet and Mariage, while American doughboys often played poker. British "Other Ranks" favoured Brag, a bluffing game that may be an ancestor of poker, Nap and Pontoon. Officers played Auction Bridge, the precursor of modern-day Contract Bridge.

There were other forms of gambling. Australians played "Two Up", which involved spinning coins and betting on whether they landed heads or tails, and American troops played "Craps", a dice-throwing game. For the British, "House" – known today as "Bingo" – was popular, but the king of gambling games was "Crown and Anchor". It was technically forbidden by the military authorities, but a blind eye was often turned. It was a dice game played on a special cloth. Typical patter of the Banker was recorded as: "Lay it [money] down, my lucky lads; the more you put down the more you pick up.

You come here on bicycles, you go away in Rolls-Royces ... Right, up she comes. Two jam tarts [hearts] and the lucky old sergeant-major [crown]."

Gambling played a significant role in British working-class culture, mainly through betting on horse racing. The endless games of Crown and Anchor, Brag and their equivalent in other armies were reminders of home, and as such an important factor in maintaining the morale of soldiers who were mostly civilians-in-uniform, in the army for "the duration". So were other forms of entertainment, such as singing. The songs were often parodies, sometimes obscene. One of the milder ones was "John Brown's Baby", sung to the tune of "The Battle Hymn of the Republic":

> John Brown's baby's got a pimple on his –shush
> John Brown's baby's got a pimple on his –shush
> John Brown's baby's got a pimple on his –shush
> And the poor bugger can't sit down

Alcohol played a prominent role for pre-war working-class males, and in estaminets, a sort of café/bar hybrid behind the lines, off-duty soldiers could drink beer (usually unfavourably compared with the beer at home), *vin rouge* and *vin blanc* (of which the word "plonk", meaning cheap wine, is said to be a corruption). Coffee and light meals, such as egg and chips were also served. John Brophy and Eric Partridge, two wartime infantryman who compiled an indispensable dictionary of soldiers' slang, wrote of estaminets that "The name had a magical quality in 1914–18 – and still has for those who survive." Many a card game was played in them, to the accompaniment of weak beer and ribald songs, giving the soldier a chance to lose himself in the pleasures of the moment.

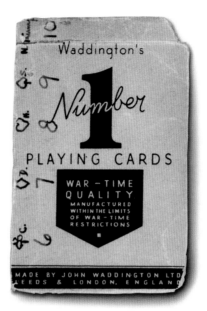

OPPOSITE: French soldiers playing cards, c.1917.

ABOVE: A complete pack of Waddington's Number 1 Playing Cards, its box damaged, used by Herbert Copestake of the Royal Flying Corps.

◼58 First-Aid Kit

The First World War is best remembered for innovations in weaponry. However, the war also saw considerable leaps forward in medical technology and technique. This was particularly true of first aid and many of the techniques pioneered in the First World War remain in use in the present day.

Every British soldier was equipped with a generic first-aid kit, which consisted of two field dressings. Soldiers were instructed on how to apply the dressing to wounded comrades to prevent blood loss and hopefully ensure the victim survived long enough to be treated by a formally trained officer. In theory, wounded soldiers would be evacuated to the Regimental Aid Post by stretcher bearers, who were equipped with a "medium first-aid kit" that contained additional dressings in a variety of sizes. Stretcher bearers usually had some basic medical training and could provide emergency treatment on the front line. Once a casualty had arrived at the Regimental Aid Post, he would be tended by the battalion medical officer, who was equipped with a more substantial first-aid kit that contained dressings, syringes, splints and morphine. After treatment at the Regimental Aid Post, unless the wounds were minor, the soldier would be sent to a casualty clearing station and thus depart from the front line.

There were a number of complications to first aid. The variety of injuries was considerable and included wounds caused by bullets, shrapnel and grenades, lacerations from barbed wire, concussion injuries from high explosives and eye and lung injuries caused by poison gas. The unhygienic conditions of the front line greatly increased the risk of infection. In many cases, treatment took place under fire, which made the work of stretcher bearers extremely dangerous. A testament to this danger is the fact that the most decorated British soldier of the war was the stretcher bearer William Harold Coltman, who, between 1917 and 1918, won the Victoria Cross, the Military Medal (twice), and the Distinguished Conduct Medal (twice) without firing a shot.

The war saw a number of important innovations in first-aid technique. In 1916, the British introduced the Thomas Splint, a traction splint designed to hold broken limbs in place. Prior to its introduction, battlefield fractures had a mortality rate of almost 80 per cent as the injured limb would be violently jolted when carried on a stretcher, aggravating the damage and causing agony for the casualty, which in turn could lead to infection or even death through shock. The introduction of the splint solved this problem by holding the limb steady and reduced the mortality rate to less than 10 per cent.

During 1915, the French Army developed the concept of triage, from the French word *trier* (to select or separate). This was the process of prioritizing the treatment of patients based on the severity of their injuries and likelihood of survival. Efforts were concentrated on those soldiers who had a chance to survive, which made treatment faster and more effective. The French also identified the importance of treating the casualty within the "golden hour", the crucial window of time after injury in which there was the highest likelihood that treatment would save the victim's life. These two related concepts would ultimately form the linchpin of first aid in both British and French armies in the First World War.

The innovations of emergency splints, triage and the "golden hour" remain a cornerstone of first aid to this day.

OPPOSITE: A dressing station in Monchy, France, where the Royal Army Medical Corps attend to the wounded coming down the line from Arras.

ABOVE: This first-aid kit was made to be carried on a horse, each box hanging down on either side of the horse's body. It contains bandages, dressings, hypodermic syringes and carron oil for burns.

59 Pozières Windmill

A few hundred yards beyond the Somme village of Pozières lie the remains of a windmill. Today it is nothing more than an uneven grassy bump in the ground with some masonry on top, but in 1914 it was a working mill, part of the landscape in a rural backwater. The windmill was progressively destroyed when war came to this area. Pozières village was located on the German Second Line of defence, and in July–August 1916 it was the scene of savage fighting as part of the Battle of the Somme. Australian flags and a commemorative plaque on the modern site are testament to the fact that Australian troops captured both village and windmill in 1916. A German assault on 7 August briefly retook the windmill, but Lieutenant Albert Jacka, who had won Australia's first Victoria Cross of the First World War at Gallipoli, organized a counterattack. In an astounding feat of personal leadership that should have merited a second VC (but did not), Jacka commanded an ad hoc group of Diggers which succeeded in repelling the asssult, recapturing the windmill, and restoring the line.

The fighting around Pozières was a microcosm of the attritional struggle on the Somme, and indeed on many other battlefields of the First World War. Given that both sides on the Western Front were broadly equally matched in terms of military effectiveness, that the temporary dominance of the defensive had brought about trench warfare with no flanks to turn and that the armies were backed by states with modern industrial economies mobilized for total war, great manoeuvre victories were impossible to achieve. Attritional strategies were thus inevitable. Not that attrition was unique to the Western Front. In the East, where a different set of tactical conditions meant that manoeuvre was possible, the Austro-Hungarian army was nonetheless worn out in a series of offensive and defensive battles.

Attrition, wearing down the enemy's physical and moral strength, is inherent in virtually all warfare. For armies to be defeated purely by superior manoeuvre is very much the exception rather than the rule. Many of the battles of Napoleon, one of the great masters of manoeuvre, ended up as attritional slogging matches; Borodino and Waterloo are cases in point. Even the Gulf War of 1991 was attritional, although the attrition was of the one-way variety, with the Iraqi forces suffering heavy losses, virtually without being able to lay a blow on Coalition forces, before the manoeuvre phase of the campaign began.

The common perception that battles of the First World War were radically different to those of the Second is wrong. While in most cases technological developments meant that battles of 1939–45 were more mobile, attrition played a significant role. Not for nothing did John Erickson entitle one section of his magisterial history of the Red Army in the Second World War "Breaking the Back of the Wehrmacht". The 1944 Normandy campaign was intensely attritional, and the four battles of Cassino were both attritional and largely static. During the Second World War, versions of Pozières were to be found on Pacific islands, in Soviet cities, North African deserts, Italian mountains, and once again in the French countryside.

OPPOSITE: Unidentified soldiers at the old mill after its recapture, photographed by an Australian official photographer on 28 August 1918.

ABOVE: British Territorials of the 48th Division fought in the Pozières sector in the summer of 1916. Here they are shown overrunning a German trench.

▪ 60 Wire Cutters

Barbed wire was invented in the late 1860s and had become widespread by the 1870s. Originally designed for agricultural purposes, it was cheap, durable and easy to erect. It was soon found to have battlefield uses, providing an obstacle that could delay the advance of attacking troops. Smooth wire had been used to strengthen defensive positions in the American Civil War (1861–65), whilst barbed wire was an essential element in the British blockhouse system during the Second Anglo-Boer War (1899–1902). In both conflicts, single strands of wire were placed at approximately knee height to entangle the legs of an attacker. The British refined the system by hanging tins filled with stones to the wire, which would alert the defenders of any attempt to cut or cross the line. Defensive wire was also employed in the Spanish-American War (1898) and the Russo-Japanese War (1904–05).

Aware of the likelihood of encountering wire in any future conflict, the British Army devised a standard pattern of hand-held wire cutters before the First World War. These were considered a highly effective tool, possessing sufficient leverage to snip wire strands, yet benefitting from a foldable design that made them compact to carry. They were standard issue to scouts, officers, gunners and Royal Engineers. In the early weeks of the First World War, these cutters were primarily used to clear away agricultural fences. During the Battle of the Marne in September 1914, British officer Captain Andrew Thorne wrote to his wife to ask her to send him a replacement "pair of wire nippers as soon as possible" as the advance was being hampered by farmer's wire.

However, by the Battle of Ypres in October–November 1914, both sides were beginning to emplace wire entanglements in front of their trenches. Initially little more

than crude single strands, these obstacles steadily grew in density and sophistication. Single strands gave way to vast belts of wire of considerable depth. Wire cutters were of little use against such complex defences, and attackers were largely reliant on preparatory artillery barrages to breach the obstacle. However, even the most intense bombardments could not completely destroy dense wire entanglements. Attackers following in the wake of the barrage needed their wire cutters to break through strands that had survived the shelling.

It is a common misconception that the entire Western Front was covered with formidable belts of barbed wire. Only important sectors benefitted from such complex defences and other parts of the line were covered by far smaller entanglements. In these areas, wire cutters proved an essential piece of equipment for scouting in no man's land or carrying out trench raids. In skilled hands, wire cutters could breach thin entanglements quickly and silently, allowing raiding parties to pass through to the enemy trenches. Aware of the dangers posed by such "cut and run" raiding, both sides frequently attached booby traps to their wire, usually a variation of the "rattle boxes" previously used by the British in South Africa, to alert the defenders of any attempt to breach the line.

Although not a glamorous or war-winning weapon, wire cutters were an essential front-line item. The British Army went through a number of revisions of its standard wire cutter design to improve weight, cost and efficiency, as well as introducing variations designed for specific duties, including cutters that could be attached to the end of a rifle. By 1916, wire cutters were standard issue to all soldiers. Such was the efficiency of the basic design that it remained in service, with minor modifications, until the 1990s.

OPPOSITE: Soldiers cutting through barbed wire defences near Oppy, France. This was a particularly heavily defended sector of the Western Front near Arras.

ABOVE: French wire cutters, manufactured by Peugeot Frères, 1916. Cutters could be easily attached to rifles.

61 Lawrence of Arabia's Arab Headdress

"Lawrence of Arabia" was one of the most glamorous figures to emerge from the war. Promoted by the American journalist Lowell Thomas, Lawrence offered a splash of romance and colour, with hints of the Arabian Nights, that contrasted with the grim reality of trench warfare. Lawrence's own books, *The Seven Pillars of Wisdom*, and the condensed version *Revolt in the Desert*, his mysterious post-war life (he joined the ranks of the RAF and the army under assumed names, and died in a motor cycle crash in 1935) all helped stoke the legend. Fascination with Lawrence continues to the present day, aided by the perennial popularity of David Lean's epic, although historically inaccurate, 1962 film *Lawrence of Arabia*.

T. E. (Thomas Edward) Lawrence was born in 1888. His mother was unmarried; his shame at his bastardy may have shaped his character. Before the war he spent time as an archaeologist in the Middle East and got to know the region well. Joining the army in 1914, he was posted as an Intelligence Officer to Cairo. In October 1916, he began the period of service with anti-Ottoman Arab Hashemite forces in the Hejaz.

Lawrence identified with the Arabs to such an extent that he frequently wore Arab robes and headdress. He was one of many Britons who fell in love with Arab culture. While his military activities were successful, he failed in his wider political objectives of promoting an independent Arabia as part of the British Empire. Lawrence wore Arab robes on campaign partly out of practical necessity, but also probably because he disliked formal uniform and what it stood for. He once recounted enraging a general by being incorrectly dressed. By wearing Arab headdress with his British army uniform at the Paris Peace Conference – Lawrence was present in his capacity of advisor and interpreter – he was making a very deliberate political point. Lawrence was deeply angered by the 1916 Sykes-Picot agreement, a secret plan to divide the Middle East into British and French spheres. Britain would gain Mesopotamia and Palestine, France would take Syria and Lebanon. This arrangement left no place for independent Arab states.

Although the regular forces of the British Empire played the primary role in the defeat of Ottoman forces in the Middle East, Arab guerrillas played a significant part in harassing and tying down enemy troops. Lawrence's exact role in the Arab Revolt is controversial. Formally a liaison officer, was he actually the effective commander of the Arab forces? In the interwar period, the military writer Basil Liddell Hart presented his friend Lawrence in an extremely flattering light, as the developer of the "first scientific theory of irregular warfare". However Prince Faisal ibn Hussein, the son of the Sherif of Mecca, was an important and effective guerrilla leader, and arguably he deserves much of the credit that has been given to Lawrence. Faisal certainly had a critical role in uniting the various tribes in pursuit of a common aim. Lawrence's version of events undoubtedly contains some, perhaps much truth, but he has been accused of exaggerating his own significance.

The creation of the modern Middle East out of the ruins of the Ottoman Empire was one of the many unanticipated by-products of the First World War, but undoubtedly it was among the most significant. By blocking the creation of the Arab state for which Lawrence and Faisal fought, France and Britain unwittingly helped shape a politically contentious region that was to become a major flashpoint in the second half of the twentieth century, and has continued to be so in the twenty-first.

OPPOSITE: Lawrence of Arabia on a camel in 1916. His post-war writing, mysterious life and early death help keep Lawrence's memory green to the present day.

ABOVE: A photograph of T. E. Lawrence taken by an American newspaper correspondent in the Middle East in 1917. The photograph gives some indication of Lawrence's charisma.

◼ 62 Kilt

erhaps the most distinctive item of uniform regularly worn by British infantry in the front line was the kilt. The kilted Highland soldier had become a Victorian icon, symbolizing the army of the wars of empire. It was no less famous during the First World War, with German propaganda often using the image of the kilted soldier. The modern kilt was a product of the attack on Highland culture following the defeat of the Jacobite Rebellions in the eighteenth century. A much simplified version of now-banned traditional Highland dress, it was designed by an Englishman, Thomas Rawlinson, in the 1720s. Although tartans were worn from at least the sixteenth century onwards, the "traditional" pairing of clans with tartans is also an eighteenth-century phenomenon.

In the late eighteenth century, the Highlander's image changed from that of wild rebel to loyal soldier. The service rendered by Highland regiments such as the 42nd Foot, or Black Watch, on battlefields from North America and India to Spain and the Low Countries contributed to the process by

which Unionism became the dominant ideology in Scotland. At the time of the Jacobite Wars, the kilt had been the dress of despised, defeated and feared rebels – by contrast, Lowland Scots troops featured prominently on the government side at the battle of Culloden in 1746 – but in time it became a symbol of the united nation of Scotland within the United Kingdom. The stand of the 93rd Highlanders at Balakava in Crimean War (1854), immortalized as the "Thin Red Line", coincided with the Victorian love affair with the Highlands, which was fuelled by the novels of Sir Walter Scott, Queen Victoria's annual residence at Balmoral and the wearing of Highland dress by the Royal family.

In 1914, the British army had five kilted Highland regiments (Argylls, Black Watch, Camerons, Gordons, and Seaforths). In addition some English regiments had

kilted "exile" Territorial battalions, such as 14th Battalion of the London Regiment (London Scottish). The vast Scots diaspora across the Empire produced kilted units such as the 43rd Battalion, Canadian Expeditionary Force, Cameron Highlanders of Canada which fought on the Western Front. On active service during the First World War, Highland troops usually wore the kilt covered by a khaki "apron".

During the First World War recruitment for the army in Scotland was extremely good: 320,589 Scots volunteered, the highest proportion in the United Kingdom. The most famous Scottish formation of the war was a Territorial one, 51st (Highland) Division. On arrival in Bedford for training in late 1914, the "kilties" caused a sensation; some locals believed that they were primitive barbarians, to the mingled amusement and annoyance of some of the middle-class volunteers.

51st (Highland) Division earned a formidable reputation as a fighting force in both world wars: the Germans nicknamed them "the Ladies from hell" (or so it was fondly believed). Like all other green divisions it took some time to find its feet, but at Beaumont-Hamel in November 1916 it did well. The well-known divisional memorial on the preserved Battlefield Park consists of a statue of a kilted soldier on a cairn, jocularly known as "the Jock on the Rock". The division's initials HD were interpreted by rival soldiers as "Harper's Duds" after its commander, Major-General G. M. Harper. In *1066 And All That*, a satirical history written by two Great War veterans, sideswipes are taken at troops that some thought got more than their fair share of the credit. These included the Americans, Australians, Canadians, "and 51 Highlanders", a backhanded compliment that illustrates that iconic status of the kilted Highland soldier, which began in the late eighteenth century, and continued during the First World War.

OPPOSITE: Men of the 2nd Battalion Argyll and Sutherland Highlanders, 19th Brigade, 6th and 7th Division, in the Bois Grenier sector, March–June 1915.

ABOVE; A French photo postcard from 1914: "Scottish soldiers arrived in France to fight alongside our soldiers." In the trenches a khaki apron was worn over the kilt.

OVERLEAF: The 2nd Battalion Gordon Highlanders marching towards the trenches of the Somme in October 1916, led by Drum-Major Kenny, VC.

⬛63 Ration Card

In 1915, British propaganda began to use the term "home front". The phrase was designed to convey the fact that the efforts of the civilian population were essential to the success of the military. Under the banner of being part of the home front, civilians were urged to support the national cause, to work hard in war industries, to maintain faith in victory and to save food. The importance of conserving food would become one of the most persistent propaganda themes of the war.

As an island Britain, was uniquely vulnerable to blockade and the government was acutely aware of the dangers of being cut off from vital maritime trade routes. Identifying the weakness of Britain's position, Germany sought to strangle British trade by imposing a U-boat blockade. Although this was ineffective in the early years of the conflict, Germany had sufficient U-boats and expertise by 1917 to make submarine warfare a serious threat to the British war effort.

The strains of war, the rising price of foodstuffs on the world market and the difficulties of importing it through the U-boat blockade all placed pressure on the British food supply.

Propaganda campaigns encouraged the population to save food, eat only what was needed, and grow vegetables in their gardens. The Royal Family were portrayed as eating frugally and cited as an example to follow. However, this voluntary approach to rationing was flawed. Those with sufficient money could buy what they wished, whilst those who were lacked funds were forced to make do with what was available; these factors fuelled resentment amongst the poorer members of society.

The initial economic response to the U-boat blockade was to increase home-based production. The government took over approximately 1 million hectares (2.5 million acres) of arable land and the wheat harvest of 1917 was the richest in British history. Nevertheless, the government knew that harvests of this quality could not be guaranteed in the future; furthermore, the latter part of 1917 saw a spate of panic buying amongst the public, which alarmed the authorities. As a result, it was decided to introduce rationing for certain foodstuffs. The foods were sugar (from 31 December 1917), butcher's meat (from 7 April 1918), butter, margarine and lard (from 14 July 1918), jam (from 2 November 1918) and tea (not rationed nationally, but distribution was limited to 2 oz (57 g) per person from 14 July 1918). Sugar and butter rationing officially lasted until 1920.

Although there were local problems, including public disturbances when rations were unavailable, the overall effect of British rationing was relatively mild. The Prime Minister, David Lloyd George, admitted that rationing was "troublesome" for the general population, but considered it a successful policy that ensured shortages did not become serious. Official figures revealed that calorie intake matched pre-war levels and in some cases exceeded them, aided by a wartime increase in real wages, which allowed civilians to purchase a greater quantity and range of food than before.

The experience of British rationing compared favourably to that of the Central Powers. The Royal Navy had instituted a blockade of Germany at the outbreak of the war, forcing Germany to introduce rationing in January 1915. German imports fell by 55 per cent over the course of 1915 and by 1916 food shortages were widespread. By late 1917 the average daily food intake amounted to just 1000 calories a day and even this limited requirement proved difficult to provide. Malnutrition and starvation was widespread, prompting food riots in German and Austro-Hungarian cities. The ruthless effectiveness of the British blockade was later judged to have been a major factor in Allied victory.

Brotkarte

Berlin und Nachbarorte

Nicht übertragbar

Nicht übertragbar

Gilt nur für die 25. Woche vom 9. August bis 15. August 1915

Rückseite beachten!

XXVIII   71581

OPPOSITE: Workers in the British Food Control Office sorting sugar ration cards, 1917. All bar one are women.

ABOVE: A German ration card for bread, dating from 1915. Bread was the first food to be rationed in Germany, and the size of the ration would be steadily reduced throughout the war.

Emperor Franz Josef's Tomb

Franz Josef I, Emperor of Austria and King of Hungary, died in the middle of the Great War, on 21 November 1916. Born in 1830, he had ascended the Habsburg throne at the age of 18 in the revolutionary year of 1848. These circumstances only reinforced his conservative character. He suffered a series of personal tragedies, including his son's death and his wife's assassination. His reign saw a series of humiliations, including military defeat at the hands of Prussia in 1866 and the granting to Hungary in 1867 of a status equal to Austria.

Franz Josef was buried in an austere, simple but splendid stone tomb among his Habsburg predecessors in the Imperial Crypt of the Capuchin Church, close to the Hofburg Palace in Vienna. He lies between his murdered empress, Elizabeth, known as Sisi (1837–98), and their son Archduke Rudolf (born 1858) who died under mysterious circumstances, probably by his own hand, in 1889. Franz Josef's funeral was one of the last hurrahs of the Habsburg empire. It was attended by a glittering assortment of European royalty (although naturally none from enemy powers), and more than 500,000 people were estimated to have lined the route of the funeral procession.

Franz Josef's passing preceded that of his Empire by only two years. While symbolically his death marked the end of an age, in reality his realm was already doomed. A multi-national, ethnically and linguistically diverse state, Austria-Hungary was under extreme pressure from separatists both within and without. It had become a de facto satellite of Franz Josef's German ally, and the take-over of Austria-Hungary was becoming a war aim of Germany. As a consequence of the often poor performances of Austrian forces, Austro-Hungarian military independence was already compromised. Germany had already begun the colonization of the Habsburg empire's armed forces, with German commanders in place right down to regimental level. Some of the damage to the Austrian army was self-inflicted. Conrad von Hotzendorff, the Chief of Staff, had launched his ill-equipped army into a disastrous series of offensives against the Russians in the Carpathians in early 1915. The army had made only modest gains and sustained huge casualties, not only from the battles but also because of the dreadful weather. Many of these casualties were experienced soldiers whom the army could ill-afford to lose. Then, in June 1916, the Russian "Brusilov Offensive" inflicted further grievous damage on his army.

Franz Josef's successor, his great-nephew Emperor Karl I, put out clandestine feelers to the Allies to see if a separate peace was possible, but they came to nothing. That Franz Josef lived to the age of 84 was in many ways a tragedy. A reactionary, Franz Josef was the wrong man to deal with the winds of change battering the Habsburg Empire. By contrast Karl was pragmatic and liberal. Had he come to the throne in peacetime, his civil and military reforms might have given the Austro-Hungarian Empire a new lease of life. By 1917–18 the time for such initiatives had passed. The various national minorities within the Empire were becoming increasingly restless, and Karl's consensual approach was at odds with that of the Germans. In May 1918, Karl was forced to agree to further measures that tightened German control over the Austrian economy and armed forces. The end of the Austro-Hungarian Empire was only six months away.

OPPOSITE: Emperor Franz Joseph I of Austria, photographed in 1914. Austria-Hungary's annexation of Bosnia and Herzegovina precipitated the Bosnian Crisis of 1908 and contributed to the outbreak of war six years later.

ABOVE: The tombs of Emperor Franz Joseph I of Austria (middle), his wife Empress Elisabeth (left) and his son Crown Prince Rudolf (right) in the Imperial Crypt in Vienna, Austria.

65 The Zimmermann Telegram

In 1914, the United States of America remained neutral. Since the formation of the Republic, the United States had striven, not entirely successfully, to stay out of foreign wars. Neutral it might have been, but America could not afford to be indifferent to the conflict being waged by the European Great Powers. Some Americans were strongly pro-Allied, even to the extent of enlisting in Allied armies. The Lafayette Squadron of American aviators flying for the French air service is the best known example, but many individuals slipped across the border and joined Canadian units or found some other way of joining the British or French forces. Other Americans, often of German or Irish descent or simply opposed to involvement in other people's wars, were determined to keep the United States out of the conflict engulfing Europe.

All this greatly reduced President Woodrow Wilson's room for manoeuvre. Personally Anglophile, he had no love for the autocracies of the Central Powers and was determined to defend the national interests of the United States in any way short of war. The country had many reasons to favour an Allied victory. Britain and France, and America's northern neighbour, Canada, were fellow democracies. Economically, British sea-power effectively prevented Germany trading with the United States, while American firms eagerly accepted Allied orders for war materiel.

Although the British strategy of blockade caused tensions with Washington, these were minor compared to the problems created by German submarines sinking neutral American shipping. The crisis, however, abated after Germany abandoned unrestricted submarine warfare in 1915. Berlin's decision after the Somme to attempt to defeat Britain by unshackling the U-boats, heedless of American reaction, made war with the United States all but inevitable. The question was, how united would be the nation that Wilson led into war?

The cause of American unity was given substantial help by an unlikely combination of the German Foreign Ministry and British intelligence. Both the British and the US State Department intercepted a cable from Arthur Zimmermann, the German Foreign Minister, to Heinrich von Eckhardt, the German ambassador to Mexico. Eckhardt was instructed to offer the Mexicans an alliance. In return for going to war with the United States, Mexico would get back the territories lost as a result of the 1848 Mexican-American War. Japan, which was actually at war with Germany, would also be invited to join the alliance. Having decoded the message, sent by submarine cable on 16 January, British intelligence exploited their coup by sending it to President Woodrow Wilson on 24 February. The "Zimmermann Telegram" became public on 1 March, appearing in newspapers across America, and caused outrage. American public fury at naked German aggression against a neutral state was intensified two days later by Zimmermann's bizarrely honest admission of the telegram's authenticity.

Relations between Mexico City and Washington were poor at this time. Only a few months earlier, Brigadier-General John J. Pershing, who was later to become famous as the commander of the American Expeditionary Forces in France, had led a punitive raid on to Mexican territory in pursuit of the revolutionary Pancho Villa. However, the Mexican government baulked at the notion of going to war with its powerful northern neighbour, even given Zimmermann's claim that Germany was winning and that unrestricted submarine warfare would soon shortly force Britain out of the war.

On 6 April 1917, the United States declared war on Germany, pushed over the edge by the activities of U-boats. The Zimmerman telegram, assisted by British intelligence, helped ensure that America went to war as a nation more united than it otherwise would have been.

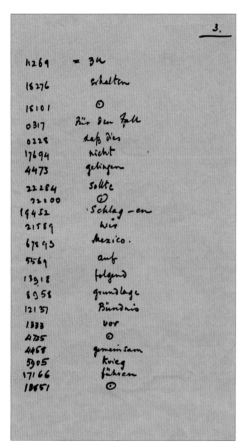

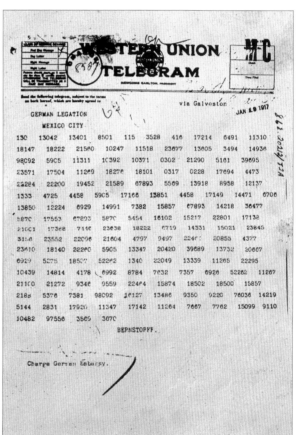

OPPOSITE: Arthur Zimmermann, State Secretary for Foreign Affairs, resigned in 1917.

ABOVE LEFT: Page 3 of the British decrypt of the Zimmermann telegram, as copied by Edward Bell of the US Embassy in London and forwarded to the US State Department on 2 March 1917.

ABOVE RIGHT: The Western Union copy of the telegram sent on 19 January 1917 by the German Ambassador in Washington, D.C., to the German Imperial Minister in Mexico City.

66 Punch Cartoon

*P*unch was a mildly liberal British humorous magazine that offered a gently satirical commentary upon contemporary events. It began publication in 1841, and within a few years had become a staple of middle-class reading. *Punch* was particularly famous for its political cartoons, and indeed the quality of the cartoonists, who included, in the First World War period, Bernard Partridge, and E. H. Shepard (who also illustrated A. A. Milne's *Winnie-the-Pooh*). Pre-war cartoons, which often featured the hook-nosed, hunch-backed Punch figure, provided comic but perceptive observations on the international scene. "Au Revoir", a cartoon of 1873, depicted a female personification of Germany saying to France, "Farewell, Madame, and if –". To which France replied, "Ha! We shall we meet again". Kaiser Wilhelm II was a regular target: as far back as 1896 he was depicted as a disruptive child, "Fidgety William", and in 1905 Partridge depicted the Kaiser as "The Sower of Tares", after the Millais painting, creating discord and undermining European peace.

The course of the war can be traced through *Punch* cartoons. The demonization of Germany is a particular feature. In August 1914, Belgium, personified as a brave farm boy, was shown blocking the path of a club-wielding, sausage-bearing, German bully. One of the most savage was "The Dance of Death" from 1917. This shows the Kaiser with a fiddle-playing skeleton. He says, "Stop! Stop! I'm tired", to which Death replies, "I started at your bidding; I stop when I choose". Among the very many of *Punch's* wartime cartoons, two from 1918 stand out for neatly capturing the near exhaustion of Britain, followed by the triumph at the defeat of Germany. The first, captioned "To All at Home", shows a soldier and sailor holding up an infant labelled "1918", who is underlining a message on a wall:

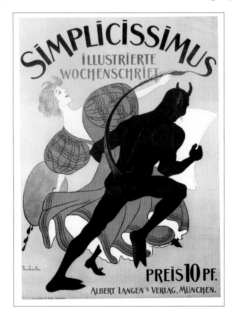

"Stick it!" The second has a mounted knight in armour with a winged figure of peace, surrounded by emblems of the Allied nations. The caption simply reads: "Victory".

A rough equivalent of *Punch* in Germany was the satirical magazine *Simplicissimus*, although this was much more radical than the British journal. The publication was noted for its "antimilitaristic, anti-nationalist" pre-war daring lampoons of Kaiser Wilhelm II, which on occasions resulted in contributors being imprisoned. However, it lost its radical edge during the war. As historian Leonard Freedman has written, "the only division on the staff was whether the magazine should cease publication because satire was inappropriate at such a time", or whether it should act as a patriotic morale booster. "The decision was that 'no German could stand aside' in a 'defensive' war."

The spread of mass literacy in Britain following the 1870 Education Act meant there was a huge demand for the printed word. Routine duty in the trenches and on board ship could leave men with much time on their hands. Many books, newspapers and magazines were sent out to the troops, many of a less elevated character than *Punch*. The magazine would have been mostly read by officers, but this was not the extent of its military readership, as significant numbers of middle-class men found themselves in the ranks. Working-class soldiers could also be voracious readers. The scurrilous journal *John Bull* was popular among the ranks, as were down-market newspapers and lowbrow thrillers such as those written by the prolific Nat Gould.

Used carefully, contemporary magazines and newspapers are an important source for the history of the war, illuminating attitudes and providing context; but it is well to remember that not everyone believed everything they read.

MOSCOW

A WALK-OVER?

THE KAISER. "THIS IS THE DOORMAT OF OUR NEW PREMISES."
EMPEROR KARL. "ARE YOU QUITE SURE IT'S DEAD?"

OPPOSITE: *Simplicissimus's* radical stire was replaced by a patriotic stance during the First World War. This cover from 1919 hints at a return to satire.

ABOVE: This *Punch* cartoon from 27 March 1918 is a comment on the recently signed Treaty of Brest-Litovsk, which had removed Rusia from the war.

67 U-Boat

One of the key factors in poisoning relations between Britain and Germany in the decade prior to the outbreak of the First World War was the creation by the Kaiser's navy of a powerful battle-fleet. The British rightly saw this as a direct threat to their security. When war came the rival battle-fleets pursued cautious strategies, and for the most part held each other in check. Under these circumstances it was the submarine, not the iconic battleship and battlecruiser, that proved to be the most potent weapon in the German naval arsenal.

The U-boat (from *Unterseeboot*) was a cheap weapon that could be produced in large quantities, but it was equipped with torpedoes capable of sinking an expensive and valuable armoured battleship. An early demonstration of the potency of the U-boat came on 22 September 1914 when *U-9* dispatched three elderly armoured cruisers, HMS *Aboukir*, *Hogue*, and *Cressy*. Fear of running into a U-boat screen was a principal factor behind Admiral Sir John Jellicoe's decision at the Battle of

64.70 m (215.5 ft) long, with a top speed of 16.4 knots (30.4 km/h) and 9.7 knots (18.0 km/h), and a crew of 35. It carried six torpedoes and could dive to a maximum of 50 m (165 ft). In all, 375 vessels were used during the war. The greatest U-boat ace was Captain Lothar von Arnauld de la Perière, who sank 194 ships. From late 1915 to March 1918 he commanded *U-35*, the most successful U-boat of the war, which accounted for 538,498 tons of shipping, 226 ships in all.

On 4 February 1915, in response to the blockade enforced by Allied navies, Germany announced that any merchant ships found in the waters around the British Isles, including neutrals – which in practice included ships of the United States – would be attacked. The strength of US protests against unrestricted submarine warfare – famously, the British liner *Lusitania* was sunk in May and 128 Americans died – forced the Germans, on 1 September 1915, to suspend the strategy. It was renewed in early 1917, in the full

Jutland on 31 May 1916 to break off the pursuit of the retreating German battle-fleet – a judgement that was controversial at the time and which still exercises naval historians a century later. Mines could be similarly destructive. The modern battleship HMS *Audacious* was sunk early in the war, although the weapon was by laid by a surface ship, not a submarine. There were also submarine minelayers. On 21 September 1915, *U-5* entered the heavily-guarded English Channel and laid a string of mines. The steamer *William Dawson* struck one of them and sank that very day. On occasions merchantmen were halted, the crew allowed to disembark, and the ship sunk by the gun with which the U-boat was armed.

U-boats came in different varieties; there were 33 classes, grouped into seven broad types. *U-35* was of the *U31* type,

knowledge that it was likely to bring the United States into the war. The gamble was that Germany could force Britain out of the war by severing her "Atlantic lifeline" and starving her population before sufficient United States troops could arrive to tip the balance on the Western Front. The gamble failed, but narrowly. The tonnage of vessels sunk in British waters in January 1917 was about 300,000, which increased to 870,000 tons in April. In the end, the U-boat was mastered by improved anti-submarine methods and, above all, by the introduction of convoys. However, surviving the First Battle of the Atlantic was a critical factor in the eventual Allied victory in the First World War. As a weapon of economic warfare, deployed to prevent food reaching the civilian population, the U-boat was a potent symbol of total war.

OPPOSITE: The engine room of a German U-boat. The submarine proved to be the *Kriegsmarine*'s most effective weapon during the First World War.

ABOVE: A submarine of the *Kriegsmarine* at sea, photographed in 1917. In this year Germany's unconditional submarine warfare campaign brought the United States into the war.

OVERLEAF: A German submarine captured by the British in 1916.

68 Rolls-Royce Armoured Car

Within the wider First World War, a number of smaller conflicts took place. One was the British campaign against the Senussi. This was a tribe in Libya which was stirred up by German and Ottoman political officers in 1915 to respond to the *jihad* ("holy war") which had been proclaimed in late 1914 to raid into British-held Egypt. This struck at a potential Achilles heel of the Allies. Both the British and French Empires contained vast numbers of Muslim subjects. The entry of the Ottoman Empire into the war on the side of the Central Powers made an enemy of the Sultan, who was regarded as the leader of the Islamic faith by millions. It seemed conceivable that Egypt could revolt, which would imperil the security of the Suez Canal, that vital artery of the British Empire. The Senussi's campaign of raiding thus had the potential to be of far more than nuisance value. Their threat was broken at the battle of Aqqaqir (26 February 1916).

Among the forces sent to fight the Senussi was the Cheshire Yeomanry, commanded by Lieutenant-Colonel the Duke of Westminster, equipped with Rolls-Royce armoured cars. The Yeomanry had conspicuous success pursuing the Senussi after Aqqaqir. As the regimental historian related, "Brave though the Senussi normally were, the spectacle of unfamiliar machines moving ... at a speed faster than anything that they had previously seen, was altogether too much for them." Those warriors who did fight back saw their bullets bounce off the armour plating, which did nothing for their morale.

Armoured cars had shown their worth at the very beginning of the war. Sent to northern France, some officers of the Royal Naval Air Service had used their private vehicles, fitted with weapons and armour improvised from boiler plate, to carry out reconnaissance and patrols from their base at Dunkirk. These men had included the Duke of Westminster and Sub-Lieutenant Lord Anglesey, descendent of Wellington's cavalry commander at Waterloo. Lord Kitchener was rather dismissive: "these irregular formations are only a means to enable certain officers and gentlemen without military experience and training to get to the front and take part in the war". The use of armoured cars was regularized by Winston Churchill's Admiralty, which placed orders for machines based on the Rolls-Royce Silver Ghost, a luxurious civilian automobile. Weighing 4.6 tons, armed with a single .303 Vickers machine gun in a turret, and 9 mm (0.35 in) of armour, Rolls Royce armoured cars were also used to great effect in the Hejaz, where from 1916 Faisal bin Hussein's forces were in revolt against the Ottoman Empire. They were supported by a squadron of Rolls-Royce armoured cars described by T. E. Lawrence ("of Arabia") as "above rubies" in value. He used them for hit-and-run guerrilla raids, attacking railway lines and bridges. Indeed, Lawrence entered Damascus in October 1918 in the course of the final and victorious campaign in a Rolls-Royce armoured car.

Rolls-Royce armoured cars also saw service at Gallipoli and in Ireland, where they were employed by the Free State forces during the Irish Civil War. The old mechanical warhorse was still use in the early stages of the desert campaigns in the Second World War, operating over much the same ground that had been familiar to its predecessors in 1916.

OPPOSITE: Belgian soldiers driving an armoured 1911 Silver Ghost by Rolls-Royce. By December 1914, the mobile period of the war was already at an end on the Western Front, limiting their use.

ABOVE: A post-war 1920 pattern, Mk 1 Rolls-Royce armoured car.

◼ 69 Lewis Gun

Although the Lewis Gun was an American invention it was not initially adopted by the United States Army. Its inventor, Colonel Isaac Newton Lewis, therefore took his gas-powered light machine-gun to Europe in an attempt to attract interest in an innovative design previously rejected by United States ordnance officials. In 1913 he departed for the industrial city of Liège, the chief centre of Belgian small arms production, where he established the *Compagnie Armes Automatiques Lewis* to facilitate commercial manufacture of the "Lewis Automatic Machine-gun". An extremely lucrative production license sold to the Birmingham Small Arms company (BSA) ensured that the means of production for what was ironically nicknamed the "Belgian Rattlesnake" was available in the United Kingdom in August 1914.

The Lewis Gun weighed just 13 kg (28 lb) with an overall length of 1,280 mm (50.5 in), and it was tthis relatively light weight as well as its impressive firepower potential (500–600 rounds per minute) that sparked interest in British ordnance circles after the outbreak of the First World War. First produced at BSA by a Belgian refugee work force, four guns were issued to each infantry battalion by June 1915. Subsequent transfer of Vickers heavy machine-gun sections from battalion to brigade command was balanced by the issue of 16 Lewis guns per battalion during the period leading up to the Battle of the Somme. Duly recognized as a "specialist weapon", the 303. calibre "Lewis Gun" was operated by a section of eight select men, each trained and cross-trained in specific tasks. The designated "Section Commander" (a Corporal or Lance Corporal) determined fire positions and issued fire control orders. The "No. 1" was responsible for carrying and firing the gun; numbers 2 and 3 each carried four of the distinctive 47-round "pan" magazines; numbers 4 and 5 acted as scouts, while numbers 6, 7 and 8 carried an additional 36 magazines between them. The amount of ammunition hauled by a Lewis Gun section was prodigious – over 2,000 rounds weighing 82.5 kg or 182 lb.

A Lewis Gun section, apart from the designated No. 1, was trained to operate as riflemen unless performing some duty in connection with the gun. Offensive tactics were embodied in a fire-and-movement section advance against obstacles indicated by the attached scouts. In defence, the Lewis was often positioned to cover vulnerable spots opposite the frontline. The main emphasis, either in the attack or defence, was on speed when engaging fleeting targets. Such was the experience of a Northamptonshire Regiment NCO at Trones Wood in July 1916. Repeated assaults against this German stronghold had failed with heavy loss before Corporal Alleway's battalion attacked under fierce rifle- and machine-gun fire. Cut-off and isolated for hours within the murky, corpse-strewn depths of the shattered forest, Alleway's half-section were rescued from imminent destruction by the timely arrival of a Lewis Gun and a man who could work it. Having immediately brought his weapon into action, the lone gunner repulsed the surrounding enemy infantry in "less time than the telling". Formidable, mobile and readily available in large numbers, the Lewis Gun became the principal firepower element of the British and Commonwealth infantry. By early 1918, there were 36 guns per battalion.

OPPOSITE: Manned by two Indian soliders, this Lewis gun has been set up for use in an anti-aircraft role.

ABOVE: A portable weapon that was effective for both attack and defence, the Lewis gun was the most successful light machine gun used by any forces during the war.

70 The Red Baron's Triplane

The single most famous aeroplane of the First World War was the red-painted Fokker Dr.I *Dreidecker* (triplane) flown by the German air ace Manfred, Freiherr von Richthofen. It gave him his nickname: "der Rote Baron": the "Red Baron". Richthofen was the highest scoring pilot of the war, credited with 80 victories. Of these "kills" of enemy aircraft, 19 were achieved while flying his Dr.I. It also proved to be the last plane that he ever flew.

The Dr.I was built as a response to the British Sopwith Triplane, which had begun to appear in the skies over the Western Front in early 1917. The Dreidecker was 5.77 metres (18 ft 11 in) long, with a wingspan of 7.20 m (23 ft 7 in). It was powered by an Oberursel Ur.II-cylinder rotary engine of 110 horsepower. Armed with two 7.92-mm IMG 08 machine guns, it had a maximum speed of 185 km/h (115 mph) at sea level, and a range of 300 km (185 miles), with a ceiling of 6,095 m (20,000 ft). Although highly manoeuvrable, the speed of the Dr.I was inferior to some rival aircraft.

The Fokker company also built some other landmark aircraft, including the 1915 *Eindekker* (monoplane). The *Eindekker*'s pilot was able to fire through the propeller arc, thus gaining a tactical advantage that triggered a period of German dominance in the air, known to the British as the "Fokker scourge".

Originally a cavalry officer, Richthofen came to the Dr.I in July 1917 after flying other aircraft, including three Albatross types: D.II, D.III and D.V. In January 1917, newly decorated with the "Blue Max", Germany's highest military award, Richthofen had become commander of *Jasta* (squadron) 11, and taken the bold decision to have his aircraft (a D.III) painted red. "After that," he was to write in his autobiography, "absolutely everyone knew my red bird." Already he had 16 kills, including the British ace Major Lanoe Hawker VC: in a short time, aided by his stand-out aeroplane and German propaganda, Richthofen passed into the realm of legend. Hailed as a hero in Germany, and admired and feared on the other side of No Man's Land, he shot down 21 planes during "Bloody April" 1917, four of them on 29 April alone.

Unlike some other aces, Richthofen was not a lone hunter. He was promoted in June 1917 to command *Jagdgeschwader 1*, a group of four *Jastas* that became known as "Richthofen's Circus". Richthofen was wounded in combat in July 1917 and hospitalized but returned to flying several weeks later, almost certainly before he was fully recovered. He was killed, flying his Dr.I, on 21 April 1918. Uncertainty surrounds his death. Initially it was thought that he was shot down by Captain Roy Brown, a Canadian Sopwith Camel pilot, but it is likely that he was killed by ground fire from Australian machine gunner, Sergeant Cedric Popkin. Either way, the most famous flight of the Red Baron's Fokker Triplane was its last.

OPPOSITE: The German fighter pilot Manfred, Freiherr von Richthofen. His fame endures as the greatest German ace of the First World War.

ABOVE: A model of the Red Baron's Fokker Dr.1 *Dreidekker* plane.

71 Lemon Squeezer Hat

The iconic slouch hat of the New Zealand soldier, with its broad brim, high crown and four dents, was inevitably nicknamed the "lemon squeezer". It was worn with a "pugaree", or hat band, in different colours to denote varying arms of service. First adopted by the Wellington Regiment before the war, the lemon squeezer spread across the entire New Zealand Division. Subsequently it came to symbolize the New Zealand soldier, and is worn on ceremonial occasions to this day. The silver fern-leaf badge, which was first used by New Zealand troops in the South African War, was another distinguishing mark; it appears on the headstones of "kiwi" soldiers in war cemeteries. The name "kiwi", from the flightless bird, was first used for New Zealand soldiers in the First World War. A giant kiwi was carved out of the chalk on a hillside near Bulford, on Salisbury Plain by men of the New Zealand Expeditionary Force (NZEF) in 1919.

Such distinctions helped differentiate the New Zealander from his Australian counterpart. The New Zealand government had decided against being included in the federation formed by the Australian colonies in 1901, but having a separate voice has long been a problem. New Zealand, of course, provided the initials "NZ" that formed part of "ANZAC" – Australian and New Zealand Army Corps" – which in lower case form became a more general term. But one often comes across the word "Anzac" being used as if it only applied to Australians. The original suggested title for the combined Australian-New Zealand formation was the "Australasian Army Corps", but this was sensibly vetoed by the New Zealanders who rightly doubted the ability of people (and the press) to differentiate between "Australasian" and "Australian". Gallipoli is seen as a key point at which the identity of New Zealanders began to

emerge, different from both the Mother Country and their cousins across the Tasman Sea.

New Zealand military forces came to prominence at Gallipoli, where a brigade fought a part of the New Zealand and Australian Division. A full infantry division was formed in Egypt in March 1916 and then sent to the Western Front. There, commanded by the formidable Major-General Sir Andrew Russell, the New Zealand Division earned a deserved reputation as an elite formation, perhaps even the best division in the British Expeditionary Force. Russell earned the admiration of Field Marshal Sir Douglas Haig, who offered him the command of a British corps (which Russell effectively declined). The New Zealand Division fought with distinction on the Somme (1916), at Messines and at Third Ypres (1917), in opposing the Germans offensives and then in the Hundred Days (1918). Other New Zealand formations included the Mounted Rifles Brigade, which fought in the Middle East.

One of the reasons why the New Zealand Division was so effective in 1918 was its size, which was greater than that of British and Australian (although not Canadian) divisions. Introducing conscription in 1916 (by contrast, Australia twice voted against conscription in referenda) and cannibalizing a brigade (in 1917 the Division had fielded four brigades instead of the standard three), it was able to maintain its manpower levels. This gave it the punch of a small corps rather than a 1918-standard division.

The commitment of New Zealand to the war effort was such that from a population of 1 million, about 45 per cent of the eligible male population served in the NZEF, and others in Australian and British forces. 18,000 NZEF members died, and another 50,000 were wounded.

OPPOSITE: New Zealand officers and NCOs being inspected by General Godley, commander of the New Zealand Expeditionary Force and II Anzac Corps.

ABOVE: The classic lemon squeezer hat as worn by New Zealand forces in the First World War.

72 Wireless Set

Guglielmo Marconi had demonstrated a functional wireless (radio) for representatives of the British army and Royal Navy in 1896. The navy had immediately seen the potential of the device and adopted it with enthusiasm. However, the army took a more cautious view. Wireless sets were too large and cumbersome to be man-portable, and they were unreliable and frequently broke down. Although the army recognized the potential of the device, it went to war in 1914 with only a handful of sets.

Other armies were experimenting with radio at this time. Famously, the Russian armies invading East Prussia in 1914 sent out messages in "plain language clear", which were intercepted by the Germans and helped shape the subsequent Tannenberg campaign. They were much pilloried for this security lapse, though the Germans were just as culpable. The interception of some 50 German wireless messages "in clear" from September to November 1914 aided French and British commanders in their decision-making at a critical phase on the Western Front. Signals intelligence – decrypting and interpreting intercepted wireless messages – played a significant but underrated role during the First World War.

The static nature of warfare from 1915 onwards prompted armies to experiment with "trench wireless", but a truly effective and portable wireless set was beyond the technology of the time. In an attempt to overcome the transport issue, the British Army began to employ "wireless tanks" in late 1917. These were conversions of older model vehicles, which replaced weaponry with communications gear. However, the vibrations inside a tank when the engine was running interfered with wireless reception, and necessitated the kit being unloaded from the vehicle prior to usage. This seriously limited their potential, although it did represent an improvement on the effectively immobile wireless of the early war.

The absence of portable wireless was a problem common to all armies in the war. The resulting mismatch between the high tempo of combat and the slow speed of communications posed fundamental difficulties that shaped the nature of the fighting. Once an attack had begun, the fog of war descended onto the battlefield as the advancing forces had no reliable means of communicating with higher command in the rear areas. In the absence of functional wireless, attackers were forced to send back runners carrying messages. However, the risks to an individual crossing the deadly battlefield were enormous and many messages failed to reach their recipients; furthermore, sending runners was a slow process and meant information could be outdated by the time it had arrived. This delay in communications meant that it was extremely difficult to exploit any success which the attackers achieved. By the time messages for reinforcements or support had arrived at headquarters, the battlefield situation had frequently already changed.

Nevertheless, although it did not solve the fundamental communication problems of the war, wireless proved valuable in specific circumstances. Aircraft were capable of carrying wireless. They were particularly useful in an artillery observation role, especially when observing fire directed deep into the enemy position. The observer could witness the fall of shells and signal back to the gunners to change their aim as required.

Wireless became more important during the Allied offensives from August 1918 onwards. The conditions of semi-mobile warfare meant that troops made comparatively deep advances and frequently outran their telephone lines. Vehicle-transported wireless allowed units to remain in contact with one another whilst new cable was brought forward for the field telephones. The full potential of wireless lay in the future, however, and it would not reveal its true value until the Second World War.

OPPOSITE: A field wireless and telegraph in operation on the Western Front.

ABOVE: A radio telephony transmitter with microphone c. 1915. Previously the only way for pilots to communicate with the ground involved hand signals and flags.

OVERLEAF: This biplane from circa 1917 was fixed with both a wireless set and a machine gun.

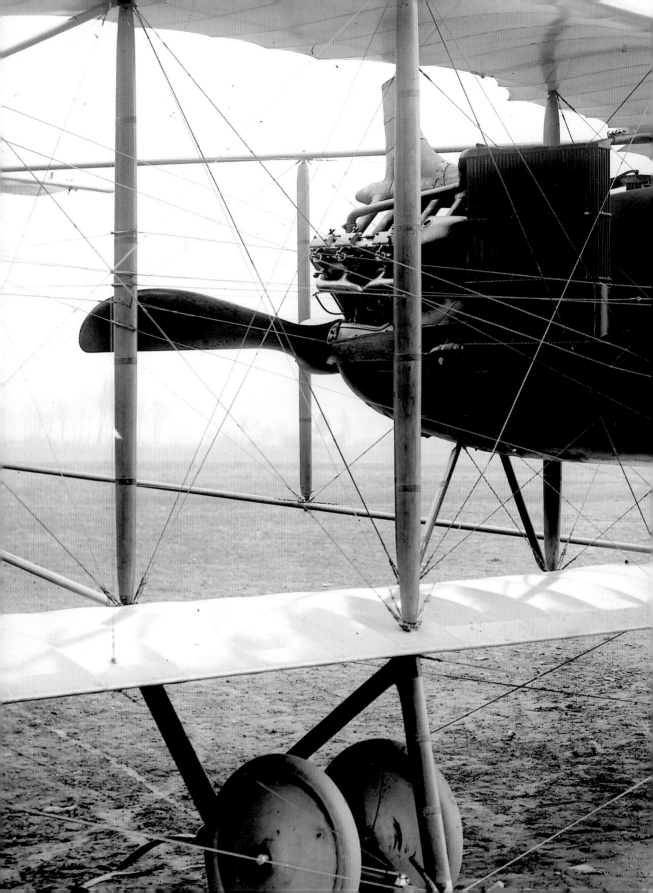

73 Siegfried Sassoon's Letter of Protest

*T*he Times of 31 July 1917 carried a statement issued by a young infantry officer, Siegfried Sassoon. Arguing that the conflict had turned from one of self-defence to one of territorial aggrandisement, Sassoon claimed, "I am not protesting against the conduct of the War, but against the political errors and insincerities for which the fighting men are being sacrificed."

Siegfried Sassoon is one of the most famous of British war poets. He was born into a wealthy Jewish family in 1886 and grew up living the comfortable pastoral life of a young squire. Fired with patriotism, he had joined the Sussex Yeomanry before the war and was commissioned into the Royal Welch Fusiliers in May 1915. Whilst serving at the front he met fellow officer Robert Graves and the two developed a close friendship.

Sassoon repeatedly risked his life leading raids and attacks, earning the nickname "Mad Jack". His courage in rescuing the wounded from no man's land during the Battle of the Somme resulted in the award of the Military Cross in July 1916. He was also nominated, unsuccessfully, for the Victoria Cross for his part in a raid on German lines. Sassoon wrote a considerable quantity of poetry during his time at the front and his early work was often patriotic and heroic in tone.

Sassoon was wounded in April 1917 and returned home for convalescence. Away from the front he had time to reflect upon his experiences and he was deeply upset by news of the death of one of his closest friends, David Thomas. He was introduced to the pacifists Robert Ross, Lady Ottoline Morrell and Bertrand Russell. With their encouragement, Sassoon chose to make a public act of protest against the war. He threw away the ribbon of his Military Cross (not the medal

itself as is commonly claimed) and wrote a letter condemning the objectives of the war entitled *Finished with the War: A Soldier's Declaration*. Russell forwarded the letter to the national press and used his connections to have the letter read aloud in Parliament. The incident sparked a furore in the press.

Rather than place Sassoon before a court martial, the authorities judged that he was suffering from shell shock and sent him for psychiatric therapy. He was treated at Craiglockhart Hospital in Scotland and whilst there he composed many of his most famous poems, which now adopted a markedly cynical tone in comparison to his earlier work. He also met and befriended fellow poet Wilfred Owen. After three months of treatment, Sassoon returned to his old regiment and was wounded again in July 1918. He was still recovering from this injury when the war finally came to an end.

Sassoon revisited his war experiences in the "fictionalized autobiography" known as the Sherston trilogy (*Memoirs of a Fox Hunting Man, Memoirs of an Infantry Officer, Sherston's Progress*), which revealed some of his attitudes about the war. In *Memoirs of an Infantry Officer* he reprinted his letter of protest verbatim, but the book also revealed something of his conflicted emotions over the incident.

Sassoon's statement has been repeatedly cited as an example of the sense of frustration and betrayal felt by the front-line soldier. However, this was a personal act of defiance and it is dangerously misleading to infer wider conclusions from a single letter. In 1945, Sassoon admitted that in retrospect it was unlikely that "a Peace negotiated in 1917 would have been permanent ... nothing on earth could have prevented a recurrence of Teutonic aggressiveness".

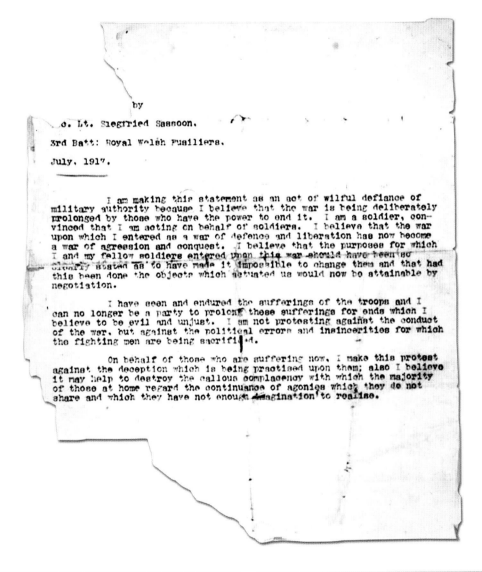

by

o. Lt. Siegfried Sassoon.

3rd Batt: Royal Welsh Fusiliers.

July, 1917.

I am making this statement as an act of wilful defiance of military authority because I believe that the war is being deliberately prolonged by those who have the power to end it. I am a soldier, convinced that I am acting on behalf of soldiers. I believe that the war upon which I entered as a war of defence and liberation has now become a war of aggression and conquest. I believe that the purposes for which I and my fellow soldiers entered upon this war should have been so clearly stated as to have made it impossible to change them and that had this been done the objects which actuated us would now be attainable by negotiation.

I have seen and endured the sufferings of the troops and I can no longer be a party to prolong these sufferings for ends which I believe to be evil and unjust. I am not protesting against the conduct of the war, but against the political errors and insincerities for which the fighting men are being sacrificed.

On behalf of those who are suffering now, I make this protest against the deception which is being practised upon them; also I believe it may help to destroy the callous complacency with which the majority of those at home regard the continuance of agonies which they do not share and which they have not enough imagination to realise.

OPPOSITE: Siegfried Sassoon, photographed in 1920. His bravery on the Western Front was exceptional, described even as "suicidal" by his friend and fellow soldier Robert Graves.

ABOVE: Written with the assistance of Bertrand Russell and the critic John Middleton Murry, Sassoon's letter was read to the House of Commons on 30 July 1917 and printed in *The Times* on the following day.

■74 Soldier's Bible

The First World War was fought by soldiers of many religious faiths and practices. The majority of troops from Britain and the Dominions were at least nominally Christian. In 1914, from a population of some 42 million in England, Wales and and Scotland, there were 2.5 million active members (i.e. communicants) of the Anglican churches, 1.2 million Scottish Presbyterians, 2 million Nonconformists, and 2.4 million Roman Catholics. Furthermore, "diffusive Christianity", the influence on wider society of Christian ethics and vague, undoctrinaire beliefs, meant that the Christian faith reached far beyond the doors of the churches.

Protestants in particular placed great emphasis on the reading and studying of the Bible. Small "Active Service Testaments" were popular with troops. These included a message from Field Marshal Lord Roberts, the archetypical Victorian Christian Warrior:

"I wish you to put your Faith in God. He will watch over you and strengthen you. You will find in this little Book guidance when you are health, comfort when you are in sickness and strength when you are in adversity."

Religion in the British Army offered a sense of community and belonging in the form of services, and the opportunity to speak in confidence to the chaplain ("padre"). Their work was often pastoral; the padre need to balance their spiritual role with what one chaplain called "Holy Grocery", the provision of comforts and acting as a welfare officer. Compared to Roman Catholic chaplains, Anglicans have had a poor reputation, but recent scholarship has demonstrated that it is largely undeserved.

Many soldiers found great solace and comfort in their pocket bibles and prayer books; the aphorism that "there are no atheists in a foxhole" is applicable to the First World

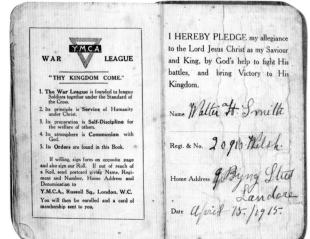

War. Many stories circulated of "lucky" Bibles that had saved a soldier's life, by perhaps stopping a piece of shrapnel or being dropped just as an enemy sniper took aim and fired into a trench.

Germany, too, was a Christian country, with Catholicism strong in Bavaria and Protestantism in the north. German soldiers also found solace in their faith. One Protestant pastor serving in a Saxon unit thought that about half of soldiers had faith of some form. Catholic soldiers built altars in rear trenches. Like the British, many German soldiers' Christianity was of the diffusive kind, rather than formal and church-based. Historian Alexander Watson has persuasively argued that "religious faith was... [very important] to the German army's ability to endure".

Many local church and chapel groups supplied their own versions of the Bible and prayer book, often with a brief inscription: "God-speed and a Safe Return from a few well wishers of Morecambe" read one. A Bible was often regarded as a "safe place" to keep photographs and letters from home. Soldiers frequently kept them as a memento of their war service when they were demobilized, and many were returned to his family as part of dead soldier's personal effects. This difficult task was often the responsibility of a chaplain, who would enclose a brief letter. These items became treasured keepsakes to be handed down through the generations. One British soldier's Active Service Testament, dated 1916, was carried by his descendants on operations in the Second World War, Korea in the 1950s, and during the Troubles in Northern Ireland. While on active service in Afghanistan in the twenty-first century, its most recent owner carried it as a talisman, tucked into his body armour.

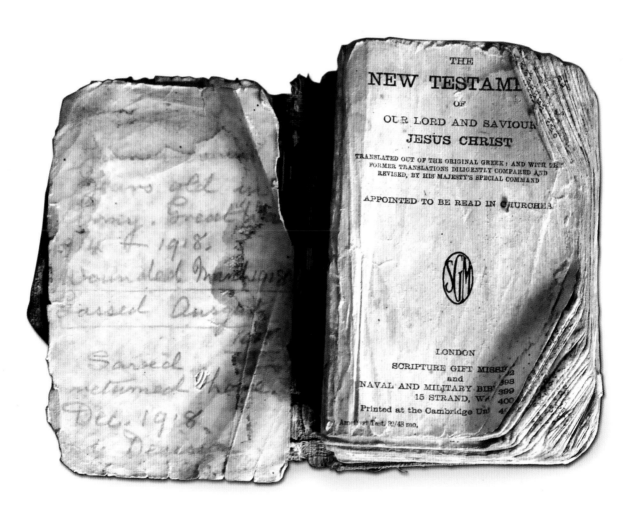

OPPOSITE: The inner pages of a handbook-size Bible issued to British soldiers. This copy belonged to Walter Smith.

ABOVE: The Bible belonging to Wilfred Ellis. He used the Bible to write notes about his experiences.

75 Toy Soldiers

Models of soldiers have been created for centuries. Examples have been found in an ancient Egyptian tomb, and European princes such as the future French kings Louis XIII and XIV played with them. However, as toys for the masses, model soldiers began to emerge about 250 years ago. *The Brave Tin Soldier*, Hans Christian Andersen's story from a century later, is testimony to the popularity of such toys. The late nineteenth and early twentieth centuries were something of a heyday for toy soldiers. Previously they had been flat figures, but the German firm of Georg Heyde popularized three dimensional models, producing a vast range. In Britain the firm of William Britain began producing hollow (and therefore less expensive) lead soldiers in 1893. This company, too, produced very many types of figure.

Boys from all parts of society played with toy soldiers. Winston Churchill had a large collection of 1,500 figures, infantry, cavalry and guns, which is currently on display at Blenheim Palace in Oxfordshire. Britain's toy soldiers were sold for prices that put them within the price range of much humbler members of society. Before the war, toy soldiers were often depicted in the splendours of full (parade) dress, or wearing uniforms of the era of Napoleon or Frederick the Great. However, the duller, more prosaic uniforms worn in the field were also represented, along with new troop types such as machine-gun crews.

The popularity of toy soldiers perhaps offers evidence of the militarization of European youth before the First World War. Militarism in this sense can be defined as a glorification of and excessive deference to the armed forces, and the permeation of military values through the state and society. The wearing of sailor suits by small boys in Britain and Germany is another example of this, as is the prevalence of uniformed youth organizations. Historian J. O. Springhall has estimated that 41 per cent of British boys were members of a uniformed organization before the First World War. Other states also had such groups: in Germany, the Pathfinders emphasized military preparedness and physical fitness. Too much can be made of this – the militarism of the Boy Scout movement can be overstated, and in Germany there were also strong left-wing youth organizations. However there is little doubt that militarism, as defined above, played a role in mentally preparing youth for war.

The British author Saki (H. H. Munro) amusingly satirized the fear of militarization through war toys in his short story *The Toys of Peace* (published posthumously in 1919). Well-meaning adults, eager to mould young minds, present two boys with a model of the Manchester Branch of the Young Women's Christian Association and lead models of John Stuart Mill and other worthies. Left to their own devices, the boys use the toys to fight a battle, with the model figures standing in for Louis XIV, Marshal Saxe and their soldiers, the French having launched a daring raid on Manchester. The disconsolate uncle slinks away, concluding that the experiment was a failure: "We have begun too late."

ABOVE: German-made toy soldiers in field-grey uniform and *Pickelhaube*, c.1914.

■76 Sandham Memorial Chapel

Tucked away in the Berkshire village of Burghclere is a building that houses some of the greatest paintings to have emerged from the First World War. The Sandham Memorial Chapel was built to honour the memory of Lieutenant Henry Sandham, who had died of disease contracted in Salonika. The artist Stanley Spencer (1891–1959), who was born in nearby Cookham and who served in Salonika, was commissioned to create a cycle of paintings. The result, painted in naive style, was a stunning visual record of a military campaign that has almost vanished from the popular memory of the conflict.

The reason why a large Allied force was established at the Greek port of Salonika lies in the decision of the French and British in 1915 to send troops to aid their Serbian allies, who were being attacked by German, Austrian and Bulgarian forces. They arrived too late to be of help to the Serbs, but although Greece was neutral, Salonika remained an Allied enclave for the rest of the war, outside the control of the Greek authorities. The size of the Allied force grew to 600,000 by 1917. The overall commander was the Frenchman, General Maurice Sarrail. One of the factors in the creation and sustaining of the Salonika "sideshow" was that the politics of the French army demanded that the influential Sarrail had a significant command away from the Western Front.

Spencer served as a humble member of the British corps commanded by General George Milne. The "gardeners of Salonika" saw intermittent action during 1916 and 1917. In November 1916, the Serbian town of Monastir was taken by the Allies. A subsequent offensive in the Monastir section in April 1917 failed, in part because of the problems of coordinating a multi-national army (in addition to the British and French, there were also Serbian, Russian and renegade Greek forces). However in the last few months of the war, under the command of the highly effective French general Franchet D'Esperey and supported by a Greek force, the Salonika army won a major victory. In September 1918, the Vardar offensive broke through the Bulgarian defences and the Allied forces drove towards the Danube. This victory was part of the cumulative pressure that brought about the defeat of the Central Powers in November.

Spencer served first as an orderly in the Royal Army Medical Corps and then in the infantry (7th Royal Berkshires). His paintings mix mundane but fascinating detail with Christian imagery: the altarpiece, *The Resurrection of the Soldiers*, has men clambering out of their graves and greeting their comrades. One winds up his puttees, needed no more. In the background, surrounded by redundant crosses, is a small figure of Christ. One wonders whether the resurrected soldiers are handing in their crosses to a heavenly quartermaster, in a respectful parody of the process of demobilization. The casualties from disease were much higher than those from enemy action (Lt Sandham died of disease), and this is reflected in Spencer's paintings. In one scene mosquito netting is being strung up in tents – Salonika was a malarial area. Climatic conditions for the soldiers were extreme, with temperatures ranging from the very hot to the very cold.

The Sandham paintings brilliantly capture the small change of soldiering, seen from the perspective of the ordinary soldier (Spencer was never commissioned). Some of the paintings recall the time he spent as an orderly in a hospital in Bristol. One has an officer reading a map while his men take the opportunity for a crafty rest. R. H. Wilenski, an art historian and critic believed "every one of the thousand memories recorded had been driven into the artist's consciousness like a sharp-pointed nail".

There is a popular view that soldiers of the First World War spent most of their time in action or in the trenches. This is wrong. Much time was spent behind the lines. From hospital beds to jam sandwiches and the minutiae of army uniforms, Stanley Spencer captured the experience of the ordinary British soldier in an extraordinary way.

OPPOSITE: Stanley Spencer. Asked initially to depict a religious service held at the front, he chose instead to show "God in the bare real things, in a limber wagon, in ravines, in fouling mule lines".

ABOVE: *Travoys Arriving with Wounded at a Dressing-Station at Smol, Macedonia, September 1916.* Spencer later said of the work, "I meant it not as a scene of horror but a scene of redemption."

77 Field Telephone

The invention of the telephone in 1876 did not have an immediate effect on European armies. Militaries around the world possessed a well developed system of communications, relying on flags, heliographs and despatch riders. The novel technology of the telephone seemed to have distinctly limited military functions, not least the difficulty in laying out the necessary cable during the midst of operations.

For the British army, attitudes began to change during the Second Anglo-Boer War (1899–1902). A turning point came when the Boer surprise attack at the Battle of Platrand (6 January 1900) caught the British defenders unawares and prompted the commander, Ian Hamilton, to telephone higher command for reinforcements. The speed of this communication played a key role in the ultimate British victory.

The army adopted a small number of telephones in the years prior to the First World War but remained cautious about their utility. The experience of fighting in 1914 proved that the caution was justified. Telephone lines were vulnerable to being cut by enemy shellfire and even when they were intact, the quality of voice communications was variable. Nevertheless, there were hints of their potential value during operations in 1914.

The imposition of static warfare from late 1914 onwards and the development of trench systems saw the field telephone increase in importance. Frontline telephones could be safely located in dugouts and the lines could be secured by integrating them into the trench network itself. When the system functioned correctly, it provided reliable and instant communication with headquarters and other rear areas, such as artillery and logistics. The German army on the Western Front in May 1917 had 515,000 km (320,000 miles) of telephone wire, with another 348,000 km (216,000 miles) on the Eastern Front.

Telephones were particularly useful for artillery. Artillery positions were some distance behind the lines, which meant the gunners were unable to observe the fall of their own shells. This problem was solved by the presence of forward observers using telephones. These observers could offer instant feedback on the accuracy of shell fire and were an essential component of the artillery branch.

The existence of the functional field telephone allowed the generals of the First World War to direct operations from behind the lines. Although the stereotypical image of the "chateau general" portrayed commanders as deliberately avoiding the dangers of the trenches, the decision to locate headquarters some distance from the front was a practical one. Through the instant communications available via telephone, commanders could be kept informed about events at the front and swiftly give orders to their subordinates. This allowed commanders to manage large battlefronts with – theoretically, at least – relative efficiency.

However, the field telephone system had its limitations. Even when integrated into the trench network, it was vulnerable to damage from enemy fire or simple mechanical failure, and thus required constant, labour-intensive maintenance. Front-line officers deeply resented the way the telephone was often used to send trivial requests from rear areas, with the frustration proving a frequent theme of parody in trench newspapers. However, the most serious limitation of the system was the inability to carry phones forward in the attack. Once the attackers had advanced into no man's land, communications became exceptionally difficult. Telephone operators in the trenches had to anxiously await the arrival of messengers from the attacking force before they could communicate information back to headquarters. The speed of telephonic communications was thus severely limited during offensive operations, with consequent problems for command and control. Communications in the midst of battle remained a problem until the advent of portable wireless.

OPPOSITE: A soldier using a field telephone in a fortified German Army shelter near Verdun, c.1916.

ABOVE: French troops using a field telephone, 1916.

OVERLEAF: An Austro-Hungarian field telephone unit in Galicia, 1915.

78 Alpini Hat

Throughout history, elite troops have worn distinctive headgear that indicated their crack status. The Alpini (Italian army mountain warfare units) wore a roughly triangular shaped felt hat with the back brim turned up. The colour was changed from black to grey-green shortly before the First World War. The front of the hat bore a badge of an eagle flying above a bugle-horn, and also featured crossed rifles and an axe. On parade and behind the lines the hat was adorned with an eagle feather on a coloured *nappina* (pompom).

When Italy entered the war in May 1915, there were 24 battalions of Alpini in an army of 36 infantry divisions. Eventually, the number of Alpini battalions rose to 64, and by late 1917, the army as a whole had increased to 65 divisions. The Italian army was poorly prepared for a major European war, being especially short of heavy artillery, the weapon which by 1915 had been recognized by the belligerents as the key to success on the modern battlefield. It also lacked sufficient stocks of machine guns, ammunition and even rifles. It did not bode well for the offensive that the Army Chief of Staff (effectively Commander-in-Chief), General Luigi Cadorna, began on 23 June 1915. This, the First Battle of the Isonzo, aimed to seize the disputed Trentino area from Austria-Hungary. Attacking uphill on to the Carso Plateau, once described as "a howling wilderness of stones as sharp as knives", Italian hopes of a rapid victory were confounded by determined Austrian resistance from strong defensive positions. It was the first of 11 Italian offensives on the Isonzo. Advances were as difficult to achieve in Italy as in France and Flanders.

The Alpini came into their own in the campaign in the Dolomites. In 1915, the Austrians retreated to make maximum

use of their height advantage, and a dreadful mountain war ensued. Soldiers of both sides had to battle the elements as well as the enemy. Snow and sub-zero temperatures were a regular hazard. Avalanches killed many. Guns and other heavy equipment had to be manhandled or laboriously hoisted up the mountainside. Alpini were often deployed in sub-units, to achieve the greatest benefit from their mountaineering skills. Mules, able to carry heavy loads to apparently inaccessible spots, were essential to conducting operations.

The terrain in the Dolomite mountains was immensely difficult, and the chances of achieving decisive success extremely remote. Historian Mark Thompson has rightly referred to the attempt to take one particular rock feature, the Castelletto ("little castle"), as a prime example of the "misplaced ingenuity and energy of the Alpine campaign". Over a period of seven months, miners from the Alpini dug a tunnel under the Castelletto, which dominated the Travenanzes valley. Although the Austrian defenders could hear the Alpini digging beneath their feet, high command ordered them to stay out "for reasons of prestige". Packed with explosive, the mine was detonated on 11 July 1916. Although a gigantic crater appeared on the position, some Austrian defenders survived and repulsed the Italian attack. As Thompson comments, the results of this vast expenditure of effort were "paltry … It took … three more months to prise the Austrians off the Castelletto".

Deadlock gripped the Italian Front until it was broken by the Austro-German offensive at Caporetto in October 1917, which hurled the Italians back. Although it is unrewarding to attempt to rank soldiers' experiences in order of hardship and misery, the Alpini and their Austro-Hungarian opponents endured conditions as grim as any in the 1914–18 war.

OPPOSITE: An anti-aircraft gun at Monte Nero, above Caporetto, probably in 1917.

ABOVE: Cesare Battisti wearing a hat of the Alpini Corps troops. An Austrian citizen, he fled to Italy at the start of the war and then fought on the Allied side when Italy entered the war.

79 Cigarettes

The First World War was won by "tea and Woodbines" [cigarettes], a British veteran once claimed. Smoking was an extremely widespread habit among soldiers of the First World War. Although pipes were popular with some, for most soldiers, cigarettes were the mainstay. Thanks to the American entrepreneur James Buchanan Duke, who created a process to mass-produce cigarettes, they were cheap enough by 1914 to allow smoking them to become a common habit among the working classes.

When women began to smoke in public during the war, it was noted as a sign of the social changes brought on by the new circumstances, a development either greeted with horror or as liberating, depending on the commentator's social and political stance. Before 1914, women smoking cigarettes was unacceptable in polite society. Indeed, in 1908 a woman was arrested in New York for smoking. However, in the 1920s tobacco firms, recognizing the important new market that had opened during the war, aimed advertising at women smokers.

At that time there was no association between smoking and serious illness such as cancer. Although maladies like "smoker's cough" were recognized, smoking was seen as manly and even health-giving – in the late nineteenth century, children suffering from asthma were sometimes given special cigarettes to smoke.

Cigarettes were smoked in their millions by the soldiers, sailors and airmen of the First World War. They were issued free or bought from canteens, and distributed by paternal officers: one celebrated British chaplain, the Rev. Geoffrey Studdert-Kennedy, was nicknamed "Woodbine Willie". British soldiers were issued with perhaps 20–30 smokes per week behind the lines, but more when in the trenches. Some brands of cigarettes were considered more desirable than others. Aside from the ever popular Woodbines, in the British army, Turkish and Egyptian cigarettes were expensive, "officer-quality"; Player's and Gold Flake were sought after; but cheap "gaspers" such as "Red Hussar" were at the bottom of the pile. Cigarettes were also closely associated with the Poilu, the ordinary French soldier. The Gauloise brand, first produced in 1910, was particularly popular. German soldiers too were inveterate smokers, but they were not as fortunate in this respect as the men on the other side of no man's land. The Allied blockade meant that Germany suffered from shortages of many things, and one consequence was the production of ersatz (substitute) tobacco. A surviving German smoker's pouch contains what is described as "coarse dark 'ersatz' tobacco with a number of large bark-like chips in it".

Aside from the fact that millions were already addicted before they put on uniform, the effect of cigarettes as a nerve steadier made "lighting up" an instinctive reaction in times of danger. Nicotine, as well as being highly addictive, helps to improve mood. To be deprived of tobacco was a real hardship for millions of soldiers, sailors, airmen, and workers on the home front. Men saved up cigarette butts for emergencies, and the shortage of genuine tobacco should not be underrated as a factor in the decline of German morale.

Cigarettes were one of the little pleasures that made life bearable for the ordinary soldier. The Tommy who declared that "tea and Woodbines" were war winners hit upon an essential truth. They were important props to morale.

OPPOSITE: In Berlin, after the war, a soldier turns cigarette trader.

ABOVE: Cigarettes were issued to sustain morale. An unintended consequence was that the use of tobacco in pipes or for chewing declined.

■80 The "Blue Max" (Pour le Mérite)

Made world famous by the 1966 Hollywood film *The Blue Max*, the distinctive enamelled sky blue and gold *Pour le Mérite* ("For Merit") was Imperial Germany's highest order for valour. Founded by King Frederick II of Prussia in 1740, the name reflects the status of French as the language of the European élite. It was originally awarded for both martial and civil achievements, and only in 1810 did Frederick William III reserve the honour for military officers only. It was not a "democratic" order, such as the British Victoria Cross, available to all ranks, and its award was originally largely confined to senior officers. Among those honoured with *Pour le Mérite* prior to 1914 were the hero of Waterloo, Field Marshal Gebhard von Blücher; the "Iron Chancellor", Otto von Bismarck; and the eminent strategist and architect of victory in the Austro-Prussian (1866) and Franco Prussian (1870–71) wars, Field Marshal Helmuth von Moltke ("the Elder").

The addition of an ornate oak-leaf embellishment by the time of the First World War indicated a higher award reserved for distinguished field commanders and noteworthy general staff officers. One third of all awards went to senior officer recipients as opposed to about a quarter that went to junior ranks primarily represented by captains and lieutenants from all branches of the service.

The *Pour le Mérite* is commonly associated with the aces of the *Luftstreitkräfte* or German Army air force. The "Red Baron" Manfred von Richthofen, aces Oswald Boelcke, Max Immelmann, Ernst Udet and Hermann Göring were among 17 pilot recipients during 1914–18. Ten *Kaiserliche Marine* or naval recipients were honoured with the order. Among them were "High Seas Fleet" architect Grand Admiral Alfred von Tirpitz; Battle of Jutland commander Admiral Reinhard

Scheer; U-boat ace Lothar von Arnauld de la Perière; and *Kapitänleutnant* Walther Schwieger, the commander of *U-20*, which sank the RMS liner *Lusitania* in May 1915. *Heer* or army recipients included Field Marshal and future Chancellor Paul von Hindenburg, controversial General Erich Ludendorff, future "Desert Fox" Erwin Rommel and celebrated East Africa guerilla warrior Paul von Lettow-Vorbeck.

The youngest and one of the most remarkable *Heer* recipients was Lieutenant Ernst Jünger (1895–1998) of the 73rd Hanoverian Fusiliers. He was an "infantry ace" by any comparable standard, and his remarkable wartime exploits were immortalized in his much-revised autobiographical classic *The Storm of Steel*. Born to a bourgeois Heidelberg family in 1895, the 17-year-old Jünger enlisted in the French Foreign Legion before, at his father's earnest bidding, returning home on the eve of the First World War. In August 1914 Jünger enlisted in the ranks and was sent to the Hanoverian Fusiliers, with whom he was wounded in April 1915. Receiving a commission, he fought on the Somme in 1916 and was awarded the Iron Cross 1st Class after the Battle of the Somme. In September 1918, he was awarded the coveted Blue Max for an action in August near Cambrai in which he was wounded. His writings are powerful evocations of combat and with their apparent glorification of war, deeply troubling to some. Although not a Nazi, Jünger's work contains some themes that come uncomfortably close to fascism. That was forgiven after the Second World War. He was congratulated on his 90th birthday, in 1995, by the French President and the German Chancellor. The last surviving recipient of the *Pour le Mérite*, Jünger died aged 102 in 1998.

OPPOSITE: Kurt Wintgens, who was awarded the Blue Max in 1916, was the first fighter pilot to hit an enemy aircraft using a synchronized gun. He was also awarded the Iron Cross.

ABOVE: During the course of the war, the number of victories required for a pilot to be awarded the Blue Max increased – from eight in

1914 to 16 in 1917 and by the war's end about 30.

OVERLEAF: The Battle of Jutland, May 1916. The creator of the German High Seas Fleet, Grand Admiral von Tirpitz and Admiral Scheer, German commander at Jutland, were both awarded the Blue Max.

81 Woodrow Wilson's "Fourteen Points" Program

Woodrow Wilson, 28th President of the United States of America, was one of the creators of the world we live in today. Although he fought the 1916 Presidential election on the slogan "He kept us out of the war", Wilson was personally sympathetic to the Entente cause. In 1915, when the German U-boat campaign and the British naval blockade both impinged upon American neutrality, his bias towards the French and the British led to tensions within his administration, and the resignation of the Secretary of State, William Jennings Bryan. Wilson unsuccessfully tried to broker peace between the belligerents, issuing a Peace Note in December 1916 that requested that the warring powers set out their war aims.

In April 1917, the would-be peacemaker became a reluctant warrior. The German campaign of unrestricted submarine warfare – which sank American ships – brought the United States into the war. But Wilson was careful to keep his distance from the Old World – the United States was an "Associated Power", not an ally. More than that, his ultimate war aims were far more ambitious than those of the Entente powers. Wilson's agenda, liberal and internationalist, was revolutionary, aimed at establishing what a later generation would describe as a new world order. Under it, the rules governing international relations would be very different from the secret diplomacy of the pre-war period.

"The world must be made safe for democracy," Wilson proclaimed, "Its peace must be planted upon the tested foundations of political liberty." As Wilson said in January 1917, in calling for "peace without victory" he believed that he spoke, not just for America, but for "the silent mass of mankind everywhere who have as yet had no place or opportunity to speak". Wilson wanted to extend the Monroe Doctrine to the entire world, "that no nation should seek to extend its polity over any other nation or people, but that every people should be left free to determine its own polity, its own way of development, unhindered, unthreatened, unafraid, the little along with the great and powerful". Wilson's idealist vision – underpinned by capitalism – reached its peak in his "Fourteen Points", issued in January 1918. These included "open covenants of peace" and an end to secret diplomacy; freedom of the seas; arms reductions; collective security; and self-determination for nationalities. Wilson's ideas went much further than anything contemplated by the British and French, and, unsurprisingly, caused friction with them.

In the short term, Wilson's vision fell well short of realization. His own country rejected much of it; thus the United States refused to join the League of Nations, which in any case was a failure as an instrument of collective security. Although Wilson was a hero in nations born out of the wreckage of European empires, the jumble of peoples was not easily fitted into discrete ethnic states, and in many countries democracy did not take root – including, disastrously, Germany.

Yet Wilson's ideology was perfectly timed. It offered an alternative to the pre-1914 imperial order, and to the Fascism that would soon emerge in Italy and Germany. Perhaps most importantly, it rivalled the new force gathering strength in Russia. As one distinguished historian, John Lewis Gaddis, has written, "Much of the subsequent history of the twentieth century grew out of the clash between these two ideologies – Wilson's versus Lenin's ..." By the end of the century, Wilson's had prevailed.

Program for the Peace of the World

By *PRESIDENT WILSON* January 8, 1918

I. Open covenants of peace, openly arrived at, after which there shall be no private international understandings of any kind, but diplomacy shall proceed always frankly and in the public view.

II. Absolute freedom of navigation upon the seas, outside territorial waters, alike in peace and in war, except as the seas may be closed in whole or in part by international action for the enforcement of international covenants.

III. The removal, so far as possible, of all economic barriers and the establishment of an equality of trade conditions among all the nations consenting to the peace and associating themselves for its maintenance.

IV. Adequate guarantees given and taken that national armaments will reduce to the lowest point consistent with domestic safety.

V. Free, open-minded, and absolutely impartial adjustment of all colonial claims, based upon a strict observance of the principle that in determining all such questions of sovereignty the interests of the population concerned must have equal weight with the equitable claims of the government whose title is to be determined.

VI. The evacuation of all Russian territory and such a settlement of all questions affecting Russia as will secure the best and freest coöperation of the other nations of the world in obtaining for her an unhampered and unembarrassed opportunity for the independent determination of her own political development and national policy, and assure her of a sincere welcome into the society of free nations under institutions of her own choosing; and, more than a welcome, assistance also of every kind that she may need and may herself desire. The treatment accorded Russia by her sister nations in the months to come will be the acid test of their goodwill, of their comprehension of her needs as distinguished from their own interests, and of their intelligent and unselfish sympathy.

VII. Belgium, the whole world will agree, must be evacuated and restored, without any attempt to limit the sovereignty which she enjoys in common with all other free nations. No other single act will serve as this will serve to restore confidence among the nations in the law which they have themselves set and determined for the government of their relations with one another. Without this healing act the whole structure and validity of international law is forever impaired.

VIII. All French territory should be freed and the invaded portions restored, and the wrong done to France by Prussia in 1871 in the matter of Alsace-Lorraine, which has unsettled the peace of the world for nearly fifty years, should be righted, in order that peace may once more be made secure in the interest of all.

IX. A readjustment of the frontiers of Italy should be effected along clearly recognizable lines of nationality.

X. The people of Austria-Hungary, whose place among the nations we wish to see safeguarded and assured, should be accorded the freest opportunity of autonomous development.

XI. Rumania, Serbia and Montenegro should be evacuated; occupied territories restored; Serbia accorded free and secure access to the sea; and the relations of the several Balkan States to one another determined by friendly counsel along historically established lines of allegiance and nationality; and international guarantees of the political and economic independence and territorial integrity of the several Balkan States should be entered into.

XII. The Turkish portions of the present Ottoman Empire should be assured a secure sovereignty, but the other nationalities which are now under Turkish rule should be assured an undoubted security of life and an absolutely unmolested opportunity of autonomous development, and the Dardanelles should be permanently opened as a free passage to the ships and commerce of all nations under international guarantees.

XIII. An independent Polish State should be erected which should include the territories inhabited by indisputably Polish populations, which should be assured a free and secure access to the sea, and whose political and economic independence and territorial integrity should be guaranteed by international covenant.

XIV. A general association of nations must be formed under specific covenants for the purpose of affording mutual guarantees of political independence and territorial integrity to great and small States alike.

OPPOSITE: Woodrow Wilson, the 28th President of the United States. For sponsoring the League of Nations, he was awarded the Nobel Peace Prize in 1919.

ABOVE: Wilson was hugely popular in Europe, but his idealism met with scepticism from other statesmen such as Lloyd George of Britain and Clemenceau of France.

OVERLEAF: Parisians line the route of President Wilson's journey through the French capital in 1918 to show their gratitude for his help during the First World War.

82 Tank Visor

"A tank is walking up the High Street of Flers, with the British Army cheering behind." This highly coloured phrase of the journalist Philip Gibbs, described the moment when British 41st Division captured the ruins of Flers. The village fell in the course of the fighting known as the Battle of Flers-Courcelette. The battle was a disappointment in operational terms: Haig had hoped for a breakthrough on a wide front, but Fourth and Reserve Armies had managed an advance of only about 2,300 metres (2,500 yards). However the debut of the tank was an immensely significant portent.

The initial tank was a very uncomfortable vehicle for its crew. The Daimler engine was in the same compartment as the crew, which meant that they breathed in an unhealthy mixture that included carbon monoxide, and the temperature could rise to 52°C (125°F). This took its toll on the crew's efficiency. Another particularly unpleasant phenomenon was "tank splash": chips of red-hot metal that flew about the interior, dislodged by rounds hitting the outside

of the tank. In order to protect the face of crew members, a chain-mail visor was introduced. Attached to a leather mask tied around the head by tape, the chains dangled in front of the eyes. This contraption was compared by one man to an African witchdoctor's mask and by another to a "crusader chain-mail helmet".

Among the fathers of the tank was Winston Churchill, who as First Lord of the Admiralty had set up the Landships Committee in 1915, but the first workable tank was designed by William Tritton and Walter Wilson of William Foster & Co., of Lincoln. The name came from a cover story introduced to maintain secrecy. The parts of the machine that were being shipped were described as being part of a [water]

tank, and the name stuck. The tank brought together existing technologies. The caterpillar track was used for tractors, and armoured cars had demonstrated the utility of bringing together a motor vehicle, armour plating, and weapons. In January 1916, the prototype tank, "Mother", was demonstrated in the grounds of Hatfield House, in Hertfordshire,

The Mark 1 tank used at Flers-Courcelette weighed 28 tons, had a crew of eight and was 7.75 m (25 ft five in) long. If fitted with a "tail" of a wheel for steering, later discarded, an extra 2.1 m (7 ft) was added to the length. The "male" version had two 6-pounder guns mounted in sponsons, plus four 7.62-mm Hotchkiss machine guns. The "female" version had four .303 Vickers machine guns and a Hotchkiss gun. Maximum armour thickness was .5 in (12 mm), and it had a top speed of 6 km/h (3.7 mph).

General Sir Douglas Haig was an enthusiast for tanks, as he was for many other types of machinery, and vainly hoped to have them ready for the beginning of the British offensive on the Somme in July 1916. In the event, tanks were available only for the major offensive launched on 15 September. Haig has been criticized for failing to use the tanks en masse. However, this unreliable and unproven weapon was available only in small numbers (of the approximately 60 tanks available in France, only 21 succeeded in crossing the start line on 15 September), and in the circumstances it was the right decision to commit the tank to battle in an infantry support role. A number of mistakes were made, including the creation of "tank lanes" – gaps in the artillery barrage along the path down which the tanks would travel – which meant that German defences were inadequately suppressed. Nevertheless, the tank had proved its potential.

▪ 83 Sir Douglas Haig's Order of the Day

This stirring message, containing echoes of Nelson's famous "England Expects" signal at Trafalgar, came from an unlikely source. Field Marshal Sir Douglas Haig, Commander-in-Chief of the British Expeditionary Force (BEF), was normally a calm, unemotional man, whose only concession to times of stress was an unconscious tugging of his moustache. But on 11 April 1918, he sensed he was close to defeat. Two days earlier, the Battle of the Lys has begun when the Germans punched through a hapless Portuguese division south of Ypres. Already, in March, the Germans had come close to beating the Allies further south, before the *Kaiserschlacht* had been halted. Now, although British troops were resisting fiercely, Haig was all too aware that a relatively short German advance would place the Channel ports in peril and risk cutting the British off from home. There was a real danger that a hasty seaborne evacuation (like Dunkirk a generation later), could be forced upon the British army in 1918 – or worse, that it would be destroyed.

Haig accordingly issued an Order of the Day, a special message from the BEF commander to the troops, calling upon them to resist the German advances and ordering "every position to be held to the last man". His rousing cry that "With our backs to the wall, each one of us must fight on to the end" has given the document its nickname, the "Backs to the Wall" order.

When officers and soldiers heard Haig's dramatic Order of the Day, reactions were mixed. Some men were stirred, their resolve stiffened. Some were alarmed – they had had no idea that things were that serious. Others shrugged their shoulders and got on with it. Haig's message of warning

mixed with hope was almost certainly aimed in part at Haig himself, a general coping with the stress of command. Curiously, in his highly detailed private diary, Haig neglected to mention his writing of the order.

This Order was the most famous thing that Haig, one of the most controversial generals in British history, ever composed. Born into a wealthy Scots family in 1861, he had a conventional army background, serving in a cavalry regiment in India, and seeing active service in Sudan (1898) and the Second Anglo-Boer War (1899–1902), where he made his name as a commander and staff officer. Haig played a major role in reforming the army before 1914, and commanded successively I Corps and First Army in France in 1914–15 before moving up to become commander of the BEF in December 1915. His strategy and tactics in the Battle of the Somme in 1916 have been hugely controversial, together with his conduct of the Third Battle of Ypres (Passchendaele) in 1917. Both were very costly in terms of lives, and gained little ground – but Haig, and some historians, argued that they wore out the German army and thus made the victory of 1918 possible.

Haig's "Backs to the Wall" order marked what was for the British army one of the most dangerous days in the entire war. But both High Command and ordinary officers and soldiers from Britain and the Empire held their nerve. Thus, the BEF weathered the storm of the Lys, and in August 1918 went onto the offensive at Amiens, winning a decisive victory. Haig's force then played a leading role among Allied forces in the Hundred Days of battles that finally defeated the German army.

SPECIAL ORDER OF THE DAY
By FIELD-MARSHAL SIR DOUGLAS HAIG
K.T., G.C.B., G.C.V.O., K.C.I.E
Commander-in-Chief, British Armies in France.

To ALL RANKS OF THE BRITISH ARMY IN FRANCE AND FLANDERS.

Three weeks ago to-day the enemy began his terrific attacks against us on a fifty-mile front. His objects are to separate us from the French, to take the Channel Ports and destroy the British Army.

In spite of throwing already 106 Divisions into the battle and enduring the most reckless sacrifice of human life, he has as yet made little progress towards his goals.

We owe this to the determined fighting and self-sacrifice of our troops. Words fail me to express the admiration which I feel for the splendid resistance offered by all ranks of our Army under the most trying circumstances.

Many amongst us now are tired. To those I would say that Victory will belong to the side which holds out the longest. The French Army is moving rapidly and in great force to our support.

There is no other course open to us but to fight it out. Every position must be held to the last man: there must be no retirement. With our backs to the wall and believing in the justice of our cause each one of us must fight on to the end. The safety of our homes and the Freedom of mankind alike depend upon the conduct of each one of us at this critical moment.

General Headquarters,
Thursday, April 11th, 1918.

Commander-in-Chief,
British Armies in France.

OPPOSITE: Haig's obituary in *The Times* said that "his war-worn soldiers loved [him] as their truest advocate and friend". This was a gross exaggeration, but he did achieve popularity after the war as President of the British Legion.

ABOVE: Special Order of the Day, issued on 11 April 1918, by Field Marshal Sir Douglas Haig.

84 Hermann Göring's Fokker D.VII

Aircraft represented the ultimate in modern technology during the First World War, and the emergence of the airman as hero had significant cultural and political consequences for the post-war world. One such hero was Hermann Göring, and his Fokker D.VIIF (No. 5125/18) biplane was representative of the finest technology German aviation had to offer. Designed and developed by Reinhold Platz, this groundbreaking all-metal fighter plane had its origins in a series of experimental "V-series" test aircraft developed during 1916–17.

The Fokker D.VII entered the skies over France and Flanders in May 1918. Powered by a Mercedes 160 hp D.III or BMW IIIa engine and armed with two fixed Spandau machine-guns, frontline pilots clamoured for the structurally robust and highly manoeuverable fighter during the final seven months of combat. Indeed, the D.VII's lauded climbing performance, disinclination to go into a spin, readily compliant stall and remarkable ability to hang on its propeller and fire upwards, led to the contemporary axiom that it could "turn a mediocre pilot into a good one and a good pilot into an ace". Approximately 3,000 to 3,300 units were manufactured in the last year of the conflict.

It was not long before what became Imperial Germany's best fighter of the war was obtained by *Oberleutnant* Göring. In 1914, the future *Reichsmarschall* was an infantry officer. He transferred to the air service, and by June 1918 he was a celebrated ace with 19 confirmed victories and, in addition to five other decorations and orders, a holder of the *Pour le Mérite*. Göring's twentieth aerial victory occurred on his first flight with a D.VII (No. 324/18) on 9 June. Victory number 21 followed eight days later on 17 June. Command of *Jagdgeschwader* I, the renowned "Flying Circus", came in July. Thereafter, administrative duties ensured he played a less active role in the fighting. A final confirmed victory, number 22, occurred on 18 July when Göring brought down a French Spad XIII. The distinctive all-white D.VII was delivered in the autumn. It is uncertain how much flying the increasingly distracted Göring actually did with this particular airplane before the armistice.

Göring was one of a large number of war veterans, fundamentally alienated from the new democratic Weimar Republic, who drifted into far-right politics. As a fully fledged war hero he was a major catch for the emerging National Socialist (Nazi) Party, which he joined in 1922. Göring's background as an aviator fitted in well with the Nazi image of modernity and technological superiority; indeed, there was a cult of the airman among fascist movements between the wars. *Triumph of the Will*, Leni Riefenstahl's film glorifying Nazism, has a scene showing Hitler flying to the 1934 Nuremberg Rally. As historian Colin Crook has noted, the cruciform shadow cast by the aircraft was symbolic of "a new Germany, reborn and free of suffering on the First World War cross of defeat and humiliation". The advanced technology represented by the airplane represented this freedom. Göring rapidly emerged as one of Adolf Hitler's principal lieutenants, acquiring vast wealth and power, becoming the chief of the *Luftwaffe* (air force) which was formed in 1933. He was convicted of war crimes at the Nuremberg trials in 1946 but committed suicide before he could be hanged.

ABOVE: The Fokker D.VII with a Mercedes engine was a single-seat fighter. By the terms of the Armistice, all examples of this formidable aircraft were surrendered to the Allies.

◾ 85 Czech Legion Flag

When the Austro-Hungarian Empire precipitated general war in 1914 it was seeking to reassert its declining influence. Instead, the declaration of war against Serbia on 28 July 1914 amounted to the death warrant of the Habsburg Empire, with a stay of execution until 1918. The flag of the Czech Legion symbolizes the forces of nationalism and the desire for national self-determination among subject peoples that finally tore Austria-Hungary apart.

Substantial numbers of Czechs were conscripted into service with the Austro-Hungarian army during the war. One of them was Jaroslav Hašek, author of *The Good Soldier Švejk*, which chronicles the career of the hapless, or possibly subtly cunning, Private Švejk. The character of Švejk is used, among other things, to show the ambivalence of many Czechs towards fighting for Austria-Hungary. Many ethnic German officers were suspicious of the true allegiance of Czech soldiers. Certainly, there were enough Czech prisoners and deserters, when added to Czech volunteers living in Russia, for the Russians to form Czech émigré units. Similar forces were established in Italy and France.

The growth of Czech formations fighting for the Allies was paralleled by the efforts of exiled Czech political leaders to achieve international support for independence. Initially, the Allied governments held the Czechs at arm's length, hoping to detach Austria-Hungary from its alliance with Germany. By 1917, the political climate had changed. Alongside the fading of hopes of a separate peace, President Wilson's Fourteen Points and Lloyd George's Caxton Hall speech of 5 January 1918, which announced support for "genuine self-government on true democratic principles" for the subject nationalities of the Habsburg Empire, opened the door to Czech self-determination.

At the end of 1917 a new Czech Legion was formed in Russia from prisoners of war, as part of a deal with Paris that recognized a Czech state. After clashes with German forces, the French ordered the Legion to go to Vladivostok, for repatriation to the West. The uneasy relationship with the Bolsheviks broke down and the Czech Legion proved to be a highly effective military force, seizing lengths of the Trans-Siberian railway and helping the anti-Bolshevik "White" forces. By late 1918, the Reds were regaining ground, and the vast majority of Czechs departed from Vladivostok by sea in 1919, returning to the new state of Czechoslovakia via the United States. The Legion's success was a factor in prompting Allied governments to become involved in the Russian Civil War, and increased the credibility and influence of Czechs in Allied capitals.

Along with exiles under Tomas Masaryk, leader of the Czech National Council in Switzerland, the Czech Legion, in historian Immanuel Geiss's words "shaped the way Czechoslovak independence emerged" at the end of the war. Revolutionary fervour was channelled into "political agreements and declarations". Domestic Czech politicians and exiles reached agreement in Geneva in late October in 1918, and on 28 October Czech independence was declared. The Slovaks joined forces, and the Allies recognized the new Czechoslovak state. Achieving independence from the old Habsburg Empire was only part of the struggle. Ethnic Germans in the Czech borderlands (later known as Sudetenland) threatened to secede, and the new Prague government took action to secure the territory. Czechoslovakia gained a defensible frontier, but stored up trouble for the future; 20 years later Hitler was to exploit the grievances of the Sudeten Germans and destroyed the new state as part of his policy of aggressively reversing the results of 1918. The Czech Legion formed the heart of the army that, as a result of the Munich agreement of 1938, had to stand by while Hitler's army began to dismember their country.

ABOVE: Legendary amongst his own people, Tomáš Masaryk enters Prague on 8 December 1918. After the fall of the Austro-Hungarian Empire, he was recognized by the Allies as the head of the provisional Czechoslovak government.

■ 86 Renault FT Tank

With its rotating turret, rear-engine compartment and tractor-based chassis configuration, the 6-ton "FT" *faible tonnage* (low tonnage) Model 1917 armoured fighting vehicle is sometimes considered to be the first truly modern tank. Designed and produced by the French automotive firm of Renault, it first saw service with French and American forces during May–November 1918. Convinced of the tactical value of light tanks as opposed to heavier British and French models, Colonel Jean-Baptiste Estienne persuaded French General Headquarters to place orders for large quantities of FTs in early 1917. Armed with a 37-mm (1.45-inch) cannon or 8-mm (0.3-in) Hotchkiss machine-gun and powered by a four-cylinder 35-hp (29-kW) engine, it was comparatively fast (with a 11 km/h [7 mph] speed as well as manoeuvrable and had an extensive (65 km/40 miles) range. In all, perhaps 3,700 Renault light tanks were produced. Some were

sent to foreign armies, including over 500 which found their way into American hands.

Major George S. Patton of the US Army encountered the FT for the first time at the French tank training centre near Compiègne in late 1917. A cavalryman by background, he became an enthusiast for the new weapon. Personally commanding from a tank turret, he practised the rough-and-ready method of maintaining direction by means of tapping the driver's head and shoulders with his foot. Test driving the novel two-man vehicle about the open expanse of the nearby proving grounds, lengthy discussions with Allied tank officers and a flying visit to the Renault factory demonstrated

how much there was to learn in the short time available. The technical and tactical lessons absorbed during Patton's useful sojourn were later recounted in an influential study that became the doctrinal foundation of United States tank operations during the First World War.

Patton was appointed to head the newly established US Army Tank Corps School at Langres not long afterwards. Training remained somewhat difficult until the delivery of 10 FTs in March 1918. Promoted Lieutenant-Colonel and given command of the 1st Provisional Tank Brigade the following August, he led the first American-crewed FT tanks during the Battle of St Mihiel (12–15 September 1918). Ordering that no tank should be allowed to fall into enemy hands, Patton showed characteristic showmanship (and courage) by walking ahead of the lumbering FTs under heavy rifle- and machine-gun fire. Of 174 FTs engaged, three were destroyed, 22 ditched and 14 broke down. The real test of battle came a fortnight later during the opening day of the costly Meuse-Argonne offensive (26 September–11 November 1918). Patton, on discovering his tanks had bogged down early in the attack, risked life and limb under murderous enemy fire to get them going again. In this, despite sustaining a crippling leg wound, he was ultimately successful, the unstuck FTs rumbling forward to help the stalled infantry secure the objective. Twenty-four years would pass before Patton experienced combat again. By that time, he was a general taking the first steps on a path that was to see him emerge as one of the most effective practitioners of armoured warfare of the Second World War.

OPPOSITE: Char FT-17 tanks in action at the Battle of Saint-Mihiel, September 1918.

ABOVE: A replica of a Char FT-17, built by Renault in 1917. Suitable for mass production, the tank was an effective weapon that was still in service with the French Army at the outbreak of the Second World War.

OVERLEAF: Renault tanks take part in a Victory Parade in 1918.

87 Advanced Gas Mask

Some of the most evocative lines in English literature were written by Wilfred Owen, who served as an infantry officer in the First World War:

"GAS! Gas! Quick, boys! — An ecstasy of fumbling/ Fitting the clumsy helmets just in time"

Owen's words brilliantly captured the fear engendered when gas shells started to fall – and the frantic struggle to get respirators out of cases before the gas took effect. These lines occur in one of the bitterest, most harrowing poems about war ever written: "Dulce et Decorum Est". The title is heavily ironic, taken from the Latin tag "Dulce et decorum est pro patria mori", or "it is sweet and fitting to die for one's country". This poem, and John Singer Sargent's famous painting "Gassed", which depicts a line of blinded soldiers shuffling along with their hands on the shoulders of the man in front, have helped promote the idea that gas attacks in the First World War were a peculiarly terrible way of making war. However, the fame of the poem and painting has tended to obscure both the low death-rate from gas –

about three per cent – and the increasing effectiveness of anti-gas measures as the war went on. By contrast, on the Eastern Front, both Russian equipment and anti-chemical training was poor, and so casualties were high.

As chemical weapons improved, so did protection against them. The British "Small Box Respirator", introduced in 1916, was a successful model that had a filter to provide uncontaminated air, which was connected by a hose to the rubberized mask. Recognizing the limitations ·of gas as a weapon, neither side made chemical warfare the centrepiece of an offensive after 1915. Chemical weapons were, however, useful when included as part of an all-arms weapons system. Mixing in gas shells with high explosive

in a bombardment forced enemy soldiers to don their respirators, which made them less efficient and tired them out. This was a particularly effective tactic against artillery crews. When at the beginning of the March 1918 German Offensive in the West, the Flesquières salient was saturated with gas shells, this was an indication that it was not about to be subjected to a major attack, for troops advancing into the gas cloud would have to wear their respirators, and this their effectiveness would have been reduced. Instead, the use of gas was intended to deny the Salient to the defenders.

Chemical shells, introduced in 1916, made the delivery of chemical munitions a much more accurate affair. Further developments in 1916–17 included the use of mortars to fire chemical rounds, and the British Lievens Projector, a type of mortar able to propel a large canister of gas. The chemical weapons themselves grew more lethal. Chlorine gas was supplemented by the much more deadly phosgene (first used by the Germans in December 1915), and then in July 1917 the Germans first used mustard gas. This amounted to a step-change in chemical warfare as mustard burns affected the skin as well as the lungs, and could remain deadly long after its initial use. Unlike earlier chemical agents, it was a "persistent" agent that took a long time to disperse and thus remained a long-term threat. The Allies were slow to respond, using mustard gas only in 1918.

Although adequate anti-gas equipment reduced the threat of chemical weapons, the fact that they remained integral to all armies' methods of fighting is an indication of their continuing utility. Against ill-equipped, poorly trained or inexperienced troops gas could be very effective indeed. No less than a quarter of United States casualties incurred in action were the result of chemical warfare.

OPPOSITE: American soldiers in France learning how to use gas masks.

ABOVE: This German gas mask is made of leather with plastic eyepieces and steel fittings. This model was manufactured between 1915 and 1918.

■88 Mark V Tank

The Battle of Amiens began at 4.20 a.m. on 8 August 1918 when 450 heavy guns opened up on the German positions. This was followed by the advance of III British, the Australian and the Canadian Corps of General Sir Henry Rawlinson's Fourth Army, supported by 552 tanks. Waiting in reserve were three cavalry divisions. To the south, French First Army, temporarily under the overall command of General Sir Douglas Haig, attacked in the Montdidier sector. By the evening, the Allied forces had advanced 13 km (8 miles) – a remarkable achievement by the standards of the Western Front. German Second Army defending this sector was shattered. Having parried and pushed back the German offensive on the Marne in July, Amiens was the point at which the Allies seized the initiative. The "Hundred Days" campaign that followed led inexorably to the defeat of the German army in the West.

Amiens was a triumph of combined arms tactics: infantry, artillery, aircraft, tanks, armoured cars and cavalry acted together as a team. However, tanks played a critical role, and indeed Amiens was the largest tank battle of the war. Fourth Army fielded 96 light Whippet tanks and 120 supply tanks, but all the heavy battalions were equipped with Mark V or Mark V*(pronounced Mark V star) tanks. The Mark V tank had the familiar rhomboidal shape (it was a development of the Mark IV), and carried a crew of eight. It weighed 29 tons, with a length of 8.05 m (26 ft 5 in) and a height of 2.64 m (8 ft 8 in). The Male version was 4.11 m (13 ft 6 in wide). With a top speed of 7.4 kph (4.6 mph), it had a radius of action of 72 km (45 miles). Male tanks were fitted with two 6-pounder guns, one mounted in

a projecting "sponson" on each side of the tank, plus four .303-in Hotchkiss machine guns. The Female version lacked the 6-pounders, but instead had six Hotchkiss machine guns. The maximum width of the armoured protection was 16 mm (0.6 in). The Mark V* was a longer, heavy version intended to carry machine-gun teams, but at Amiens, the combination of fumes, motion sickness, and the temperature inside the tank rendered them "unfit for action".

Never again during the Hundred Days were the British able to concentrate such a large number of tanks for a single offensive. Amiens was succeeded by Third Army's attack at Albert. On that occasion only 156 tanks were available. That, and the fact that the majority of the attacking formations were ordinary British divisions, makes this battle, in its way, as remarkable an achievement as Amiens. The failure of GHQ to mass tanks for offensives was not, as has been suggested, because of a move back to "traditional" away from "mechanical" warfare. The operational tempo of the BEF in the Hundred Days was such that the demand for tanks outran the supply, particularly given how prone they were to breakdown and the German use of anti-tank weapons. British High Command was not opposed to the use of tanks and such tanks as were available were committed to operations. With the Germans on the back foot, it would have been unrealistic and counterproductive to ease the unrelenting pressure by pausing operations to allow tanks to be concentrated for a fresh offensive.

American troops also used the Mark V in action in 1918, and Mark Vs also saw service in the Russian Civil War.

OPPOSITE: British tanks moving forward from Bellicourt on 29 September 1918, carrying the cribs that they used to cross the Hindenburg Line.

ABOVE: This Mark V tank participated in the Lord Mayor's Show of 1918.

▪89 58ᵗʰ (London) Division Memorial

58ᵗʰ (London) Division's memorial at the village of Chipilly, near the River Somme, is one of the most attractive and touching on the Western Front. Erected by the people of Chipilly, it was designed by Henri Désiré Gauquié (1858–1927). It consists of a white stone sculpture of an artilleryman with his arms around the neck of a wounded horse. As a statement of the bond between soldier and animal in war it is difficult to fault. Gauquié's most famous work is probably his 1896 monument to the eighteenth-century French artist Jean Antoine Watteau in the Jardin du Luxembourg in Paris. He was an appropriate choice of sculptor: his home village Flers-lez-Lille, was occupied by the Germans in October 1914 and liberated by the British army four years later.

58th (2/1st London) Division was a Territorial formation formed in 1914 as the "second line" of the more famous 56th, or 1st London, Division. Its infantry consisted entirely of battalions of the London Regiment, although the 4th Suffolks was posted in as the Divisional pioneer unit in 1918. Arriving in France in 1917, 58th Division saw extensive action at the Third Battle of Ypres (Passchendaele) in 1917 and in the battles of 1918. It was fairly typical of the unshowy but reliable British divisions that made up the bulk of the BEF in 1918. On 9 August 1918, as part of III Corps's operations to secure the northern flank of the Allied operations during the battle of Amiens, 58th Division captured Chipilly village.

It is very appropriate that the memorial should be located on this battlefield. The Battle of Amiens (8–11 August 1918), launched by the British III, Australian and Canadian Corps, and French First Army, saw the employment of an extensive range of advanced military technology. Over 500 tanks were used and large numbers of aircraft were deployed in support of the ground forces. The RAF lost 17 aeroplanes in attempting to bomb the Somme bridges. This was an primitive attempt at interdiction which pointed the way to future warfare; for instance, the havoc

wrought by aircraft in Normandy on the retreating Germans at the Falaise Gap in 1944. The most sophisticated technology was employed by the Royal Artillery. The devastatingly effective use of Allied artillery at the beginning of the battle was founded on the use of aircraft to provide targeting intelligence for the gunners, along with advanced techniques of flash spotting and sound ranging to allow accurate shooting "off the map" – that is, without alerting the enemy by firing preliminary ranging shots. In this way surprise was achieved. The Allies won a decisive victory at Amiens, advancing 13 km (8 miles) and inflicting 27,000 casualties on the enemy.

Yet the 58th Division monument is a reminder that the armies which won the victory, although immensely "hi tech" in comparison to those at the beginning of the war, still relied heavily on the muscle power provided by horses. Under the right conditions, horsed cavalry still had a part to play on the Western Front – at Amiens the British cavalry proved very effective – but the vast majority of horses were draft animals, used for pulling wagons or artillery. At its strongest, the cavalry only ever accounted for six per cent of the BEF's equine strength. Horses retained their key function in armies for many years after the First World War. By 1939, the British army was virtually completely mechanized, having gone further than any other army in that regard. By contrast, the German army was heavily reliant on horse-drawn transport, and remained so until the very end of the Second World War.

ABOVE: British tanks in the destroyed town of Bapaume in August 1918.

OPPOSITE: The 58th (London) Division Memorial, Chipilly. This division fought in III Corps on the northern flank of the Allied attack at Amiens, 8 August 1918.

H. GAUQUIE

AUX MORTS DE LA 58ᵉ DIVISION BRITANNIQUE

LONDON DIVISION

PRO·DEO·PRO·REGE·PRO·PATRIA

LA 58ᵈᴹᴱ DIVISION BRITANNIQUE FUT UNE DES SEULES DIVISIONS
ANGLAISES QUI EN COOPÉRATION AVEC L'ARMÉE FRANÇAISE ET LES
CORPS D'ARMÉE AUSTRALIENS ET CANADIENS RÉUSSIT A PÉNÉTRER
LES DÉFENSES ALLEMANDES ENTRE LE QUESNOY ET MONTDIDIER
LE 8 AOÛT 1918 DÉTERMINANT LE COMMENCEMENT DE LA RETRAITE
ALLEMANDE QUI SE TERMINA PAR L'ARMISTICE DU 11 NOVEMBRE 1918.

■ 90 Bellicourt Tunnel

The Belgian and French countryside over which much of the fighting on the Western Front took place was criss-crossed by a complex network of canals. These provided useful defensive obstacles and they featured prominently during the battles of movement in 1914 and 1918. The first engagement of the British Expeditionary Force, the Battle of Mons (23 August 1914), was fought using a canal as a defensive position. Conversely, in 1918, the advancing Allies were forced to fight their way across a number of canal lines that the Germans had prepared for defence. Such operations were always challenging.

The Bellicourt Tunnel formed part of the St Quentin to Cambrai Canal. In late 1916, the Germans had begun constructing a defensive line in this area, known as the Wotan Line, itself a subsection of what the British called the Hindenburg Line. The formidable position was designed and constructed to be capable of resisting the very best that the Allies could deploy against it.

The Bellicourt Tunnel was incorporated into this design. The tunnel was vast, running for approximately 5,700 metres (6,250 yards). Its spacious interior allowed the Germans to convert narrow boats and moor them inside, using them as accommodation for the defending troops. This allowed them to rest in safety from any Allied bombardment of the position above. The hillside itself was filled with a maze of passages that permitted the defenders to reach the surface or defensive positions at the either end of the tunnel quickly. German troops living inside the tunnel found it a surprisingly congenial environment. The air was cooler and fresher than in a standard dug out and the sleeping accommodation was spacious.

However, despite the efforts to place the area in a state of defence, the presence of the tunnel represented a point of vulnerability for the Germans. The hillside effectively provided a land bridge across the canal which would allow an advancing army to cross quickly and without the need for bridges. The Germans had therefore prepared the area around the tunnel with a formidable array of defences, including deep wire entanglements, concrete bunkers, hidden machine-gun nests and carefully ranged artillery pieces.

On 29 September 1918, the imposing position was attacked by a multi-national Anglophone force consisting of British, American and Australian troops. Supported by 150 tanks, American and Australian troops bore the brunt of the fighting for Bellicourt Tunnel itself. The battle was costly, particularly for the tank crews and inexperienced American soldiers. Of 39 tanks assigned to support the attack of the 27th (United States) Division, only a single vehicle survived to reach the crest. But 46th (North Midland) Division had remarkable success on the right flank. It attacked across the open canal, with some soldiers wearing lifebelts; crucially, a party seized the key bridge at Riqueval. Thus, the Allies succeeded in fighting their way onto the hillside above the tunnel and had captured the position by nightfall.

The victory on 29 September represented a stunning military success. The German High Command had pinned much hope on being able to hold the Hindenburg Line for several months, but the position had been fatally breached in just a single day. The success at Bellicourt Tunnel, itself part of a wider victory in the Battle of the St Quentin Canal (29 September–10 October), allowed the Allies to advance into the open country beyond and forced the Germans into a retreat that would continue until the end of the war in November 1918.

OPPOSITE: Victorious troops of 137 Brigade after their crossing of the St Quentin Canal. This took place on the right of the Bellicourt Tunnel.

ABOVE: The Bellicourt Tunnel, photographed on 1 November 1918. The attack was the first time that a large cohort of Americans had fought under British command. Inexperienced, they fought alongside combat-hardened Australian troops.

91 Bolshevik Poster

The poster opposite exhorts workers to struggle against one of the principal bogies of the Russian Bolshevik regime: international imperialism. On coming to power, Bolshevik leaders were faced with myriad problems. Not only was Russia at war with Germany, but the authority of the new government over its own people was fragile. Before long, a state of full-blown civil war was to emerge, complicated by the intervention of United States, French, British Empire and other forces. However, the upheaval in Russia was believed to be merely the precursor of proletarian uprisings across Europe, as a new social and economic order emerged from the ruins of war and revolution.

The war with Germany was ended by the Treaty of Brest-Litovsk, signed in March 1918. Lenin's lieutenant, Trotsky, led the Bolshevik negotiating team. His tactics of prevarication in the hope that a revolution would break out in Germany failed, and Berlin insisted on very harsh terms. The cession of 3.4 million square km (1.3 million square miles) in Finland, Ukraine, part of Belorussia, Poland and the Baltic provinces meant that a good part of the most productive agricultural land and industry of the old Russian Empire was lost. Some, but not all, of this territory was regained following the German defeat in November 1918.

The Bolsheviks accepted the treaty to give themselves a free hand to cope with domestic problems. But Brest-Litovsk actually intensified the simmering civil war as "White" forces, assisted by foreign troops, sought to overthrow the Bolsheviks. Trotsky was able to fashion an effective military force, the "Red Army", underpinned by Political Commissars, which successfully defended the Bolshevik heartland and was eventually able to take the offensive and defeat the Whites, who were divided among rival groups and generally poorly led. In 1921, the Red Army achieved victory.

Domestically, Lenin at first adopted a policy of handing over land to peasants and the nationalization of land and large industrial concerns. "War Communism", introduced in June 1918, nationalized all firms, and foodstuffs were requisitioned from the peasants, often violently. This in turn led to resistance. Peasants grew crops solely for their own needs, and in some cases rose in revolt. With the economy in desperate trouble, War Communism was replaced by the "New Economic Policy" in 1921, which contained some elements of capitalism.

Outside Russia, there was much high-level fear of "Bolshevism". Some events appeared to show that such anxiety was well founded. In 1919, Béla Kun established a short-lived Communist regime in Hungary. The Spartacists, headed by Rosa Luxemburg and Karl Liebknecht, staged a revolt in Berlin in January 1919, which was swiftly crushed by right-wing paramilitary "Freikorps" and government forces. In the anarchic conditions, right-wing groups also flourished in Germany, most famously, the fledgling National Socialists under Adolf Hitler, who launched the abortive Beer Hall Putsch in Munich in November 1923. However, the Weimar Republic gradually established its authority, albeit tenuously, and it was democracy, not communism, that prevailed in Germany. The same was true in Western Europe, although conditions were unstable for some time after the war. In Britain, the moderate, reformist Labour Party attracted working-class votes. Elsewhere, during the interwar period, authoritarian governments of the right became the norm.

The failure of the Russian Revolution to trigger widespread insurgency was tacitly recognized in the policy of "Socialism in One Country" introduced by Josef Stalin, who eventually succeeded Lenin after the latter's death in 1924. However, in the years between the wars, the Soviet Union remained a pariah state, treated with the deepest suspicion by conservative politicians in the West.

СМЕРТЬ МИРОВОМУ ИМПЕРИАЛИЗМУ

OPPOSITE: Vladimir Ilyich Lenin urges on the forces of the Revolution.

ABOVE: "Death to worldwide imperialism": workers fight a green monster that is strangling a factory.

OVERLEAF: Diplomats and officers of the Central Powers and Russia signing the Treaty of Brest-Litovsk which ratified the exit of Russia from the First World War on 3 March 1918.

228

92 Influenza Mask

This face mask was one of a number of types used to try to avoid being infected with influenza. Commonly known as "Spanish flu", or "the Spanish lady", the disease was first detected in February 1918 in San Sebastian, in Spain. A month later there was a case in the United States, and influenza had reached the Western Front by the first days of April. The pandemic, which lasted from 1918 to 1920, killed far more people than died on the battlefields of the First World War. Although figures are notoriously imprecise, there were perhaps 10 million military dead. A low estimate of total deaths from the influenza pandemic would be in the order of twice that figure. Conceivably, as many as 100 million died of Spanish flu, 12–16 million in India alone. Nearly 730,000 influenza cases were recorded in the United States Army and Navy, with the death rate running at 7.2 per cent. An analysis of 1,043,653 British casualties admitted to medical units in 1916–20 showed there were 94,989 influenza cases.

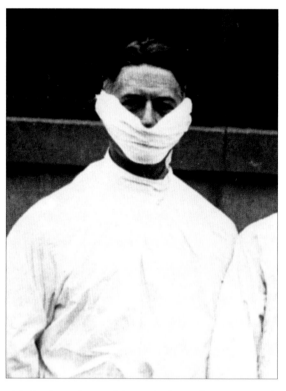

The war did not "cause" the pandemic. Poor nutrition was not responsible for the virulence of the flu (wealthier, better fed people died just as readily as those from poorer classes), although undoubtedly the sudden onset of the disease exacerbated the strains of war. In Germany, where the population was suffering from severe food shortages, the death rate among females had climbed by 23 per cent, thanks largely to tuberculosis and pneumonia, even before the flu pandemic began. The first strain of Spanish flu, which lasted until summer 1918, was relatively mild.

It was unusual for victims to die from the disease. This strain was succeeded by another, much more dangerous variety. It killed young and old, fit and unfit alike. Adults between 20 and 40 were particularly vulnerable, and the impact of Spanish flu was magnified by the fact that large numbers of young men were cooped up together in military units, making transmission easier. Survival appeared to be a matter of chance. The death rate per week in Britain was running at 7,000 people by the end of October.

A variety of prophylactics were used. Each country used a different type of face mask. Disinfectant was squirted in public places, leaflets advising precautionary measures were distributed, but none of these precautions made any difference.

Spanish flu had a direct influence on military operations. Flu swept through the ranks of all armies in 1918, but it seems that the Germans were particularly badly affected. At the Battle of Amiens, 8 August 1918, their divisions were already understrength because of the heavy losses sustained in the severe fighting in the spring and summer, which could not be fully replaced. The effects of influenza made a bad situation far worse for the Germans. British Fourth Army's divisions were around 7,000 strong (the Canadian Divisions were much stronger); German divisions generally consisted of between 3,000 and 4,000 men. The full impact of Spanish flu on the fighting has yet to be assessed by historians.

OPPOSITE: The masks used by medical staff to try and avoid the Spanish influenza varied in style from country to country.

ABOVE: Doctors, army officers, and reporters wear surgical gowns and masks while touring a hospital to observe the treatment of patients with Spanish influenza, 1918.

■93 Railway Carriage, Compiègne

A railway carriage in a clearing in a forest near Compiègne, in eastern France, was the setting for the formalities that brought the killing on the Western Front to a conclusion. There, on 8 November 1918, representatives of the new German republic, led by Matthias Erzberger, the Centre Party leader, met Marshal Foch, who presented them with the armistice terms. These included evacuation of all occupied territory and the west bank of the Rhine, and the surrender of weapons and railway rolling stock. Foch made clear that there was no room for negotiation. The Germans had until 11 November to reply. With no choice, the Germans complied. The armistice came into force on 11 November, at 11 a.m.

A British delegation was present at Compiègne, but the show of apparent unity masked divisions between the victors. There were no commonly held set of war aims. As German defeat became more likely in 1918, this led to an increase of tension between the coalition partners. One of Britain's vital interests, seen as critical to national naval security, was the expulsion of Germany from Belgium. The security of the Low Countries was a traditional British objective, as was the maintenance of the balance of power in Europe. Britain had fought Revolutionary and Napoleonic France for 25 years over precisely these issues. In addition, there was a vague but nonetheless real aim of punishing German aggression. Also as in previous wars, Britain wanted to acquire territory overseas. In the aftermath of the Great War the British Empire reached its greatest ever extent, enlarged with ex-German colonies and territory taken from Germany's ally, Turkey.

France's central war aim in the First World War was to remove German forces from its territory. Beyond that was a desire to reclaim the provinces of Alsace-Lorraine, which France had been forced to cede to Germany in 1871 after defeat in the Franco-Prussian War. It was by no means guaranteed that Paris would receive the support of its principal allies in Washington and London in its efforts to achieve that aim, although this was eventually achieved in the 1919 Treaty of Versailles. France also sought to expand its empire, effectively dividing up colonial spoils with Britain.

One radical idea favoured by some of the French camp was to remove Germany as a threat by breaking it up into smaller states, effectively turning the clock back 100 years. This alarmed the British, who did not want France to emerge from the war as the unchallenged dominant European power. Both France and Britain also looked with suspicion on the United States, fearing with some justification that President Woodrow Wilson was operating to a very different agenda (see Woodrow Wilson's "Fourteen Points" Program, page 202).

This dissension during the final days of the war prefigured the collapse of the wartime coalition after victory had been achieved. As a result, the Versailles Treaty could not be properly enforced. In the late 1930s, the British and French were reluctantly forced to reactive their alliance in the face of a renewed German threat.

The railway carriage had another part to play in the turbulent history of the twentieth century. On 22 May 1940, following Germany's remarkable victory over France and to emphasize the reversal of the humiliation of November 1918, Hitler had the carriage unearthed from a museum and brought back to the clearing near Compiègne where the Armistice had been signed. There, the French representatives signed the formal terms of surrender. The carriage was taken in triumph back to Germany, where it was destroyed in 1945. Today, a replica stands on the original spot at Compiègne.

OPPOSITE: Marshal Foch (second from right) holding the text of the Armistice that ended the war, on 11 November 1918. He later said of the Treaty of Versailles, "This is not a peace. It is an armistice for twenty years."

ABOVE: The interior of the railway carriage where the Armistice was signed in 1918 – and the surrender of France, on 21 June 1940.

■94 Kaiser's Abdication Proclamation

Kaiser Wilhelm II's Abdication Proclamation, issued on 9 November 1918, marked a staging point on his road from "All Highest" to an ex-monarch in exile in a foreign land. The end had come with brutal rapidity. As recently as mid-July, the German elite could treasure at least the illusion that victory was at hand. Foch's counter-offensive on the Marne (18 July), followed by Haig's victory at Amiens (8 August) ushered in the Hundred Days of Allied victories. Defeat on the battlefield was accompanied by collapse on the home front. More concerned with saving the army than the state it served, the German High Command sought to transfer the blame. Prince Max of Baden, a liberally inclined aristocrat, was brought in as Chancellor and opposition Social Democrats entered the government. The seeds of the post-war "stab in the back" myth were planted.

On 9 November, General Groener, who had succeeded Ludendorff on 26 October, bluntly told Wilhelm, "Sire, you no longer have an army … it no longer stands behind Your Majesty." Wilhelm dithered over whether or not to abdicate, toying with the idea that he could step down as Kaiser but remain King of Prussia, but his hand was forced. The same day, the government issued the abdication decree without consulting the Kaiser. He left for exile in the Netherlands.

Wilhelm was born in 1859. He was the son of Crown Prince Friedrich Wilhelm, the heir to the Prussian throne, and Victoria, the eldest daughter of her namesake, Britain's Queen Victoria. Wilhelm grew up fluent in English and came to have an ambiguous relationship with his mother's country, both admiring and envying Britain. His birth was difficult, resulting in a withered arm and possibly brain damage. Wilhelm underwent some horrendous and unsuccessful treatments as a child to correct his deformity, which may

have contributed to the development of his character. He grew up to be a difficult, arrogant man who never matured. Some who met him thought he was deranged.

Wilhelm's father succeeded as Kaiser and King of Prussia in 1888, but reigned for only three months before he died of cancer. As Kaiser, Wilhelm was determined to make his mark. Dismissing the long-serving "Iron Chancellor", Otto von Bismarck in 1890, Wilhelm changed the course of German foreign policy. Bismarck had smashed the existing balance of power in the course of his German Wars of Unification (1864–71) but then had settled within the new one. In pursuit of Wilhelm's *Weltpolitik*, Germany ceased to be a status quo power. Following Wilhelm's failure to renew a treaty with Russia, the Russians allied with France in 1892. At the turn of the century, Wilhelm's sabre-rattling over the Boer War, and Germany's building of an impressive navy that attempted to rival Britain's, alienated London. The British were turned within a decade from potential allies to potential enemies. Wilhelm must bear a share of the blame for bringing about the coalition that went to war against Germany in 1914.

Once at war, Wilhelm was in theory Germany's Supreme War Lord, although in reality he was pushed into the background by the military. He did, however, retain important influence over senior appointments; for instance, Falkenhayn was Wilhelm's appointee. For the most part, however, the Kaiser was a marginal figure in decision-making. His son, Crown Prince Wilhelm commanded an army group, paired, in the usual German fashion, with a professional officer as chief of staff.

In spite of demands that he be handed over for trial as a war criminal, Wilhelm lived quietly in exile in the Netherlands until his death in 1941.

Ich verzichte hierdurch für alle Zukunft auf die Rechte an der Krone Preussen und die damit verbundenen Rechte an der deutschen Kaiserkrone.

Zugleich entbinde ich alle Beamten des Deutschen Reiches und Preussens sowie alle Offiziere, Unteroffiziere und Mannschaften der Marine, des Preussischen Heeres und der Truppen der Bundeskontingente des Treueides, den sie Mir als ihrem Kaiser, König und Obersten Befehlshaber geleistet haben. Ich erwarte von ihnen, dass sie bis zur Neuordnung des Deutschen Reichs den Inhabern der tatsächlichen Gewalt in Deutschland helfen, das Deutsche Volk gegen die drohenden Gefahren der Anarchie, der Hungersnot und der Fremdherrschaft zu schützen.

Urkundlich unter Unserer Höchsteigenhändigen Unterschrift und beigedrucktem Kaiserlichen Insiegel.

Gegeben Amerongen, den 28. November 1918.

OPPOSITE: Wilhelm II leaves Berlin on 31 October 1918, heading into exile in the Netherlands, which had remained neutral throughout the war.

ABOVE: The abdication proclamation, formally published on 28 November 1918. The Treaty of Versailles provided for his prosecution as a war criminal, but the Dutch refused to extradite him.

⬛95 **Fascist Black Shirt**

The Fascist black shirt offers mute testimony to the fact that war often brings about unintended consequences. When Italy entered the war in May 1915, it hoped to capture territory inhabited by Italian speakers who had remained outside the united state created as a result of the *Risorgimento* – "revival" – in the 1860s and 1870s. The phrase "unredeemed Italy" gave birth to the word "irredentism", referring to the desire to incorporate these "lost" territories into Italy. Peace settlements at the end of the war left irredentist dreams only partly fulfilled for Italy. Although it made some solid gains, including part of South Tyrol and Trieste, important land such as Dalmatia went to the newly created state of Yugoslavia, and Fiume became a Free State.

Italian aspiration for territory in Asia Minor and Africa were disappointed. Italians were frustrated and resentful, believing that they had been let down by their allies, and that the vast sacrifices made by the nation had not been justly rewarded.

The Italian army had mounted a series of attritional offensives against Austro-Hungarian forces. Attacking in mountainous terrain that greatly favoured

the defender, the Italians made little headway. Although the Central Powers launched a devastating attack at Caporetto (October 1917), which forced the Italian army back in rout, the Italians won an impressive battle at Vittorio Veneto (November 1918) after being reinforced by British and French divisions. The cost of the war to the Italian army had been high: some 460,000 killed, 950,000 wounded, and half a million men taken prisoner.

The war had done terrible damage to the cohesion of Italian society. It cost Italy 148 billion lira to fight the war. Taxes were not increased, resulting in enormous levels of debt and significant inflation. The credibility, even the legitimacy, of the liberal, quasi democratic state was dangerously undermined. The Fascist Party, led by a

journalist, renegade socialist, and combat veteran, Benito Mussolini (1883–1945), took advantage.

Mussolini, who had fought with the army on the Isonzo front, became Italy's leader in 1922. A right-wing extreme nationalist, he formed a paramilitary group, the "Blackshirts" in 1919, and two years later founded a parliamentary party, the Fascists; the name came from the "fasces", a bundle of sticks with an axe blade protruding, used as a symbol of authority in ancient Rome. In 1922, with Italy in political turmoil, he was appointed prime minister. Three years later he established a totalitarian state, with himself as "Duce" (leader).

As the Fascist Party's uniform of a black shirt indicates, Mussolini's Fascists were one of the new type of mass member totalitarian political parties that were such a striking feature of the first half of the twentieth century in Europe. Adolf Hitler learned much from the Italian example. Superficially, Mussolini's Italy contrasted strongly with the regime it had supplanted. In reality it had a number of defects, not least a failure to deal with Italy's chronic economic backwardness, which would greatly reduce its effectiveness in the Second Word War.

Mussolini's later failures as a war leader, when he became a figure of fun, are remembered by posterity. Less familiar is the fact that in the inter-war period, when democracies struggled to cope with the many challenges – economic, social and political – with which they were faced, Italian fascism, with its emphasis on military virtues and order, seemed an attractive and plausible alternative. Mussolini had a number of admirers outside Italy, some of whom, like Winston Churchill, would later be embarrassed by their enthusiastic words. Fascism was a product of the Great War, which had fatally weakened a liberal state that entered it to make territorial gains – an unintended consequence indeed.

OPPOSITE: Mussolini alongside fellow Nazis in Naples, on the evening before the March on Rome, October 1922.

ABOVE: Mussolini, head of the Italian Combat Veteran's League, on the way to the Augustus Theatre to attend the first Fascist meeting in Rome, 1919.

◼96 CWGC Headstone

ommonwealth War Graves Commission (CWGC) cemeteries are to be found all over the world. These "silent cities" vary greatly in size. Some are very small. Hunter's Cemetery, on the 1916 Somme battlefield, contains 46 graves. Tyne Cot at Passchendaele in Belgium, by contrast, is vast. Over 11,500 men are buried there, and nearly 35,000 names of those who have no known grave are commemorated on a memorial to missing.

Although there are local variations, most contain the familiar upright white headstones, engraved with the rank and name of the individual whose remains lie beneath, the date of death and often an inscription suggested by the family. These, such as the many variants on the theme of "much loved father/son/brother", can be almost unbearably poignant.

The headstones, originally made of Portland stone but now of Botticino limestone, are 81 cm (2 ft 8 in) high and 38 cm (1 ft 3 in) wide, and they bear the badge of the unit in which the serviceman, or sometimes servicewoman, served: a fouled anchor for the Royal Navy, the eagle with outstretched wings for the Royal Air Force, and a huge variety for the army. 1914 was the heyday of the county regiment, and walking around a CGWC cemetery one sees badges of infantry regiments long disbanded or amalgamated: the antelope of the Royal Warwickshires; the tiger and rose of the Hampshires (known as the "cat and cabbage"); and the crossed machine guns of the Machine Gun Corps, a war-raised unit that did not survive long into peacetime, among very many others. New Zealanders, who, as their war memorials proclaim, came from "the uttermost ends of the earth" to fight, have a fern leaf on their headstones; Canadians a maple leaf; South Africans a springbok; Australians their Rising Sun badge. The headstones are marked by a religious symbol such as a

cross or a Star of David, or occasionally left blank.

Original battlefield graves were usually marked by a rough wooden cross with the soldier's name written on it in indelible pencil. The Imperial (later Commonwealth) War Graves Commission was created in 1917. It owed its existence to Fabian Ware, who developed the work of graves registration while serving with a Red Cross unit and went on to play an immensely important role in the new organization. Sir Reginald Blomfield designed the "Cross of Sacrifice", which combined the Christian symbol with a sword. Another prominent architect, Sir Edwin Lutyens, produced the design for the Stone of Remembrance, to be found in larger cemeteries. Rudyard Kipling, whose son John was posted as "missing, believed killed" at Loos in 1915, took a great interest in the activities of the Commission. He suggested the phrase "Known unto God" which appears on the graves of unknown soldiers, as well as the words on the Stone of Remembrance: "Their name liveth for evermore".

The impression striven for, and generally created no matter how alien the flora, is of an English country garden, an oasis of calm and tranquillity. The impression is very different from gloomy, sombre German war cemeteries, with their dark-coloured crosses, or United States cemeteries, which celebrate America. Today, CWGC cemeteries, invariably immaculately tended, are a visible reminder of the human cost of the wars of 1914–18 and 1939–45 – and, by implication, subsequent conflicts. King George V's words during his "pilgrimage" to France and Flanders in 1922 remain powerful: "I have many times asked myself whether there can be more potent advocates of peace upon earth through the years to come than this massed multitude of silent witnesses to the desolation of war."

OPPOSITE: Ari Burnu cemetery at Gallipoli, Turkey. It is just one of 31 Commonwealth War Graves Commission cemeteries in the area.

ABOVE: Grave of Private L. A. Cox, Royal Army Medical Corps, who died on 9 December 1917. Like most early headstones erected by the Commonwealth War Graves Commission, it is made of Portland stone.

OVERLEAF: A German wartime military cemetery, circa 1919.

97 Hall of Mirrors at Versailles

The Palace of Versailles is a reminder of the ebb and flow of European history and power over the last 300 years. The Palace was extensively rebuilt between 1678 and 1684. It was intended to glorify Louis XIV, the "Sun King", whose armies carried out a series of wars of conquest that enlarged his territories and made France the military superpower of the day. The magnificent Hall of Mirrors, with its 357 looking-glasses, was the scene of two events that helped define modern Europe. On 18 January 1871, in the aftermath of the Franco-Prussian War, the King of Prussia was proclaimed Kaiser (Emperor) Wilhelm I of Germany.

For a united Germany to be inaugurated at a symbol of former French greatness was a terrible humiliation for France. Another turn of the wheel and on 28 June 1919, the Treaty of Versailles, which formally brought to an end the war with Germany, was signed in the Hall of Mirrors. Having humiliated France, Germany in turn was receiving the same treatment.

The Treaty of Versailles imposed reparations of £6,000 million on Germany. Alsace-Lorraine, annexed by Germany in 1871, was returned to France. Other territory was awarded to Poland to give the newly created state access to the sea. Perhaps the most bitterly resented part of the Treaty was Article 231, the so-called "War Guilt Clause", which saddled Germany and her allies with responsibility for the outbreak of war.

The Treaty of Versailles received withering criticism on economic grounds from John Maynard Keynes. Between the wars, liberals in the United States and Britain became uneasy at the perceived injustices suffered by the Germans at the hands of the victorious powers that had framed the Treaty.

Thus, the moral authority, even the legitimacy, of Versailles was called into question. Critics of the Treaty unwittingly aided the rise of Adolf Hitler; attacks on Versailles were a major part of his programme. But the simplistic idea that the Versailles Settlement "caused" the Second World War does not hold water. Significant revision took place before Hitler came to power in 1933, for instance in the area of reparations, and Weimar Germany was largely reintegrated into the international community. The convincing case has been made that the 1929 Wall Street Crash, which plunged the world in economic crisis, was more important than Versailles in bringing about the Second World War. It was this that paved the way for Nazi government in Germany, and Adolf Hitler was always determined to wage ideological war of conquest.

Given the scale of destruction and suffering caused by the First World War, the punitive peace imposed on the defeated power – which was believed to have begun a war of aggression – does not seem disproportionate. It was less harsh than the Peace of Brest-Litovsk forced on the Russian Bolshevik regime by Germany in 1918, and pales into insignificance when compared with what happened to defeated Nazi Germany in 1945. An ideal peace in 1919 would have been mild, to give the new democratic German government a chance, but this was politically and psychologically impossible in the febrile atmosphere of 1919. Alternatively, it should have been much harsher, to destroy Germany's ability to make war for decades to come. In the event, the Treaty signed in the Hall of Mirrors at Versailles was harsh enough to cause resentment, but not sufficiently severe to prevent a resurgent Germany from waging a war of revenge 20 years later.

OPPOSITE: German delegates receiving the terms of the peace treaty from the Allies at Versailles on 7 May 1919.

ABOVE: The Hall of Mirrors, where the Treaty of Versailles was signed – a location chosen because it also saw the conclusion of the Franco-Prussian War in 1871, which had been a humiliating defeat for France.

◼98 Tomb of the Unknown Warrior

The Tomb of the Unknown Warrior in Westminster Abbey is the final resting place of an anonymous British soldier of the First World War. The tomb serves as a memorial to the dead of the war who were never identified, or who have no known grave.

The idea of a tomb to commemorate unknown casualties was the brainchild of British Army chaplain Reverend David Railton. In 1916, he was deeply moved by the sight of a crudely made wooden cross that carried the words "An Unknown British Soldier". The image left a lasting impression, and in August 1920 he suggested the creation of a permanent memorial to commemorate the unidentified British dead of the war. The cause was taken up by the Dean of Westminster, Herbert Ryle, who used his personal influence and considerable energy to turn the proposal into reality. The idea received support from the Prime Minister and the King.

The selection of the unknown warrior was the source of some debate, with the suggestion that the tomb should hold an unknown casualty from each of the three major services. However, this was rejected: a single corpse was exhumed from each of the areas where the British Army had seen major combat; the Aisne, Arras, the Somme and Ypres. The four bodies were covered with British flags and laid in the chapel at St Pol near Arras. Brigadier-General L. J. Watt, who was the General Officer commanding British troops in France at the time, was then asked to choose one of the four. He closed his eyes and selected one of the soldiers at random. This body was placed in a coffin whilst the remainder were reburied.

The casket carrying the unknown soldier was constructed with oak taken from a tree grown at Hampton

Court Palace. Atop the coffin was laid a 16th-century sword chosen by George V from the Tower of London collection, and surmounted above this was an iron shield that bore the words "A British Warrior who fell in the Great War 1914–1918 for King and Country". The coffin was transported to Boulogne. Marshal Ferdinand Foch presented a military salute to the coffin as it was carried aboard HMS *Verdun*. The ship was specially chosen as a mark of respect for the French sacrifice at the battle of the same name.

On 11 November 1920, the coffin was placed on a gun carriage for its final journey. Senior figures of the British military served as pall bearers, including Sir David Beatty, Sir Douglas Haig and Sir Hugh Trenchard. After pausing at the unveiling of the cenotaph, the casket led a procession consisting of the royal family and members of the cabinet to Westminster Abbey. A guard of honour of 100 Victoria Cross holders flanked the coffin as it was carried into the abbey. After the coffin was laid to rest, the grave was filled using 100 sandbags of French soil. Following burial, the tomb was capped with a Belgian black marble stone.

Enormous crowds were present in London for the procession, and the ritual surrounding the burial of the unknown soldier was a deeply emotional experience. Many historians have seen this as an important cathartic event for the British public. By 1920, the initial euphoria of victory had begun to fade. In its place the nation had fallen into a "state of emotional shock" and was in need of an outlet for both collective and individual grief. The bereaved could hope – or as some cases passionately believe – that the Unknown Warrior was their son, husband or brother.

BENEATH THIS STONE RESTS THE BODY
OF A BRITISH WARRIOR
UNKNOWN BY NAME OR RANK
BROUGHT FROM FRANCE TO LIE AMONG
THE MOST ILLUSTRIOUS OF THE LAND
AND BURIED HERE ON ARMISTICE DAY
11 NOV: 1920, IN THE PRESENCE OF
HIS MAJESTY KING GEORGE V
HIS MINISTERS OF STATE
THE CHIEFS OF HIS FORCES
AND A VAST CONCOURSE OF THE NATION

THUS ARE COMMEMORATED THE MANY
MULTITUDES WHO DURING THE GREAT
WAR OF 1914-1918 GAVE THE MOST THAT
MAN CAN GIVE LIFE ITSELF
FOR GOD
FOR KING AND COUNTRY
FOR LOVED ONES HOME AND EMPIRE
FOR THE SACRED CAUSE OF JUSTICE AND
THE FREEDOM OF THE WORLD

THEY BURIED HIM AMONG THE KINGS BECAUSE HE
HAD DONE GOOD TOWARD GOD AND TOWARD
HIS HOUSE

Grave of the
Unknown Warrior 1920   27

OPPOSITE: The coffin of the Unknown Warrior lying in Westminster Abbey before burial. The Unknown Warrior symbolized the dead of the British Empire who had no known grave.

ABOVE: The body of the Unknown Warrior, which lies in Westminster Abbey, was brought back from France and buried on 11 November 1920, two years after the war's end. It contains soil from France and the black marble is Belgian.

OVERLEAF: Many countries had their unknown warrior. Here a two-minute silence is observed after the burial of Belgium's unknown warrior on 12 November 1922.

◾ 99 *All Quiet on the Western Front*

Erich Maria Remarque's novel *All Quiet on the Western Front* was a literary sensation. It was first published in Germany in January 1929, under the title of *Im Westen nichts Neues*. Translated by A. W. Wheen, the book made an immediate impact on its publication in the Anglophone world later that year. Aided by an effective advertising campaign, the book sold two-and-a-half million copies in 18 languages in the first year-and-a-half after it was first published.

All Quiet on the Western Front graphically tells the story of a young German soldier, Paul Bäumer, who is sent to the front, endures a number of horrible experiences, sees his friends killed, sheds his initial patriotism and becomes utterly disillusioned with the war. Paul is killed near the end of the war, the pointlessness of his death being underlined by the statement issued by the military about the lack of major operations that day, which gave the book its ironic title. Remarque's purpose in writing the book is stated very early on:

> "This book is to be neither an accusation nor a confession, and least of all an adventure, for death is not an adventure to those who stand face to face with it. It will try simply to tell of a generation of men who, even though they may have escaped shells, were destroyed by the war."

The publication of *All Quiet* was the most important event at the beginning of what historians have referred to as the "great war books boom". This was a remarkable outpouring of memoirs, novels and published diaries that began in the late 1920s (Siegfried Sassoon's *Memoirs of a Fox Hunting Man* appeared in 1928) and continued until the mid-1930s. British examples included Robert Graves's Goodbye to All *That* and Richard Aldington's *Death of a Hero* (both 1929); in the United States, Ernest Hemingway's *A Farewell to Arms* also appeared in that year. The stage and screen also contributed to the genre. R. C. Sherriff's play *Journey's End* was first staged at the end of 1928, and the Hollywood film version of *All Quiet* was released in 1930.

The significance of this deluge of literature was considerable. It appeared to reflect widespread disenchantment with the First World War, and in fact with war in general: pacifism briefly appeared to be a major force in Britain. In 1931, the American novelist William Faulkner claimed "America has been conquered not by the German soldiers that died in French and Flemish trenches, but by the German soldiers that died in German books."

As historian Dan Todman has shown, the embittered tone of *All Quiet* owed more to the failures experienced by Remarque after the war than what actually happened to him on the Western Front. Remarque did not speak for all war veterans. His book was banned by the Nazis when they came to power in 1933. War was very much part of their agenda for Germany. Some British war veterans criticized the picture of relentless misery which, they argued, did not represent the true experience of the Western Front. As the distinguished historian and combat veteran Cyril Falls put it, "Every sector is a bad one ... no one ever seems to have a rest." Many, probably most, British veterans did not come to view the war as futile. However grim their post-war experience, they continued to see Imperial Germany as a dangerous and aggressive enemy and Britain's war as a fundamentally defensive and just one.

ALL QUIET ON THE WESTERN FRONT
ERICH MARIA REMARQUE

OPPOSITE: Erich Maria Remarque, photographed around 1930. Injured by shrapnel, he was repatriated to an army hospital in 1917, where he spent the rest of the war.

ABOVE: The first US edition of *All Quiet on the Western Front*, published in 1929. The story was first published in a German newspaper *Vossische Zeitung*, November–December 1928.

100 Käthe Kollwitz's Statues

Käthe Kollwitz (1867–1945) was a highly acclaimed German artist noted for her etchings and sculptures. In the years prior to the First World War, her work explored themes such as poverty, hunger and anger. She was particularly fascinated by the struggles of the downtrodden against what she perceived to be bourgeois oppression. She attracted great praise for her cycle of work *The Weavers*, which portrayed the failed Silesian uprising of 1842. She followed this with a cycle illustrating the bloody German Peasants' War of 1524–26.

The experience of the First World War left Kollwitz with deep psychological scars. Her youngest son, Peter, enthusiastically volunteered for the German army at the outbreak of war. On 23 October 1914, his patriotic but inexperienced unit was hurled into action at the First Battle of Ypres, as the Germans launched a series of frontal attacks against well-placed Belgian defences at Dixmude. The assaults were repulsed with severe losses and 19-year-old Peter was killed in action.

Peter's death was a terrible loss for Kollwitz and caused her to enter a deep depression. Trying to make sense of the death of her son and many of his young friends, she began work on a monument to commemorate their deaths. Her design proceeded slowly. In 1919, she abandoned work on the memorial but noted in her diary, "I will come back, I shall do this work for you, for you and the others." In the years that followed, she focused her energies on anti-war woodcuts and posters.

However, she returned to the memorial project in 1925. This time she was able to complete the work to her satisfaction

and the result was *The Grieving Parents*. Although the figures were based on Kollwitz and her husband, she intended the memorial to represent a universal sense of loss. Completed in 1931, the work was exhibited in Berlin before being placed at the German cemetery at Esen, Belgium in 1932. In the 1950s, the cemetery was relocated to Vladslo, Belgium and the sculptures were moved to this new location, where they remain to this day. The statues are placed so that the eyes of the father figure rest on the headstone of Peter Kollwitz.

Adolf Hitler became chancellor of Germany less than a year after the first placement of the sculpture. The emotional force of the memorial and their evocation of tragic loss stood in stark contrast to the heroic portrayals of the war favoured by the Nazi government. As a result Kollwitz's art was deemed "degenerate" and she was forbidden from exhibiting any of her works. Kollwitz and her husband were persecuted by the Nazi authorities throughout the 1930s and threatened with deportation to a concentration camp. In a cruel twist, the duty of organizing the commemoration of the battle in which Peter had fallen was given to the Hitler Youth, who portrayed the event as a triumph of nationalism and heroic sacrifice. Her sculptures had no place in this politicized portrayal of war.

The defeat of the Nazi regime saw her work returned to prominence in post-war Germany. *The Grieving Parents* remains one of the most emotionally affecting memorials of the First World War. Its unique sense of parental loss has made it a pan-European symbol of the casualties of the conflict.

OPPOSITE: Käthe Kollwitz, whose youngest son Peter was killed in October 1914. Peter's death traumatized her and influenced the rest of her artistic career.

ABOVE: *Die Trauernden Eltern* (The Grieving Parents), in Vladslo, a German war cemetery in West Flanders where lie the remains of 25,644 soldiers. The grieving father gazes at the headstone in front of him, on which Peter's name is written.

Bibliography

Air Historical Branch, *The Royal Air Force in the Great War* (Battery Press Inc., 1996)

Ross Anderson, *The Forgotten Front 1914-18: The East African Campaign* (Tempus, 2007)

Vince O. Armstrong, *World War One Soldiers: Training, Trenches and Weapons* (Createspace, 2009)

Max Arthur, *When This Bloody War is Over* (Piatkus, 2001)

Stéphane Audoin-Rouzeau and Annette Becker, *1914–1918: Understanding the Great War* (Profile, 2002)

C.E.W. Bean, *Official History of Australia in the War 1914–1918 Vol. III: The A.I.F. in France 1916* (Angus & Robertson, 1934).

Ian F.W. Beckett, *The Home Front 1914–18: How Britain Survived the Great War* (National Archives, 2005)

Ian F.W. Beckett, *The Great War 1914–1918* (Person, 2001)

Martin Blumenson, *Patton: The Man Behind the Legend, 1888–1945* (William Morrow & Co., 1985).

Brian Bond, *Survivors of a Kind: Memoirs of the Western Front* (Continuum, 2008)

John Bourne, *Britain and the Great War 1914–1918* (Edward Arnold, 1989)

John Bourne, *Who's Who in World War One* (Routledge, 2001)

John Brophy and Eric Partridge, *The Long Trail: What the British Soldier Sang and Said in the Great War of 1914–18* (Andre Deutsch, 1965

John Buckley, *Air Power in the Age of Total War* (Indiana University Press, 1999)

Stephen Bull, *Stosstrupptaktik: The First Storm Troopers* (Spellmount, 2007).

Mike Chappell, *The British Soldier in the Twentieth Century 4: Light Machine Guns* (Wessex, 1988).

Peter Chasseaud, *Topography of Armageddon: A British Trench Map Atlas of the Western Front* (Mapbooks, 1991)

Peter Chasseaud, *Artillery's Astrologers: A History of British Survey and Mapping on the Western Front 1914–1918* (Naval & Military Press, 1999)

Roger Chickering, *Imperial Germany and the Great War, 1914–1918* (Cambridge University Press, 1998)

Anthony Clayton, *Paths of Glory: The French Army 1914–18* (Cassell, 2003)

Deborah Cohen, *The War Come Home: Disabled Veterans in Britain and Germany, 1914–1939* (University of California Press)

Nik Cornish, *The Russian Army and the First World War* (Spellmount, 2006)

Colin Cook, 'The Myth of the Aviator and the Flight to Fascism', *History Today* Vol. 53, No. 12 (2003).

Rose Coombs, *Before Endeavours Fade: A Guide to the Battlefields of the First World War* (After the Battle, 1983).

Gordon Corrigan, *Sepoys in the Trenches: The Indian Corps on the Western Front 1914–1915* (Spellmount, 2006)

Daniel G. Dancocks, *Welcome to Flanders Fields: The First Canadian Battle of the Great War: Ypres 1915* (McClelland & Stewart, 1988).

Joseph Darracott and Brenda Loftus, *First World War Posters* (Imperial War Museum, 1972)

Robet A Doughty, *Pyrrhic Victory: French Strategy and Operations in the Great War* (Belknapp Press, 2005)

William M. Easterly, *The Belgian Rattlesnake – The Lewis Automatic Machine Gun: A Social and Technical Biography of the Gun and Its Inventor* (Collector Grade Publications, 1998).

James Edmonds, *Military Operations: France Belgium 1915 Vol. I* (Macmillan, 1928).

James Edmonds, *Military Operations: France and Belgium 1916 Vol. I* (Macmillan, 1932).

James Edmonds, *A Short History of World War I* (Oxford University Press, 1951)

Max Egremont, *Siegfried Sassoon: A Life* (Farrar, Straus & Giroux, 2005)

Cyril Falls and A.F. Becke, *Military Operations Egypt and Palestine Vol. II* (HMSO, 1930)

Bernard Fitzsimons (ed), *Warplanes and Air Battles of World War I* (Beekman House. 1974).

Lucien Fornier, 'Carrier Pigeons in the French Army, *Scientific American*, 12 July 1913, at http://www.pigeoncote.com/sa/sa.html

Norman Franks & Hal Giblin, *Under the Guns of the German Aces* (Grub Street, 1997).

Leonard Freedman, *The Offensive Art: Political Satire and Its Censorship around the World from Beerbohm to Borat* (Praeger, 2008)

Immanuel Geiss, 'Armistice in Eastern Europe and the Fatal Sequels: Successor States and Wars 1918–23' in Hugh Cecil and Peter H Liddell, *At the Eleventh Hour: Reflections, Hopes and Anxieties at the Closing of the Great War, 1918* (Leo Cooper, 1998).

Martin Gilbert, *Winston S. Churchill: The Challenge of War 1914–1916* Vol. II (Houghton Mifflin, 1971).

Lucinda Gosling, *Brushes & Bayonets: Cartoons, Sketches and Paintings of World War I* (Osprey, 2008)

Adrian Gregory, *The Last Great War: British Society and the First World War* (Cambridge University Press, 2008)

Adrian Gregory, 'Railway stations: gateways and termini' in Jay Winter and Jean-Louis Robert, *Capital Cities at War: Paris, London and Berlin 1914–1919* (Cambridge University Press, 2007, 2 vols.)

Jeffrey Grey, *A Military History of Australia* (Cambridge University Press, 2008)

Paddy Griffith, *Forward into Battle* (Crowood, 1990)

Paddy Griffith, *Fortifications on the Western Front 1914–18* (Osprey, 2004).

Mary Guatt, 'Better Legs: Artificial Limbs for British Veterans of the First World War', *Journal of Design History*, Vol. 14, No.4, 2001

Brian Hall, 'The British Army and Wireless Communication 1896–1918', *War in History*, Vol. 19, No.3, 2012.

Paul G. Halpern, *A Naval History of World War I* (UCL Press, 1994)

Sir John Hammerton (ed), *'The Great War … I Was There!' Undying Memories of 1914–1918 Vol. 2* (Amalgamated Press, 1939).

Neil Hanson, *The Unknown Soldier* (Doubleday, 2005)

Mark Harrison, *Medicine and Victory: British Military Medicine in the Second World War* (Oxford University Press, 2004)

Mark Harrison, *The Medical War: British Military Medicine in the First World War* (Oxford University Press, 2010)

Michael Haselgrove & Branislav Radovic, *The History of the Steel Helmet in the First World War: Austro-Hungary, Belgium, Bulgaria, Czechoslovakia, France, Germany* (Schiffer, 2006).

Ian Hogg, *Grenades & Mortars* (Ballantine, 1974).

Tonie Holt & Valmai Holt, *Till the Boys Come Home: The Picture Postcards of the First World War* (Deltiologists of America, 1977)

Tonie Holt, *Major and Mrs Holt's Battlefield Guide to the Somme* (Pen & Sword 2008)

Richard Holmes (ed.) *The Oxford Companion to Military History* (Oxford University Press, 2001)

Alistair Horne, *The Price of Glory: Verdun 1916* (Penguin, 1994)

Alvin Jackson, *Home Rule: An Irish History 1800-2000* (Oxford University Press, 2003)

Herbert Jäger, *German Artillery of World War I* (Crowood, 2001).

Fred T. Jane, *Jane's Fighting Ships* (Sampson Low, 1911)

Ernst Junger, *Storm of Steel* (Penguin, 2004).

Alan Krell, *The Devil's Rope: A Cultural History of Barbed Wire* (Reaktion Books, 2002).

Lee Kennett, *The First Air War: 1914–1918* (Free Press, 1999).

Rudyard Kipling, *The Irish Guards in the Great War: The Second Battalion* (Sarpedon, 1997).

Tony Lane, 'The Merchant Seaman at War', in John Bourne, Peter Liddle, and Ian Whitehead (eds.) *The Great World War 1914–1945* (2 vols. , Harper Collins, 2000–01).

Tony Lane, 'The British Merchant Seaman at War', in Hugh Cecil and Peter Liddle, (eds.) *Facing Armageddon: The First World War Experienced* (Leo Cooper, 1996)

Witold Lawrynowicz, *French Light Tank Renault FT US Six Ton Tank 1917* (Model Centrum Proges, 2006).

Edward G. Lengel, *To Conquer Hell: The Meuse Argonne 1918, the Epic Battle that Ended the First World War* (Holt, 2009).

Philip Longworth, *The Unending Vigil: The History of the Commonwealth War Graves Commission* (Pen and Sword, 2010)

George McMunn and Cyril Falls, *Military Operations Egypt and Palestine* Vol. I (HMSO, 1928)

Arthur Anderson Martin, *A Surgeon in Khaki: Through France and Flanders in World War 1* (Bison, 2011)

W.E. Mason, *Dogs of all Nations* (Mason, 1915)

Bruce W. Menning, *Bayonets before Bullets: The Imperial Russian Army 1861 - 1914* (Indiana University Press, 2000)

Martin Middlebrook, *The First Day on the Somme* (Allen Lane, 1971)

Martin Middlebrook, *The Kaiser's Battle* (Allen Lane, 1978)

Martin and Mary Middlebrook, *The Middlebrook Guide to the Somme Battlefields* (Pen and Sword, 2007)

Allan R. Millett and Williamson Murray (eds.) *Military Effectiveness* Vol. I *The First World War* (Unwin Hyman, 1988)

T.J. Mitchell and G.M. Smith, *Medical Services: Casualties and Medical Statistics of the of the Great War* (Imperial War Museum/Battery Press, 1997)

Stuart C. Mowbray & Joe Puleo, *Bolt Action Military Rifles of the World* (Mowbray Publishing, 2009).

Michael Moynihan, *Black Bread and Barbed Wire: Prisoners in the First World War* (Leo Cooper, 1978)

David Nicolle, *The Ottoman Army 1914–18* (Osprey, 1994)

David Nicolle, *The Italian Army of World War I* (Osprey, 2003)

John Parker, *The Gurkhas* (Headline, 2000)

Major E. Penberthy, 'British Snipers: An Account of the Training and Organisation of Snipers in the British Armies in France', *The English Review*, September 1920

Major Hesketh Vernon Hesketh-Prichard, *Sniping in France* (Hutchinson & Co., 1920)

Stephen Pope and Elizabeth-Anne Wheal, *The Macmillan Dictionary of the First World War* (Macmillan, 1995)

Ian Porter and Ian Armour, *Imperial Germany 1890–1918* (Longman, 1991)

Stephen Thomas Previtera, *Prussian Blue: The History of the Order Pour le Mérite* (Winidore Publications, 2005).

R.E. Priestly, *Breaking the Hindenburg Line: The Story of the 46ᵗʰ (North Midland) Division* (Fisher Unwin, 1919)

Robin Prior, *Gallipoli: The End of the Myth* (Yale University Press, 2009)

Mick J. Prodger, *Flying Helmets before the Jet Age* (Schiffer Military/Aviation History, 1995)

David Ramsay, *Lusitania: Saga and Myth* (W.W. Norton & Company, 2002)

Paul Reed, *Walking the Somme* (Pen & Sword, 2011)

Robert Rhodes James, *Gallipoli* (Batsford, 1965)

Donald Richter, *Chemical Soldiers* (Leo Cooper, 1992)

Anthony Saunders, *Weapons of the Trench War 1914–1918* (Sutton, 1999)

Anthony Saunders, *Dominating the Enemy: The War in the Trenches 1914–1918* (Sutton, 2000).

Siegfried Sassoon, *Memoirs of an Infantry Officer* (Faber & Faber, 1931)

Gary Sheffield, *Leadership in the Trenches* (Macmillan, 20000

Gary Sheffield, *Forgotten Victory: The First World War – Myths and Realities* (Headline, 2001)

Gary Sheffield, *The Chief: Douglas Haig and the British Army* (Aurum, 2011)

Dennis E. Showalter, *Tannenberg: Clash of Empires* (Brassey's 2004)

Ian Skennerton, *An Introduction to British Grenades* (Greenhill, 1988).

Stephen Skinner, *The Stand: The Final Flight of Lt. Frank Luke Jr.* (Schiffer, 2008).

Joseph E. Smith, *Small Arms of the World* (Stackpole, 1969).

Leonard V. Smith, Stéphane Audoin-Rouzeau and Annette Becker, *France and the Great War 1914–1918* (Cambridge University Press, 2003)

Roger Smither & Stephen Badsey (eds.), *Imperial War Museum Film Catalogue ,The First World War Archive Vol. One* (Flicks Books, 1993)

Michael Snape, *God and the British Soldier: Religion and the British Army in the First and Second World Wars* (Routledge, 2005)

Michael Snape and Edward Madigan (eds.) *The Clergy in Khaki: New*

Perspectives on British Army Chaplaincy in the First World War (Ashgate, 2013)

David Stevenson, *1914–1918: The History of the First World War* (Penguin, 2004)

John Still, *A Prisoner in Turkey* (John Lane, 1920)

Hew Strachan (ed.), *The Oxford Illustrated History of the First World War* (Oxford University Press, 1998)

Hew Strachan, *To Arms: The First World* War Vol. I (Oxford University Press, 2001)

Nigel Steel and Peter Hart, *Jutland 1916: Death in the Grey Wastes* (Cassell, 2003)

Ian Sumner, *They Shall Not Pass: The French Army on the Western Front 1914–1918* (Pen & Sword, 2012).

A.J.P. Taylor, *The First World War: An Illustrated History* (1966)

John Terraine, *Business in Great Waters* (Wordsworth, 1999)

Owen Thetford & Peter Gray, *German Aircraft of the First World War* (Bodley Head, 1970).

Mark Thompson, *The White War: Life and Death on the Italian Front 1915–1919* (Faber and Faber, 2008)

Dan Todman, *The Great War: Myth and Memory* (Hambledon and London, 2005)

Charles Townshend, *Easter 1916: The Irish Rebellion* (Allen Lane, 2005)

Charles Townshend, *When God Made Hell: The British Invasion of Mesopotamia and the Creation of Iraq 1914–1921* Faber and Faber, 2010)

Deltert Trew, *War Wire: The History of Obstacle Wire Use in Warfare* (DRM Publishing, 1998).

Barbara Tuchman, *The Guns of August* (Macmillan, 1962).

Spencer C. Tucker (ed.) *The European Powers in the First World War: An Encyclopedia* (Garland, 1996)

Spencer C. Tucker (ed.) *The Encyclopedia of World War I* (ABC Clio, 2005, 5 vols.)

Alexander Watson, *Enduring the Great War: Combat, Morale and Collapse in the German and British Armies, 1914–1918* (Cambridge University Press, 2008)

Alan Weeks, *Tea, Rum & Fags: Sustaining Tommy 1914–18* (The History Press, 2009)

Ian Westwell, *The Illustrated History of the Weapons of World War One* (Southwater, 2011)

Thomas Wictor, *German Flamethrowers in World War I* (Schiffer, 2007)

John Williams, *The Other Battleground. The Home Fronts: Britain, France and Germany 1914–1918* (Henry Regnery, 1972)

Craig Wilcox, *Red Coat Dreaming* (Cambridge University Press, 2009)

Dale E. Wilson, *Treat 'Em Rough!: The Birth of American Armor 1917–20* (Presidio Press, 1990).

Graham Wilson, *Dust, Donkeys and Delusions: The Myth of Simpson and his Donkey Exposed* (Big Sky 2012)

Trevor Wilson, *The Myriad Faces of War* (Polity, 1986)

Jay Winter, *Sites of Memory, Sites of Mourning* (Cambridge University Press, 1998)

Jay Winter & Emmanuel Sivan (eds.), *War and Remembrance in the Twentieth Century* (Cambridge University Press, 2000)

Sarah Womack, 'Ethnicity and Martial Races: The Garde indigène of Cambodia in 1880s and 1890s', in Karl Hack and Tobias Rettig (eds) *Colonial Armies in Southeast Asia* (Routledge, 2006)

John Yarnall, *Barbed Wire Disease: British and German Prisoners 1914–1919* (Spellmount, 2011)

Mitchell A. Yockleson, *Borrowed Soldiers: Americans Under British Command 1918* (University of Oklahoma Press, 2008)

Erik Zürcher, 'Little Mehmet inn the Desert: The Ottoman Soldier's Experience' in Hugh Cecil and Peter Liddle, (eds.) *Facing Armageddon: The First World War Experienced* (Leo Cooper, 1996)

Some useful websites

http://www.1914–1918.net [The Long, Long Trail]

http://www.cwgc.org/ [Commonwealth War Graves Commission]

www.GermanColonialUniforms.co.uk

www.militaryheadgear.com/garments/19-Flight-Helmets

http://info-poland.buffalo.edu/classroom/JM/monument. [Tannenberg memorial]

http://smsmoewe.com/ships/smsms10.htm

http://www.stanleyspencer.org.uk/

http://www.uboat.net/

http://www.winston-churchill-leadership.com

Index

Picture Credits

The publishers would like to thank the following sources for their kind permission to reproduce the pictures in this book.

AKG-Images: 18-19, 24, 64, 75, 166, 190, 196, 198, 200-201; /Bildarchiv Monheim: 251; /Marc Deville: 243; /Erich Lessing: 164, 227, 234, 235; /IAM: 165, 227; /Interfoto: 22-23, 29, 118, 186-187; /NordicPhotos: 106; /RIA Nowosti: 88; /Ullstein Bild: 242; /Alamy: AKG-Images: 20; /The Art Archive: 159; /Martin Bennett: 5, 171; /CBW: 77; /David Crossland: 15; /Hemis: 215; /Hiberniapix: 184; /Interfoto: 16, 38 (top), 55, 162; /Masterprints: 31; /Oleg Mitiukhin: 79; /Patrick Nairne: 223; /The Print Collector: 146; /Tony Roddam: 14; /VPC Travel Photo: 161; /Australian Railway Historical Society, NSW Division: 117; /Australian War Memorial: 76 (JO6392), 102 (PO9591.046), 103 (H03231), 122-123 (RELAWM03709-1), 132, 148 (E03375); /Balcer via Wikipedia: 51; /Battlefield Historian: 225; /The Bridgeman Art Library: City of Edinburgh Museums and Art Galleries, Scotland: 43; /Archives Larousse, Paris, France/Giraudon: 10; /National Army Museum: 149; /Private Collection: 213; /Karl Bulla: 78; /© Canadian War Museum: 34 (bottom) CWM 19440025-009,; /George Metcalf Archival Collection 34-35 (top) CWM 1992004-282, 133; /Corbis: Bettmann: 230, 231; /Hulton-Deutsch Collection: 222; /Piotr Naskrecki/Minden Pictures: 126; /Getty Images: Apic: 26; /Jacques Boyer/Roger Viollet: 119, 180-181; /Buyenlarge: 95; /FPG/Hulton Archive: 50, 110-111; /Fotosearch: 204-206; /General Photographic Agency: 90, 198; /Hulton Archive: 36, 42, 44-45, 58-59, 72, 84, 92-93, 170, 202, 210, 240-241; /Keystone-France/Gamma-Keystone: 208, 237, 248; /Imagno: 174, 250; /IWM: 54, 206; /Keystone: 96-97; /Peter Macdiarmid: 73; /Mondadori Portfolio: 120, 228-229; /Horace Nicholls/IWM: 63; /Photo12/UIG: 124; /Popperfoto: 68-69, 91; /SSPL: 134; /Topical Press Agency: 86, 158, 236; /© James G. Howes, 1998: 89; /Imperial War Museums, London: 37 (CO 3392), 40 (Q 56658), 46, (FEQ 802), 48 (PST 13672), 49 (EPH 3813), 57 (Q 58467), 101 (MUN 1362), 113 (WEA 2225). 125 (Q 32002), 127 (EQU 3855), 137 (MISC2152_005323), 151 (FEQ 465), 172 (Q 24660), 173 (FIR 9220), 189 (ART 2268); /Library of Congress/Harris & Ewing Collection: 160; /National Library of Ireland: 121; /Head Quarters, New Zealand Defence Force Library, permission of the New Zealand Defence Force Library: 176; /Mary Evans Picture Library: 135; /Guy C. Powles from The New Zealanders in Sinai and Palestine Volume III Official History New Zealand's Effort in the Great War: 116; /Private Collection: 183; /Rex Features: Stuart Clarke: 185; /Science & Society Picture Library: 56, 85, 99, 107, 147, 168-169, 179, 192-193, 197, 207, 219, 232, 233; /Solo Syndication: 87; /Surrey History Centre: 140, 141; /Oliver Thiele: 175; /Topfoto.co.uk: 6-7, 46, 52, 60, 62, 74, 80, 81, 82-83, 104, 108, 112, 122 (bottom), 138, 178, 194, 203, 209, 211, 216-217, 220, 221, 224, 244, 245, 246-247; /The Granger Collection: 12, 67, 163 (left & right), 182, 218, 249; /The Print Collector/HIP: 17, 66, 98, 114, 150, 153, 154, 156-157, 239; /Roger-Viollet: 11, 28, 38 (bottom), 61, 70, 71, 109, 115, 129, 144, 214; /Ullstein Bild: 8, 9, 21, 53, 191, 195; /World History Archive: 30

Every effort has been made to acknowledge correctly and contact the source and/or copyright holder of each picture and Carlton Books Limited apologises for any unintentional errors or omissions, which will be, corrected in future editions of this book.

Specially photographed with kind permission from the following:
Historial de la Grande Guerre Château de Péronne/Photograph by Carlton Books Limited: 139
In Flanders Fields Museum/Photograph by Carlton Books Limited: 177
Musée du fort de la Pompelle/Photograph Carlton Books.: 13, 105 The publishers would like to thank the following sources for their kind permission to reproduce the pictures in this book.
AKG-Images: 18-19, 24, 64, 75, 166, 190, 196, 198, 200-201; /Bildarchiv Monheim: 251; /Marc Deville: 243; /Erich Lessing: 164, 227, 234, 235; /IAM: 165, 227; /Interfoto: 22-23, 29, 118, 186-187; /NordicPhotos: 106; /RIA Nowosti: 88; /Ullstein Bild: 242; /Alamy: AKG-Images: 20; /The Art Archive: 159; /Martin Bennett: 5, 171; /CBW: 77; /David Crossland: 15; /Hemis: 215; /Hiberniapix: 184; /Interfoto: 16, 38 (top), 55, 162; /Masterprints: 31; /Oleg Mitiukhin: 79; /Patrick Nairne: 223; /The Print Collector: 146; /Tony Roddam: 14; /VPC Travel Photo: 161; /Australian Railway Historical Society, NSW Division: 117; /Australian War Memorial: 76 (JO6392), 102 (PO9591.046), 103 (H03231), 122-123 (RELAWM03709-1), 132, 148 (E03375); /Balcer via Wikipedia: 51; /Battlefield Historian: 225; /The Bridgeman Art Library: City of Edinburgh Museums and Art Galleries, Scotland: 43; /Archives Larousse, Paris, France/Giraudon: 10; /National Army Museum: 149; /Private Collection: 213; /Karl Bulla: 78; /© Canadian War Museum: 34 (bottom) CWM 19440025-009,; /George Metcalf Archival Collection 34-35 (top) CWM 1992004-282, 133; /Corbis: Bettmann: 230, 231; /Hulton-Deutsch Collection: 222; /Piotr Naskrecki/Minden Pictures: 126; /Getty Images: Apic: 26; /Jacques Boyer/Roger Viollet: 119, 180-181; /Buyenlarge: 95; /FPG/Hulton Archive: 50, 110-111; /Fotosearch: 204-206; /General Photographic Agency: 90, 198; /Hulton Archive: 36, 42, 44-45, 58-59, 72, 84, 92-93, 170, 202, 210, 240-241; /Keystone-France/Gamma-Keystone: 208, 237, 248; /Imagno: 174, 250; /IWM: 54, 206; /Keystone: 96-97; /Peter Macdiarmid: 73; /Mondadori Portfolio: 120, 228-229; /Horace Nicholls/IWM: 63; /Photo12/UIG: 124; /Popperfoto: 68-69, 91; /SSPL: 134; /Topical Press Agency: 86, 158, 236; /© James G. Howes, 1998: 89; /Imperial War Museums, London: 37 (CO 3392), 40 (Q 56658), 46, (FEQ 802), 48 (PST 13672), 49 (EPH 3813), 57 (Q 58467), 101 (MUN 1362), 113 (WEA 2225). 125 (Q 32002), 127 (EQU 3855), 137 (MISC2152_005323), 151 (FEQ 465), 172 (Q 24660), 173 (FIR 9220), 189 (ART 2268); /Library of Congress/Harris & Ewing Collection: 160; /National Library of Ireland: 121; /Head Quarters, New Zealand Defence Force Library, permission of the New Zealand Defence Force Library: 176; /Mary Evans Picture Library: 135; /Guy C. Powles from The New Zealanders in Sinai and Palestine Volume III Official History New Zealand's Effort in the Great War: 116; /Private Collection: 183; /Rex Features: Stuart Clarke: 185; /Science & Society Picture Library: 56, 85, 99, 107, 147, 168-169, 179, 192-193, 197, 207, 219, 232, 233; /Solo Syndication: 87; /Surrey History Centre: 140, 141; /Oliver Thiele: 175; /Topfoto.co.uk: 6-7, 46, 52, 60, 62, 74, 80, 81, 82-83, 104, 108, 112, 122 (bottom), 138, 178, 194, 203, 209, 211, 216-217, 220, 221, 224, 244, 245, 246-247; /The Granger Collection: 12, 67, 163 (left & right), 182, 218, 249; /The Print Collector/HIP: 17, 66, 98, 114, 150, 153, 154, 156-157, 239; /Roger-Viollet: 11, 28, 38 (bottom), 61, 70, 71, 109, 115, 129, 144, 214; /Ullstein Bild: 8, 9, 21, 53, 191, 195; /World History Archive: 30

Every effort has been made to acknowledge correctly and contact the source and/or copyright holder of each picture and Carlton Books Limited apologises for any unintentional errors or omissions, which will be, corrected in future editions of this book.

Specially photographed with kind permission from the following:
Historial de la Grande Guerre Château de Péronne/Photograph by Carlton Books Limited: 139
In Flanders Fields Museum/Photograph by Carlton Books Limited: 177
Musée du fort de la Pompelle/Photograph Carlton Books.: 13, 105